KING OF THE BEGGARS
SEAN O'FAOLAIN

POOLBEG

First published 1938
First paperback edition published 1980 by
Poolbeg Press Ltd.,
Knocksedan House,
Swords, Co. Dublin, Ireland.
This edition published 1986

© Sean O'Faolain 1980

ISBN 0 905169 83 2

*Cover illustration "Ireland without the Repeal" (detail), Irish
School 19th Century, courtesy the National Gallery of Ireland.*

Designed by Steven Hope
Printed by The Guernsey Press Co. Ltd.,
Vale, Guernsey, Channel Islands.

ACKNOWLEDGMENTS

I am grateful to Dr. Richard Hayes, Mr. C. P. Curran, Frank O'Connor, and Mr. M. J. Farrell, who read the proofs and made several helpful suggestions. Mr. Brinsley MacNamara has been particularly interested and patient in this matter, and I am under a special debt to his kindness. Dómhnall O'Súilleabháin has kindly permitted me to make use of his Gaelic life, *Beatha Dhómhnaill Ui Chonaill*. Mr. J. M. Hone was instrumental in getting me some information about Miss Rose MacDowell. Frank O'Connor has given me permission to quote his translation, "Farewell to Patrick Sarsfield." I have read with profit every biography pertaining to O'Connell, and although I base the course of the narrative on the older Lives, I must make special mention of the more recent ones by Denis Gwynn and Michael MacDonagh. The debt of every biographer of O'Connell to Arthur Houston for his edition of the O'Connell *Diary* is so obvious that it hardly needs further mention. One debt every Irish writer on general subjects must always acknowledge, and I do so in all gratitude, is to the staffs of the National Library and the Central Students' Library, Dublin.

To Mr. John Hampden I owe a particular and personal debt for his encouragement in the earlier stages of the book.

S.O'F.

Contents

		Page
I.	Proem: 1691/1775	13
II.	1775/1798	39
III.	The Bar and Politics: 1798/1813	91
IV.	The Man of the People: 1814/1829	191
V.	The Sphinx: 1830/1840	241
VI.	The "Come-Back"; 1840-1847	284
Index		331

HISTORICAL NOTE

From the Norman invasion, resistance, at first desultory, later more persistent, on occasion national, had been offered by the Irish chiefs to English efforts at conquest, colonization, and absorption. The seventeenth century saw the most effective and bloody efforts to expel the English: the Rising of 1641 under the great O'Neill, the Cromwellian conquest and plantation, and then the final effort to hold Ireland for the Stuart king, James II, ending with the Battle of the Boyne and the Siege of Limerick, 1690–91. That siege, which ended the Jacobite War, ended the protracted effort of the old Gaelic world to protect itself.

From that on an "Ascendancy" Parliament controlled the country until the "Act for the Legislative Union of England and Ireland"—commonly called the Union—in 1800. After that Ireland was ruled from Westminster.

This history begins with the miserable days after the fall of the old Gaelic state in 1691. The population was then not much over a million—the great majority wretchedly poor, living in cabins, sleeping on straw, living mainly on milk and potatoes. They were treated by the Williamite conquerors as helots under the infamous code known as the Penal Laws. Through the eighteenth century this helot population multiplied. They numbered seven millions by the end of the century; eight by the end of the first quarter of the nineteenth.

It was these people, without hope, without a leader, without the slightest political sense, slaves in their own land—a glance at any history will appal by the severity of the Penal Laws—whom O'Connell took and fashioned into a modern democracy.

The Ireland of the present day may therefore be best appreciated in terms of this period and this man.

I went to visit old Roderick O'Flaherty who lives very old in a miserable condition at Park, some three hours west of Galway, in Hiar or West Connaught. I expected to have seen here some old Irish manuscripts but his ill fortune has stripped him of these as well as his other goods so that he has nothing now left but some few of his own writing and a few old rummish books of history, printed In my life I never saw so strangely stony and wild a country.

> THOMAS MOLYNEUX: *A Journey to Connaught: April 1709* (*Miscellany of Irish Archaeological Society,* Vol. One, page 171. Dublin, 1846).

I never will get half credit enough for carrying Emancipation, because posterity never can believe the species of *animals* with which I had to carry on my warfare with the common enemy. It is crawling slaves like them that prevent our being a nation.

> O'Connell to his friend P. V. Fitzpatrick.
> *May* 14, 1839

La plus grande charité envers les morts, c'est de na pas les tuer une seconde fois en leur prêtant de sublimes attitudes. La plus grande charité, c'est de les rapprocher de nous, de leur faire perdre le pose.

> FRANÇOIS MAURIAC: *La vie de Racine* (Paris, 1928).

for Frank O'Connor

I : PROEM

1691–1775

I

THE wild geese come in their thousands with the October moon. They blacken the sky, and they cry the coming of Autumn. Where there are low marshlands, or sloblands, they settle down, and then the cabins are cooking them with much butter or grease in the bastables all the winter. About the estuary of the Shannon, and all up the river into Limerick, they must have whizzed and moaned, that winter of 1691, when Ginkel offered the terms that ended the Jacobite War, and started bitter quarrels among the tired and tattered Irish. The flying Irish, down the Shannon or down the Lee with Sarsfield, looked up at the skies, and took the name, The Wild Geese. It was the end of a period. It was all but the end of a race.

Some remained, but most went to France under their gentry, the Fitzgeralds or the Mountcashels—Ireland's first French legionnaires. But older men remembered what had happened when thousands went to Spain after the Eleven Years' War, and, remembering, they cursed at one another all along the battered bastions of Limerick, while the women, who had so gallantly flung down bricks and bottles at the attackers, sat and smoked, and were sullen. When those earlier Wild Geese had fled, in 1652, the Cromwellian whores had taken the women and children and sailed them down the Shannon and the Lee to the Barbados. In their tens of thousands they had turned black under the sun—cooked in a Barbados bastable; or dead, their bodies blacker, or rebellious, their Irish bodies red from the whips. *Wild* Geese, indeed! Up and down they cursed, and quarrelled, and argued. There were Diehards among them, "No surrender" men, gunmen who were to become Raparees, and rove the hills, and raid the settling conquerors, and sleep and be cold and hungry under the trees. But whatever they did—it was the end. They could not know that. It was, just the same, the end. For while Limerick emptied, whether to France or to the woods, Ireland was draining her jugular into the past. It might have been better for her if she had died outright. Instead she kept it up for a hundred years, the awful slow withering-away of the eighteenth century. Limb by limb she began to rot. Every single historian of that century has spoken of her in terms of some disease, and the best phrase of all says that she was like a body dragging itself about with one half already dead. That dead half was her past, alive only in the memory, and slowly rotting even there.

2

THERE was at least one man alive then, who is able to say to us what it felt like. He knew Limerick well, Connello Upper and Connello Lower, Shanid and Glenquin, that border Kerry and Cork. He knew Sir John Fitzgerald well, had been boarded and clothed by him, and wept when he went beyond the sea. O'Bruadair was his name—David O'Bruadair, the poet. Nobody knows where he was born, and nobody (naturally) knows where he died, or when, or how; for he died after the siege of Limerick, when death was as common as "Get Out," and he may well have died of the plague and stiffened in a ditch like the Yellow Bittern, with his toes to the sky. It is significant that he spent his last years, not in composing poetry, but in transcribing it. And you can always smell disaster when a poet begins to transcribe; he is garnering in the past; he smells the darkness. Once before, in Ireland, the poets did that in a body—in the twelfth century, the age of the great manuscript collections, the leatherbound books, the vellum epitaphs, the last will and testament of the men who were waiting for the Norman knocking at the door. O'Bruadair is worth a glance. He sums it all up— that end of the old Ireland on which O'Connell turned his back.

Take him one night before the end falls on his Gaelic world. It is a wet night of 1674, and he is tramping northward on the road from Youghal, to Cahirmoyle in the County Limerick. As he goes he is weaving two poems. One is to excuse him to a lawyer down in Cork for something said in his drink. The other is a queer, mad, arcane Walpurgisnacht of an Epithalamium—all so local, parochial, traditional, allusive, conventional, so very Irish of the Bardic Irish, that it is now half unintelligible and seems to be somewhat obscene. As he passes Two Pot House, and Mallow, and crosses to Limerick, that he knows as well as the lumps on his mattress, or his cock and hen, or his three-legged stool, he adds line to line. He is walking into the dark, with empty pockets, and God knows if the thing he is making up in his queer brain, for he had a very queer brain, could ever be called poetry. (Poetry itself is on the decay.) Even as he looks around that Limerick he seems to make up images of the general crapulousness that is about to invade Ireland:

> Knockawnroo, up there, is raining,
> And Knockfierna is showery, too,
> And Mayne blinking at the bogs,
> And Dromanee under a shroud of mist,
> From noon to noon.
> Like Kilawley, grumbling in pain,
> Kilmichael is weeping wearily. . . .

It hurts us to read that litany, knowing how unevocative those names are to our times—how utterly all those local pieties have been blown to bits by the Williamite guns, how dead are those antique memories of the Gaelic past that once enriched poverty with love. What touched the *O'Bruadairs* will touch anglicized *Brodericks* no more.

As he tramps on, this figure out of the old order that O'Connell is to replace by a new order warms himself with thoughts of the fire, the wine, the applause, the shocked laughter that will rise when he sings the happy pair to bed. He will say (he plans to himself):

> Here I put the gentle maiden
>   gently up
> with her man in bed,
>   no bed of straw,
> and loosen knees
>   to furrow flesh,
> and loose the austere belt
>   until doors unlatch
>   with kisses,
> and there's blanket sport
>   under the rose. . . .

And then (he plans) he will talk of the cheese-stacks, the "wharf-tierces," the wine, the walled mansions. He will sing nonsense-verses in between to tickle the jovial and addle the prim, with jingles on top of all for the sake of good measure. . . . (How could it go?):

> He's a bodach
> Who'd lift his stick
> To make a smack
> Or a saucy crack
> On his wife's back
> When it was all
> Pronocum and Potato
> For Saluta
> When he was courting her. . . .

His patrons sum him up, as he sums up his period in that ancient convention that is about to die. They are one Oliver

Stephenson and one Eleanor Burke. Queen Elizabeth had settled the Stephensons in Ireland; but that does not bother O'Bruadair. After all, that same conquering Stephenson had a son who
died fighting on the side of Ireland in the wars of 1642, and his
son, in turn, fell also under the Irish flag. As he fell, he killed
with a blow a son of the Earl of Cork. Equally impartial on that
side, O'Bruadair had been, a few years before, singing at a wake
in the house of one of the Irish Barrys, who was a brother-in-
law to that son of the Earl of Cork whom Stephenson killed.
And, to add to the confusion, Barry was a half-brother to his
slayer, Stephenson. . . .

We need not try to disentangle these interlockings of family
and political history; the point is that, up to the siege of Limerick, O'Bruadair and all he stood for did manage, however am-
biguously, and in whatever makeshift way, to keep the old order
alive, and that he and his kind did manage, all through the
seventeenth century, to link up in memory and loyalty, pure
Irish, Anglo-Irish, half-Irish. The Burkes, the Browns, the
Roches, Boyles, Barrys, Fitzgeralds, MacCarthys, Stephensons,
and a dozen more were all one. Colonists and natives still lived
in a makeshift kind of unity, at least a tolerance, up to the end of
the seventeenth century. After it—after O'Bruadair—that all
came to an end. The new division is a social one—the conquerors
and the conquered.

He has a leg, too, in the century of death. For it is the typical
ragged-breeches of the eighteenth century who, at the end of
the journey, sings so light-heartedly and vulgarly at the wedding:

> So here I am at last tonight
>   with torn feet,
> And a borrowed breeches
>   on my rump.
> I am hairy, and hungry from the road—
>   so long, so cold, so wet.

What am I but an eerie, stumbling pilgrim
   visiting a gentle maiden,
Up to the waist potation full
   and then, ear to the wall, laid out,
Who slept last night in the woods
   after a dreggy drunk? . . .

That is sheer Happy-Go-Lucky, almost a forecast of Handy
Andy, with his shirt through his tail. It has the lazzarone touch.
But it has more. Like the leitmotiv from Roderick O'Flaherty
that I have put at the head of the chapter (a bit from 1709), it
is in the vein, also, of self-pity, self-drama, and the sense of self
as symbol. Later, all that becomes the identification of the poet
with the ruin of his country, and gives even to the most drivelling
poetasters of the eighteenth century a dignity not their own.

At the risk of being wearisome about O'Bruadair, there is one
other thing one must say about him and his work, and, after all,
he is so typical that he is worth attention. It is that he has in his
work something of the homely realism of the century following—the century of Dan O'Connell (who was nothing if not
homely and realistic). Though in the main a conventional bard,
O'Bruadair could, in a typical elegy on Maurice fitz Edmund
fitz John, Lord of Castle Lisheen, say, for example:

Every little creature turned colour when he died. The hound and
the cat and the horse and the salmon shed tears for him. *Aye, even
the hens felt it.*

His bardic rivals, buckram snobs, were aghast at this undigni-
fied reference to hens, and old O'Bruadair had to defend himself
for his simple fancy. That realism is the best thing in him. It is
as if he had the wit to forecast a time when ruin turned every
hen into a swan, and a man was lucky if he had a hen-egg for
his breakfast.

Yet, though he forecast that end of glory, it was an end he
never really had the courage to face; and small blame to him.
When the end really came, with black poverty, and the death of

all patrons after the flight of the Wild Geese, and the iron heel of the last invaders on his people, he lapsed back into a conventional bardism. (Men always lapse back into the womb in times of stress.) The poor wretch shirked the reality when he saw himself threatened by an anonymous grave. That wet night of 1674 (he knew) he held together three planes of Irish life and history, many classes, a variety of life that was not merely self-contained because it contained nothing—like the later Ireland—but self-contained because it contained everything natural to a civilized life in at least some kind of harmony. But on that endless night after Limerick, he realized that he no longer held anything at all together. He realized that it was all scattered to the four winds of heaven by King Billy's Orange guns.

What does he say then? What he says ends the summary of what his life expresses. The man actually turns savagely on the common people—on the Raparees, on the men and women sullenly arguing under the broken walls of Limerick. He is furious because so many of them refuse to fly like the Wild Geese, refuse to leave their women, their children, and their land to the mercy of the English. "What do you mean?" he cries. "Do you mean to desert my patron, Sir John Fitzgerald? Do you mean to desert the gentry?"

The sullen Limerick men turn from him without an answer. They turn their eyes where the wind fills the sails of Château-Renault's thirty-eight ships on the Shannon—those ships that came too late to relieve Limerick, to win Ireland for James the Second—Jim Dung, as he is for ever reviled in Irish memory.

"But tell me! Answer me!" babbles the poor, bothered poet. "Why do you not go with Sir John Fitzgerald to France?"

The starved Limerick women can only cry into their fists.

"I don't understand," mutters O'Bruadair. "It seems to me no shame to go abroad with the gentry. *Why do you not go with Sir John Fitzgerald to France?*"

He gets no reply, and wandering away he is lost to us. We

read little more about him, except when he, this Gaelic poet, this symbol of the ancient and lineal Gaelic race, writes down something that we can read now only in the most utter amazement:

If the story of the fight [he says] were set down on paper, without bitterness, or vanity, and the names of all the Irish gentry who were lost in it, it wouldn't be a sin to put down in a song that the bargain they made was not a coward's compromise.

The gentry who followed the cause, and in spite of hardships suffered the slippery hills—I really cannot see where the shame was for them to go over the sea in spite of the concessions offered them at home.

But from the time the children of serfs [i.e., the men and women of Limerick; the common folk] *began to grow proud, neither woodland nor bawn has been safe from their billeting. Alas, that nobody punished the rapacity of the Raparees: until those they ruined were driven to the wilds.* . . .

There it is, out at last. The gentry fly. The Diehards, the first Common Irish, the first tough bits of an Irish Democracy, remain behind to spit contempt on him and all he stood for.

And yet, he could have said as well (and had he said it, this Ireland would have begun with him and not with O'Connell):

Guerrillas, children of serfs, to the hills! Beggars now in your own land, begin the building of a new nation out of your own four bare bones—out of your bitter courage neither to submit nor yield. Gaeldom is over. . . . Let Ireland begin. . . .

No! He despises the people. He thinks of them precisely as his fellow Gaelic poet, Egan O'Rahilly, thought of them later, saying:

They are boors who never used elegant, digestible food, or sweet, intoxicating drink, or clean, lovely clothes, but wore shirts of tow—thin, coarse-woven rod-coats of the rotten hair of puck-goats, with boots of putrid, untanned leather, and crooked, ugly, long-eared caps, without shape or form, and stumpy, rusty, ugly clogs, *and as Saint Patrick ordained for them, waited, and tended, and ploughed, and harrowed for the nobles of every reign from time immemorial, obeying the kingly laws as was their duty.*

So the Gaelic poet, one of a clan that in the time of defeat whimpered, and cadged from, and praised any man who would create about them the flea-bitten simulacrum of the old aristocratic patronage.

There is but small respect due to the end of the old order of Gaeldom, to that eighteenth-century collection of the *disjecta membra* of an effete traditionalism. There is respect due to but one man. We must respect Dan O'Connell, despite all his faults, all his mean lawyer's tricks, all his ambiguity, all his dishonesty, evasiveness, snobbery, because he, at least, he alone, had the vision to realize that a democracy could be born out of the rack and ruin of Limerick and 1691, out of the death and decay of antiquity—and it decayed rather than died, for it was rotting before it disappeared, and it stank before it was buried.

He, a Kerry peasant, one of the people, to be acknowledged and entitled *The Man of the People*, took the beggars of Limerick and gave them a kingdom of the mind. All he said to them was that they were not a rabble, and that they could, out of their own strength, make themselves into a nation.

With his tall hat cocked on the side of his curly head, his cloak caught up in his fist, a twinkle in his eye, he became King of the Beggars. The dates merge: 1691, and he that came at the close of the century after, and won out by 1829. The dates merge, for less than one hundred years after he had emancipated his people, this modern Ireland came into being.

3

It may be, in one sense, unfortunate that in considering a piece of political history we should thus have to find our evidence for the condition of the national mind in poetry rather than in State Papers. Still, apart from the fact that there is no choice (because there are no Irish state documents for this period of ruin), a great deal may be gathered from a literature so public, if not popular, as that poetry. It was written by men who regarded themselves as part of a traditional institution, and they wrote not for private joy so much as for public entertainment and instruction. *They* felt themselves as men who expressed the national political mind. They have no modern equivalents.

It is with that national, political mind we are concerned, with its decay, or with its growth, with its disintegration, or with its birth. In so far as these poets illustrate it they are useful. In so far as they express something else that is out of touch with that mind —express, for example, a conventional, or an unrealistic way of thought, or the attitude of a class rather than the whole people, that is less useful but still illuminating. In any case we have no other entry into the mind of the race, and it is to that mind we have to come sooner or later, the inward building or breaking of its molecules, their clustering and rushing in search of a nucleus, their collapse or their cohesion. The outer degradation—the dirt, or the hunger, or the starvation, terrible and horrible as it was —all comes down in the end to this condition of the national spirit that, after Limerick, was either doomed to pulsate or stop pulsating. It reminds one of an operating theatre where the body lies swathed in red-stained bandages, and the surgeon almost lies down on the victim to hear the heart say "I will," or "I surrender."

So, when O'Bruadair has vanished into the dark after Limerick, we must watch the next "eerie pilgrim" stagger into the century of defeat, and wonder what kind of racial inwardness he will reflect.

4

THERE were many successors to O'Bruadair, and as time goes on the distinction between poet and peasant vanishes, for the "poet" is not now supported by rich and intelligent patronage, but has to work like any other man for his living. The songs heard in the cabins of the eighteenth century were composed over the spade-handle by men who were job-gardeners like the northern poet Art MacCooey, or day-labourers like Eóin Rua O'Súileabháin, or composed over the rent-collector's ledger by a Pierce Mac-Ghearailt, or into the mouth of a postman's bag by a Tomás Rua O'Súileabháin—a protégé of Dan O'Connell.

What they brought in the way of distraction to the people from 1700 onward is the subject of that unique book *The Hidden Ireland* by Daniel Corkery; as he pointed out, such men might be addressed by any foreign traveller without being recognized as the lineal descendants of the old bardic line, the proud possessors of an aristocratic tradition of literature. Here, however, it is not the literary value of the work of these men that is in question. We are interested only in the light these semi-popular songsters throw on the political thought of the people who heard them, and presumably applauded them on occasion, even as they were doubtless occasionally comforted by them in the midst of lives so exiguous as to be miracles of endurance.

From this point of view it is correct to speak of them as "semi-popular" because their songs reveal a division in Irish life in the eighteenth century which has, hitherto, hardly been recognized at all; a division identical with that we have already observed in the sympathies of O'Bruadair. For one thing it is patent that these singers did not, at the beginning of the century, think in the least of a popular audience, however willing they were, equivocally, to be supported by popular sympathy. O'Bruadair has shown how that naturally occurred; how the old order was chained by its memories to a wish-fulfilment concept of reality. His contemporary, who lived on to 1730, O'Rahilly, has likewise, in all his work, but two main ideas—that the Stuarts will return, and that the old patronage will return with them. But so long as that patronage of the nobility comes back there is not a line to suggest that O'Rahilly cares two pins what will happen to anybody else.

Take, for example, the poem in which he visits Castle Tochar. It was once held by his lieges the MacCarthys, Lords of Muskerry, whose "capital" was Blarney. Pretending that Theigue MacCarthy is still in possession, he eulogizes the hospitality he has received there. But he well knows that the MacCarthys are long since laid low, and accordingly his poem must next pretend that he has suddenly been informed of the change-over. He is told that Castle Tochar is now in the hands of an English usurper, named Warner, who has displaced the old Gaels; whereupon O'Rahilly, the Gael, is faced with the fact that he has been eating Saxon food and swilling Saxon drink. Does he at once rise up in anger and protest? On the contrary (after O'Bruadair we cannot say "to our surprise") he whines out:

> It is God who has created the world
> And given us one generous man for another who died,
> One who gives gifts to families, scholars, and bards,
> A champion not false but great of heart. . . .

If one swallow made a summer we should need to say nothing further. We should need only to say that these semi-popular poets who carried on the bardic line into the eighteenth century clearly think solely in terms of their own narrow class, have no conception of the hopeless condition of the mass of the people, and have no message for them. But let us see a few more examples. His elegy on the death of one William Gould, a man interested in the old learning, is typical of the Gaelic hatred for realism.

In that convention a man had to be praised for his generosity in bestowing things he never bestowed, and for his lineage which nobody would sensibly wish to prove. William Gould did not in this convention bestow possible things like pennies, or bacon, but silks, wines, jewels, steeds, cloaks, gold in abundance, silver and arms for heroes, with one single word *clothes* to indicate the frieze coat that Gould probably had at some time or other given to the poet. More interesting is the list of people who have lost

by the death of Gould. In a series of rhetorical questions the poet
tells us who they are:

> What has brought the poets to hapless durance?
> And nobles to dungeons long without release?
> The friars to straits, the clergy and the learned?
> Heroes, and seers, and bards without a meal?

That is "Ireland" to this so-called poet of the people—"poets, nobles, friars, clerics, learned folk, heroes, seers, bards." Five times
in five quatrains he mentions the bardic tribe; twice the clergy;
twice the nobles. *Never once the peasant!*

One tries to defend him and his tradition, perhaps, by saying
that this is, after all, a convention and nothing more. But what
does that mean? It means either that these semi-popular poets
had nothing to say to the people that was related to their real
political and social condition; or else it means that the people
were themselves living in a conventional attitude of mind, asked
for and desired no realistic songs, had no wish for a faithful
image of their appalling conditions—were, in one word, sleep-
walking. Either conclusion means that four million helots, of
whom Chesterfield said that they were treated worse than Negroes, and for whose masters Lecky had no milder word than
"Anti-Christ," were living in a state of political obfuscation, not
indeed ripe for a realistic political leader, but badly in need of
one.

Actually, however, there is no reason whatever to suppose
that the people ever heard these conventional poets reciting their
conventional poems, or if they by chance heard them, heeded
them. Why should they? The whole tenor of these poets' complaints is that their poems are not heard or heeded. They constantly bewail the passing of a time when bookish men did hear,
heed, understand, and reward. As early as 1603 the poet Eochaidh
O'Heóghusa was bewailing the effects of the downfall of the
old aristocracy, saying that henceforth all he can hope to write
—if he wishes for reward—is "free and easy verse on the open

road," which was, says his editor, Dr. Osborn Bergin, "as if a poet laureate had to seek engagements at a music-hall . . . competing with strolling singers." Later, the last official poet of those dethroned MacCarthys of Blarney, whose usurper O'Rahilly saw fit to praise, wrote:

> My craft is withered with the change of
> rule in Ireland.
> My grief that I must henceforth take to
> brewing.

That cry is one of the commonest among these hapless men whose songs, so late, so out of tune with the times, are like the troubled cries of birds nesting in a wintry season.

Such conventional verses have never been gathered from the mouths of the people as have been the later, more simple songs that came home to their hearts and their lives from singers who had learned, in accepting the inevitable, the first lesson in political wisdom. These later singers did not so much write as sing, however mournfully, and they sang with more verve and more truth, like O'Rahilly's successor Sean Clárach MacDomhnaill, whose verses reflect the realities of that eighteenth century so well in the lines,

> *Atá mo chóraid gan fuithin*
> *'S mo chuingir gan féar gan fás . . .*

> My cattle are shelterless,
> My team without grass do not thrive.
> My people are in misery
> With their elbows out through their clothes.
> The pack is after me
> At the command of the law.
> My boots are in bits
> And I haven't a copper to pay to repair them. . . .

From that, to go back to another of O'Rahilly's elegies, this time on one O'Callaghan of Clare, is surely to go back from intelligence to somnambulism. Here, again, it is the friars, and the clerics, and the bards who have lost. Here, again, the dead hand of the past is trying to write on a page that has been already scarred and blotted by brutal conquest. While his people are, like those wretches whom the American traveller, Asenath Nicholson, found in Omey, living in burrows in the sand; or, as a hundred travellers found them, starving in windowless, chimneyless hovels that they shared with their lean beasts, O'Rahilly is fantastically listing, over and over, the glories of O'Callaghan's house, glories in which we do not find, once, a homely detail, a thing we could take as a fact, one item to make us feel that we are not being taken by the hand into a complete dream-world.

He goes fondly through his list—wines; viands; coverlets; sweet odours "from the breath of the trumpeting bands"; airs played on harps; "the wise and learned reading histories," and there we get, again, a glimpse of what really matters to O'Rahilly —"books in which there is an accurate record of each great family that rose in Europe"; and then the list goes on, waxlights, soldiers, silver goblets, speckled silks, satin garments, "invalids drinking mead," heroes playing chess . . . all from a patron whose line has been traced back, in verse after verse, through Phœnix, Mercury, Pan, Ceres, Cairbre, Lugh, Ionnadmhar, Adhamar, Mogh Corb, Cobhthach, and five and fifty more until we come to Noah, Magog, Methuselah, and, lastly, Adam.

Well indeed does Professor Corkery say in *The Hidden Ireland* that "from the view of history the value of such verse is inestimable," though not exactly, or solely, as he has measured it. Its value is rather a negative value. Its value is to underline the one thing with which we are here properly concerned—that chasm which was breaking apart the old world from the new, Gaeldom with all its irreality and make-believe from the modern democratic Ireland that, in the torment of slavery, presently opened its bloodshot eyes to a realization of the state to which all that old Gaelic make-believe had reduced it.

Perhaps the most revealing of all O'Rahilly's poems—the last of its kind we need consider—is one in which he bewails the death of John Blennerhasset of Ballyseedy in County Kerry. These Blennerhassets had been vaguely connected with the Jacobites, but took no part in the Jacobite Wars. In writing of them O'Rahilly suddenly does remember the poor.

Young Blennerhasset, he says, is:

> A loss to stately maidens,
> A loss to lovely princely ladies,
> A loss to the weak, severe loss to the learned,
> A very great loss for ever to the bards.
> An utter loss to the poor of the land,
> Ruin to children and lone mothers,
> A loss to the English, their leader and chief,
> A loss to the Irish for ever and ever. . . .

For the moment we may stay our puzzlement at this curious impartiality which finds that a man can be equally a loss to the enemy and to the native; for if we are to be puzzled let us be well puzzled. He goes on with his old formula—"their" shield is lost; "their" helmet; "their" light, support, leader, prince, defence, key, true king, sun, champion, spear, gate, watchman, protector, glory, apostle, joy, guard, knight, fighting cock. . . . But there we stop. "Whose?" we ask. "Whose protector, king, key, defence? *Whose?*" The poet mumbles, much as old O'Bruadair had mumbled, before him, to the men of Limerick:

> Englishmen were wont to visit him,
> Poets, bishops, princes, viscounts. . . .
> This lion who was a lion of the seed of
>   high England. . . .

We throw up our hands. It is only too plain that if this man were indeed a poet of the people, then the people were well called by their saviour O'Connell—"crawling slaves." And that is his only link with O'Connell, though a priceless link, that O'Connell did well to kick him and his like out of the way when he turned to the emancipation of his people.

This is something so necessary to know (if we are to understand O'Connell's politics) that it is as well to enlarge it by saying that in emancipating his people O'Connell had to emancipate them as much from their own outdated loyalties as from the
unwilling loyalties forced on them by their English masters. Had
he not done so he would never have released their natural ener-
gies. Hypnotized by the Past, yet never fed by it, hypnotized
first and then abandoned, they would have been such easy prey
for the colonists that there is no saying how far—however slowly
and unconsciously—they would have gone towards absolute acquiescence in their own extermination as a distinct people. Having no political sense, no absolute sense of *themselves* as a nation, they might have become, but for him, like the Welsh and
Scots, picturesque appendages of England. O'Connell abandoned the picturesquerie, the outer trappings of Gaeldom. He
held and developed the distinctive mind.

5

THAT distinction between the picturesque trappings and the distinctive mind has long occupied the attention of modern Irishmen. It was Frank O'Connor who first pointed out that the trappings belong to an effete, aristocratic order, and that the distinctive mind was the mind of a popular democracy that then
began to raise its head in Ireland, for the first time, in the
eighteenth century. In his essay on *Democracy and the Gaelic
Tradition*, which may well mark an epoch in the development
of modern democratic Irish thought, he quoted those insulting
verses of O'Bruadair's on the Raparees which we have already
seen, and went on to make a contrast so striking that I must
quote it in turn:

From the same place [writes O'Connor], occasioned by the same
event, the flight of the Wild Geese, perhaps even written in the

same place as O'Bruadair's crabbed lines, comes a song of absolute simplicity in the Irish of the people.

Do I deceive myself in thinking that into it goes the whole thwarted genius of the Irish people, the genius which has as yet grown to nothing like its full height? O'Bruadair is enveloped in deception, while the soldier goes straight for actuality, the thing poor Irishmen and Irishwomen, slinking away to the English towns, had for generations been seeking.

That poem ("a hundred O'Bruadairs never wrote anything as good as it") is the Irish song "*Slán le Pádraig Sairséal*" ("Farewell to Patrick Sarsfield"). It goes:

> Good luck, Patrick Sarsfield, wherever you may roam;
> You crossed the seas to France and left empty camps at
>> home
> To plead our cause before many a foreign throne,
> Though you left ourselves and poor Ireland overthrown,
>> Och, ochone!
>
> Patrick Sarsfield, 'tis yourself that was sent to us by God,
> And holy is the earth that your feet ever trod;
> May the sun and the white moon light your way,
> You trounced King Billy and won the day,
>> Och, ochone!
>
> Patrick Sarsfield, with you goes the prayer of every man,
> My own prayer, too, and the prayer of Mary's Son,
> As you passed through Birr, the Narrow Ford you won,
> You beat them back at Cullen, and took Limerick town,
>> Och, ochone!
>
> I'll climb the mountain, a lonely man,
> And I'll go east again if I can,
> 'Twas there I saw the Irish ready for the fight,
> The lousy crowd that wouldn't unite,
>> Och, ochone!
>
> Who's that I see, now, yonder on Howth Head?
> "One of Jamie's soldiers, sir, now the king has fled:
> Last year with gun and knapsack, I marched with joyous
>> tread,

And this year, sir, I'm begging my bread,"
> Och, ochone!

Great God, when I think how Diarmuid was taken,
His flesh wrenched asunder, his standard broken.
And God Himself couldn't fight His way through,
When they chopped off his head and held it up to view,
> Och, ochone!

The fumes were choking when the house went alight,
And Black Billy's heroes were warming to the fight,
And every shell that came, wherever it lit,
Colonel Mitchell asked was Lord Lucan hit,
> Och, ochone!

Many and many a soldier, all proud and gay,
Seven weeks ago they passed this very way,
With their guns and their swords and their pikes on show.
And now in Aughrim they're lying low,
> Och, ochone!

Kelly has manure that's neither lime nor sand,
But sturdy young soldiers stretched over his land,
The lads we left behind us in Aughrim that day,
Torn like horsemeat by the dogs where they lay,
> Och, ochone!

Well may that simple, heart-breaking song be put beside the
strange animosities of the bardic poets; and well may we, in
underlining that robust note of the folk-mind, say with Frank
O'Connor that therein "Irish democracy has been born."

Or we may put that "Farewell to Patrick Sarsfield" beside
O'Rahilly's angry pretence that the common folk are now hail-
ing Cromwell, because

> He freed the fellow with the flail
> And left the landed heir with nothing,

since we find in that same opposition of classes the combustion
of the new Irish nation.

Small help then from these despising poets for the unhappy

hut-dwellers drooping by their peat fires. Had there been no O'Connell to call them, there was no other man out of their own class, no other man who knew them and understood them, no man who spoke their Gaelic and knew their history, to bid them raise a hand. Only in the east coast, as far as possible from the forts of Gaeldom, or in the North, in the city of Belfast, were there a few men—Wolfe Tone and the United Irishmen, or John Keogh, the Dublin shopkeeper, or the pikemen of Wexford and Wicklow at the end of the century—to give them a lead; and then, in Kerry, one of their own, at long last, whom, when he came, they hailed with an extravagant but just delight as The Man of the People.

6

ALL through the century it is the same. We can see these four and a half million helots finding no practical aid from the traditions of the old world that is ended. It was not possible that they should, for that old world was not a democratic world, and they had never shared much in its good things, and they had, as a class, never got much out of it. It had not been organized for them. It had been chiefly an aristocratic order, and its figureheads had been those people whom O'Rahilly listed as the losers by its fall—the clerics, the learned, the chieftains, the bards, the nobles. How much the plebs lost is impossible to say. They do not make many appearances in the annals of the old Irish world; indeed I do not know a single indigenous Irish piece in prose or verse, composed before 1600, which deals with the life and interests of what we may call the lower orders; whereas elsewhere one thinks readily of scores of things that record, or were written to please, humanity in its humblest station—all those *fabliaux* that were a revolt against the rigidity and conventionality of the knightly life, the heartily vulgar tales of Chaucer, the saga of *Havelok the Dane*, where the hero is the ward of a common fisherman, and where the life of the fisherman is recorded with evident delight, the whole satire of Langland, all those popular German tales like *Tyll Eulenspiegel* or *Reynard the Fox*. . . . Of that direct reflection of a popular form of life, nothing was ever preserved in Ireland. We do not even know how the people dressed; or where they lived before the thatched, white-washed cabins were built.

That contempt for the people continues well into the eighteenth century. It goes on, indeed, right to the end, a little beaten down by the harshness of the times, but never exterminated. Yet the thing is pathetic too. It was bad enough to turn Mr. Warner into a Gaelic patron. But when it is not a castle but a farmhouse that becomes a "court," or a "walled mansion" where "wine" is drunk and "harps" played, the snobbery and the lack of realism become a matter for despairing laughter.

So Art MacCooey (1715–73), carting manure for the local rector, in speaking of his "lord" O'Neill, talks of the "court," the harp-strings, the young steeds prancing, the wine on the shining board, and the inevitable loss to the bards. Pierce MacGhearailt (1709–98) solemnly signs himself High Sheriff for the South of Ireland; and as solemnly issues now a warrant for the arrest of a blasphemous schoolmaster, now a passport for a travelling pedlar. Sean O'Murchú (1700–62) writes a begging verse to the tithe-collector, one Mark Carew, and he at once becomes "Marcus of the proud blood of the Carews." Had these snobs even clung absolutely to their delusion of grandeur there would have been something magnificent in their intransigence, but it is that same MacGhearailt who writes a pandering poem to one Squire Freeman, which ends with the flattery of a pimp and the folly of a slave (it is interesting to note that this song is to this day published in song-books for Irish schools, so persistent is somnambulism):

> He was pressed from the blood of heroes
> Who once held sway in London;

With Carew's blood he is well endowed,
Blood of Barry, Burke, and Power,
And every gallant Grecian flower
Who levelled Troy in thunder.
Of Leinster's land the kings by right,
Crosby, Hazard, Synan, White,
Has sprung the lord I sing tonight
Squire Freeman, Ireland's wonder.

That is just as shameful as the horrible story—horrible to us, amusing to him—that Sir Jonah Barrington records in his *Memoirs* of the "poet" Daniel Bran, who was kicked into the mud by the local Squire Flood, and, as he sprawled there on his back, roared out:

There was Despard the brave
The son of the wave
   And Tom Conway the pride of the bower,
But noble Squire Flood
Swore God damn his blood,
   He'd drown them all in Delower.

An example of human (let alone Irish) degradation painful to recall.

So they drag on debasing themselves in their (not unnatural) efforts to curry favour with their slave-drivers. At the same time they try to keep a leg in with their own folk. We find one poet writing verses to a parson, offering to turn Protestant for money:

The Protestants in their courts and coaches
   Say I'd get a vote with their faith,
Free land to own, and guns for poaching,
   And my hat arrayed with the crossed cockade,
Wines and feasting, arranged in portions
   While I lodge in ease to the end of day,
And wouldn't that be better for me to go with
   Than live an idler with the desert Gaels?

We find another now writing a Litany to the Virgin in sorrow for having read the Lutheran creed on conforming to the same religion, now following it up by a set of verses damning a Father MacAirt who had done exactly the same thing.

Yet that same poet who fawned on Freeman wrote one of the finest songs of the whole century, the "Battle-Song of Munster" (even if it is politically fatuous to have been singing songs for the Stuarts so many years after the '45). It is impossible to give any idea of the vigour of that song in translation, but the contrast is too informative not to quote a verse or two.

> I saw it myself, by the ice and the cold,
>   And Thetis in storm all over the sea,
> By the cries of the birds, so sweet and so bold,
>   That my Cæsar and King was come back to me.
>   To Munster no muster could sound half as sweet
>   No wonder, no thunder, no warning,
>   As that slash of the sleet on the Jacobite fleet
>   And the crack of their sails in the morning.
>
> Then gather every man who's bursting with rage,
>   Ground by their laws, robbed by their lies,
> Each nerve and each sinew at last we'll engage
>   To hack them and hew them 'till every cur flies.
>   To Munster no muster could sound half as sweet
>   No wonder, no thunder, no warning,
>   As the slash of the sleet on the Jacobite fleet
>   And the crack of their sails in the morning.

That, in Irish, is a fine song, and we may be sure the rag-tags in their hovels ground their lean fists to hear it. Would that the Gaelic world always sang at least with the same gusto. Alas, they did not; and even that Jacobite poetry soon settled into its own convention, and, reality lending it no blood, rotted in it.

7

IT is not necessary to emphasize the point further; although it could be illustrated over and over again from the writings and lives of these eighteenth-century Gaelic poets. It must be left to

some scholarly historian to elaborate the fact that the Gaelic order was undemocratic, unrealistic, and nostalgic.

To annotate this particular kind of trepanning, however
(which concerns itself only with the political aspect of things),
the reader should, in justice, not fail to go to that other book I
have already mentioned, *The Hidden Ireland*. It sins from over-
softness, and from romanticism, as this survey sins, perhaps, from
harshness, or impatience, due to a deliberate insistence on political realism. In that book will be found a tribute to the real
and (from the O'Connell point of view) only value of these old
traditions—their literary power to distract the hovels from their
misery, and to keep, at whatever cost of illusion, their native
pride alive. There the old order performed a useful work when,
on the collapse of all other patronage, its poets came in the end
into line with the people. They never wholly admitted that they
were doing so, and always they tried to keep up the pretence
that they were superior to the hovels. Their last little dying spurt
was probably in 1827, when they held a Great Bardic Convention in Dundalk, when the final competitors were a Dr. Woods
(a chemist who collected manuscripts and sometimes composed)
and one Art Mór O'Murphy, Great Art O'Murphy, of Grotto
Castle. (The castle, of course, was a hovel.) The set subject,
ironically, was "A Welcome to Dan O'Connell." There the poets
come into line with the folk, and there they, about to die, salute
their exterminator.[1]

That levelling of the old order, under the pressure of hard

---

[1] The following, which is one of the latest and best specimens of the nostalgia-
fantasy complex, is from *Annals of the Irish Harpers* by Charlotte Milligan
Fox (London, 1911), page 157:

"The O'Connors were the kingly family of Connaught. . . . The title of
O'Connor Don is still retained. . . . In 1895 the Royal Society of Antiquaries
of Ireland, making a western tour, was entertained by the O'Connor Don to a
hospitable luncheon within the walls of Ballintubber Castle. The O'Connor
Don on that day was jubilant over the fact that he had recently acquired this
castle, which had been out of the family for a length of time, and it evidently
delighted him, in his character of an Irish chieftain, to feast upwards of a
hundred guests within the ancestral walls. *The marquee in which the luncheon
was served was pitched inside the ruin.*"

facts, is a phenomenon in Irish history. For it *is* a phenomenon to see Irish poets singing of the simple day-by-day affairs of the public—a hurling-match, an avaricious priest, a bailiff's death, a stolen goat, a priest's horse. That popular literature helped to enliven the whole life of the countryside, and had it come earlier might have merged into the life of the democracy O'Connell created.

But it was too late. Literature must inform life, reveal its bones, or else become a mere distraction or amusement. That last was all these poets and these traditions could now do, and since one amusement is as good as another, these hut-dwellers accordingly took these singers lightly. They found the revelation not from the Gaelic order but from the English or the French order, as interpreted by their leaders. The literature of the French Revolution, the English Radicals, Godwin, Tom Paine, the French Deists, Adam Smith, Mary Wollstonecraft—these assimilated and adapted by O'Connell, put into words of one syllable, were what really interested the poor people of Ireland.

Popular poets, indeed! They were as popular as a modern detective story is popular, and no more. The people had in their own folk-tales, *which were never used as the subject of any poet's verse*, a truly popular literature, in the best sense, and one which they constantly adapted, with the natural realism of the peasant, to the conditions of their lives.

With a similar genius for adaptation, the common folk made one other great use of these poets, and it amply defines their attitude towards them and theirs. They used them as schoolmasters to teach English to their children, and with it, mathematics and trigonometry and book-keeping, so as to be able to measure their land, and talk to the bailiff, and understand the machinery of their oppression. From these hedge schoolmasters their children sometimes also learned Latin—but not often, and only if there was any hope of making a boy into a priest or friar.

If O'Connell had any influence at all over the people, he must have imbued them with his own opportunism on this as well as on so many other things. ("I am a confirmed Benthamite," he once said.) His attitude to the old Gaelic world is clear enough. "I am sufficiently utilitarian," he said, speaking of Gaelic, "not to regret its abandonment. It would be of vast advantage to mankind if all its inhabitants spoke the same language. Therefore, though the Irish language is connected with many recollections that twine around the hearts of Irishmen, yet the superior utility of the English tongue, as the medium of all modern communication, is so great that I can witness without a sigh the gradual disuse of Irish." He often addressed meetings partly in Gaelic; he never wrote a line in it. He, at least, had no doubts that Ireland was beginning all over again.

So the people set out on their long journey with but one possession, a not inconsiderable inheritance—their religion. They had not, under the heavens and on the earth, one single other weapon; not land—for they were allowed by law to own none; not schools —for they were allowed by law to enter none; not position—for they were allowed by law to accept none; not so much as a gun —for they were allowed by law to possess none; not so much as a horse—for unless it was worth less than five guineas (and what animal was worth so little!) they were allowed to possess none. They had no churches—even after the great Volunteer Reform of '82 they could not build a steeple, so that to this day all the older churches in Ireland are without one. Neither had they any episcopacy, or other church organization, except what they were able to preserve underground, and they had for nearly a hundred years to smuggle their priests from abroad. They had, in a word, with that one exception of their faith, nothing, neither a present, nor a past, nor a future. They had no parliament, no vote, no papers, virtually no books, no leaders—no hope. One other thing only they had. They had a cry that brought them back to first causes. That was: *Remember Limerick!*

They were slaves with a thirst for revenge.

II

~~~~~~

1775-1798

"A Radical I am, and ever shall remain."
O'CONNELL to Lord Cloncurry,
November 16, 1820.

I

BALZAC said well that O'Connell incarnated a whole people, and O'Connell's germinal chemistry was such that he
could not have done otherwise. With his ancestry, embedded
where he was in time and place, he could not but have been a
recomposition of the diverse elements of his race. His emotional
instinct for life was their instinct. He vibrated as they vibrated.
He was like the shell taken from the sea—and he himself liked
the lines:

And it remembers its august abodes,
And murmurs as the ocean murmurs there.

No one of his family but shared the strength and weakness of
Ireland with his neighbours, as children share the strength and
weakness of their mother. He was a potential conspiracy from
the day of his birth because he spoke the secret language of fel-
lowship in helotry. No Irishman before or after him did that but
Michael Davitt and, to a far less degree, Michael Collins.

His brother Maurice, who began life step in step with him,

39

then joined the Irish Brigade and died in the West Indies in 1797, was not less one of that freemasonry of helots for having evaded their lot—the tradition of foreign soldiering was an old and acknowledged one by '97—but it did mark a difference in him. For whoever evaded any of the conditions of Irish life had to discard some of the characteristics it fostered: it is the mark of all our colonials, all our exiles. Whereas Dan consolidated those things that the wilder Maurice either lacked, or despised, or could not use—such as resilience, bottom, endurance. By making Ireland *do*, Dan made these qualities that Ireland's terrible conditions had created *do* for him. He turned her infirmities and handicaps into his virtues and advantages; and in doing so showed his people how to do it too. In that sense he never left his base.

This does not mean that he was not, also, something of a solitary. Like most great men he nurtured the essential separateness of the human species—most separate in men of genius—in a perpetual loneliness of mind. He lived among men all his life; he had followers by the million; thousands of acquaintances; there is not a letter of his extant to any man, except possibly Fitzpatrick his treasurer, that is the letter of a friend to a friend. Tradition is satisfied that he had many women: Mercer Street in Dublin is still pointed out as his own private brothel-quarter—with what truth I do not know. But he never had a love affair after marriage until he was seventy and doting; and there never was a man who rejoiced more, and in all honesty, in the privacy of his domestic circle. The only really passionate letters we have from him are to his daughter, or when one of his grandchildren dies. His diary is a wail of grief when Maurice perishes in the Indies. Yet this domestic creature was, as a child, fostered out to a herdsman's wife, and called her "Mother," and spoke distantly of his father as "Morgan O'Connell." He was early taken under the wing of his uncle Count O'Connell, as if he were an orphan. That Count O'Connell kept nagging at Dan's other uncle Maurice, called Hunting Cap—a shrewish, hard-fisted old smuggler—

until he persuaded him to adopt Dan as his protégé. He adopted young brother Maurice as well; but as Maurice was wild and displeased Hunting Cap, Dan was soon left without his only comrade. From that on he was cut off by the difference in his aim and station from his brothers and sisters. His grandmother, a great old character, and some say his true progenitor, died when he was a lad. His father died when he was barely come of age. All told, his childhood, youth, and manhood were a more lonely business than one would have expected.

He used to hide when other children wanted him to play among the rocks of Darrynane. He would sit, like a tailor, cross-legged in a window-recess that later became converted into a press in the housekeeper's room at the "Abbey," and there he would—he told it himself—devour, and even blubber over, Cook's *Voyages round the World.* . . . Below him the Atlantic wailed among the rocks.

Besides, Darrynane Abbey itself was cut off, to some degree at any rate, from the wretched cabins about it—cut off by its ambitions rather than its superiority—for it was a house that, like a few other such Catholic Big Houses, had managed to side-step the worst evils of the Great Defeat, and intended to keep on side-stepping them. What land went with it was held on a very ancient lease. Indeed it stood for so much of the history of O'Connell's people that, like Herbert's image of man, it was a flask wherein lay his world's riches that he was to contract into a span. Its owners—his grandmother Máire Duv, and her eldest son Maurice—had managed to hold it only by those communal elements of character that he inherited and so magnified—prudence, forethought, resource, doggedness, tortuosity, a great deal of close-mindedness, and a gift for silence; and above all, and to crown all, that so typically Kerry-ish form of silence, an affluence of volubility. What we know of them marks their type. No modern Irishman needs to be told what that type is like. We know our Kerrymen.

Though the building was not an old house in his time—it was begun around 1745, and he was born in '75—it was an old house in the genealogical sense, and its history and its appearance were well matched. Family and building alike are so full of outcroppings and juttings as to induce one to think that Dan was not so much bred there as outcropped in his turn. The history of the O'Connells is in that way like a geologist's map, with a layer thrusting out at Aughrim, another cropping up at Limerick, another that is lost at the Boyne—dived and disappeared, though doubtless emerging somewhere later in the rubble of poverty that has no genealogy. That fatal word "disappeared" has to be used often by the historian of even the most sturdy Irish families of the seventeenth and eighteenth centuries.

This geological map was well known to Darrynane. They would have remembered, for instance, the fate of their collateral Maurice O'Connell of Caherbarnagh, which is three miles east of Waterville, and north of Loch Currane. This Maurice had been a constable in a castle of the MacCarthys (O'Rahilly's patrons, whom Warner replaced at Blarney) until Cromwell packed him off to the bogs of Clare. The old man had set out one December day, with his cows and his chattels, tramping across Limerick to the Shannon, just like O'Bruadair in '74. He had died by the roadside on his way into exile, as, it seems, his line died on the roadside of history soon after. Nothing so toughens the gut as a memory like that, handed down from generation to generation like an embalmed mummy—a memory and a warning of death. Beside it was the opposite kind of lesson, learned from Daniel O'Connell of Aghavore, who managed to hold on to his bit of land by holding tough in the Forty-One.

Not that Darrynane needed such memories: examples of ruin packed them round. Neither the fighting O'Donoghues of Glenflesk, nor the great O'Mahony with, in Froude's language, his three thousand cut-throats, nor even the great Kenmares managed to hold their possession through the eighteenth century.

With them all, like O'Rahilly's MacCarthys, it was a case of "Laune, and Lene, and Lee diminished of their pride." History alters the position but the lesson always impinges. "Are you a Sinn Feiner?" an old man was asked in Clare, a hundred and fifty years after. "Why wouldn't I? I might have my house burned over my head if I wasn't."

The crafty O'Connells, wise as the old dog on the hard road, observed and remembered that kind of thing. Though tucked away behind the shadows of their mountains on their lonely peninsula that is the heel of Ireland they exchanged the dangerous, because precarious, tradition of farm-work for the methods of modern business. They bought, and sold, and smuggled. They made money and put it safely away. They bided their time.

They might almost be said to have played a double game, or as the kindly will call it a prudent game. Uncle Maurice was more than prudent. He supported the Union. He was one of the first to bring information to the government supporters of the danger of Wolfe Tone's landing in Bantry with the French fleet; he may well have lost a peerage by arriving late with the news; for White of Bantry, who arrived at Cork City twenty-four hours before him, became a peer soon after. He was a Justice of the Peace in Kerry. On the other hand he warmly supported Dan in his Catholic Emancipation campaign, even if he did almost threaten to disinherit him for joining the Lawyers' Corps of Volunteers around the time of Ninety-Eight, or again, though a J.P., never halted his smuggling. It was a matter of adapting oneself to hard times, and a matter on which the conscience had to bend or break. Dan's father, though a good Catholic, had to be married in a Protestant church. The General Count O'Connell, though one of the highest officers in the French service under the Bourbons, moving on terms of equality with the nobility of France, had to become, after the Revolution, a colonel in a British regiment; as did his young relative Colonel Eugene MacCarthy, who died fighting under the English flag. The whole career of Dan O'Connell himself is, in his most intransigent period, ambiguous in the same way. The Irishman had always cantered, since these days, on the buoyant cushion of a caoutchouc conscience. It is recorded of the dreaded Donal O'Mahony of Dunglow, with his thousands of lawless "fairesses," that he always carefully paid his rent.

2

To this Darrynane Abbey the child was early removed from his birthplace at Carhen. It is today a dark, half-empty house in which few people would care to live—it is especially chilling if one sees it on a wintry day, among its dark shrubs, with a wild sea before it and wild mountains closing it in from every side. Yet, in the eighteenth century, when Hunting Cap's father built it around a smaller house (using local stone) and weather-slated it against the storms with thick, veined slates from the local quarries; and especially when it was added to, later on, a bit here and a bit there, and the low, dark rooms became panelled with oak from the last woods about, and it became crowded with "the multitude of our followers and fosterers," it must have seemed a tremendous place in the eyes of young Dan—the only slate-roofed house in the whole district. So bright must it have seemed to a traveller into those wilds that one might easily forgive a romantic poet for talking of it in extravagant terms, with the labourers coming and going, the local craftsmen each at his own particular loom or bench, beasts lowing to the lanterns in the byres, and the tang of the turf and the wood-smoke spreading in the air outside. The best way to think of it is to compare it with the kind of picture we get from Aksakov in his *Chronicles of a Russian Family*—something half-way between the ark of a patriarch and the stronghold of a feudal tyrant. To this day the Kerry people preserve the memory of its first owner—Máire Duv, or Máire ni Dhuiv, O'Connell's grandmother, because her

muscular intellect, caustic tongue, and power of invective turned
her into a folk-legend almost while she lived. She was a poetess,
too; she sang the future Count O'Connell out of Darrynane har-
bour, along with four other nephews and eighteen others, all of
them recruits for the Brigade in France.

Both she and Hunting Cap, its second owner, and her contemporary, were a mixture of tough business-folk and antique
patriarch. If he had a dispute to settle between any of his "fosterers and followers" he would produce his famous *skean*, the
"Crooked Knife," the symbol of his authority, take the skull of
a monk said to have been murdered by one of Cromwell's soldiers, place it in the hands of one of the disputants, and bid him
speak on the skull. One poor woman was so frightened that she
let it fall; it broke into pieces on the flags, and had to be buried
reverently in the little ruined monastery on the island below the
house. Máire Duv had a sly and slightly ominous way of paying
the servants. She put the money into their hands with, "God
prosper your wages, my love—*or otherwise*, according as you
earned them."

Dan, who owed his whole career to Hunting Cap, had taken
his measure very early in his career. His extremely diplomatic
letters to his patron show a healthy respect for that shrewd, cautious, generous, and highly intelligent old man, and the old man's
own letters are just as revealing. Here is a portion of one he
wrote about young Daniel's holidays at Darrynane:

Your son [he is writing to the boy's mother] left this ten days
ago, and took with him my favourite horse. Had it not been for that
I might have dispensed with his company. He is, I am told, *employed*
at visiting the seats of hares at Kularig, the earths of foxes at Tarmon,
the caves of otters at Bolus, and the celebration of Miss Burke's wedding at Direen—useful avocations, laudable pursuits, for a nominal
student at law!

The many indications he has given of a liberal mind in the expenditure of money has left a vacuum in my purse, as well as an impression on my mind, not easily eradicated.

One could very easily imagine that old devil not thinking twice about laying a whip across his servants' backs like any of his contemporaries in Russia.

Had he chosen to do it there was nobody to stop him. Kerry, like most wilder districts in Ireland, however carefully considered from the major point of view of confiscation, still lived, to a large degree, outside the empire of the common law. Privateers and pirates sheltered in the bays. Young Dan was once carried by his foster-mother to see John Paul Jones's vessel riding there at anchor. Deserters and other lawless men found the mountainy districts a safe place to "go on the run." We may presume the usual swarm of more or less tractable mendicants who infested Ireland all through the period, and if there were no highwaymen about—though there may have been, for they were as common as milestones elsewhere—it was only because they were all, in a sense, unprofessional highwaymen themselves. (Morgan O'Connell was tried for his life for inciting his people to half-murder a customs officer who had caught him in the act of landing a contraband cargo, and he was acquitted by a Protestant jury composed mainly of his customers.) To that kind of semi-lawless, *Beggar's Opera* atmosphere, add the real misery of the wandering peasants who, without fixed tenure in any patch of land, drove their black Kerry cows hither and thither, erecting a hut on a mountain-top in the late spring, planting the praties—compelled to pay rent, of course, as soon as they were observed to have alighted on somebody's land—and then disappearing between crops, either in search of easy plunder (*crelaghs* they called such cattle-rustlers in Iveragh) or attaching themselves as casual labourers to any rock that would tolerate such battered barnacles. "Mine" and "Thine" were thus terms whose solemnity was not measured solely by poverty. They were also subject to humane interpretation: again the necessary elasticity. Once while Dan was still on fosterage with the herdsman, his father, Morgan O'Connell, asked him if he ever got any meat to eat. "Yes," said the child, "my *father* stole one of *Morgan O'Connell's* sheep, so we had mutton for a while." At which his father laughed heartily.

In brief, the landlords enforced the law where it paid them. The people were always fighting it. They had laws of their own composite of a balance between Charity and Necessity. It is the only kind of law that is ever really regarded in Ireland, or is ever likely to be regarded in Ireland. It is, in fact, a kind of local and imaginative codification of the Catholic belief that there is no Justice where there is no Charity to temper it. All that has to be borne in mind when we come to O'Connell's ambiguous political morality; it has always hitherto been judged by the rather crude standards of English justice, where the tempering element is not so patent, but is sufficiently powerful to have given more imaginative races as many opportunities for speaking of English hypocrisy as Irish ways have given English critics for speaking of Irish dishonesty.

That kind of natural justice is, inevitably, a dangerous God to serve—one that can quickly disintegrate all conscience. There were times when O'Connell went far towards self-disintegration in this way, playing for what he would no doubt have called an Ulterior Truth, and killing Truth in the process. But in so chaotic, so inchoate a world as that beginning Ireland, one could not have expected either more or less than a good deal of moral confusion. There, for example, was Morgan smuggling happily on the ground that the Law was a tyrant: but when some "crelaghs" who sold Kerry cattle in Clare, and Clare cattle in Kerry, stole fourteen of his cows on the ground that the Law had also made outlaws of them, he called out his retainers, with their long knives stuck in their belts, forayed to the mountains, and killed two of the robbers. Some time after they ambushed him, and he had to fly with the bullets around his head. There was Justice running wild.

The general position may be summed up in the story of the

visit paid by the historian Smith to Darrynane. Under the potency of the usual semi-feudal welcome, and packed to the brim with Hunting Cap's arrogant stories about the greatness of his forebears, Smith promised to blazon the greatness and goodness of the Clan Conaill in his next book.

No, no! [Hunting Cap is supposed to have said.] No, Mr. Smith. We have peace and comfort here, and amidst the seclusion of these glens we enjoy a respite from persecution. But if you make mention of me or mine, the solitude of the sea-shore will no longer be our security. The Sassenach will scale the mountains of Darrynane, and we, too, will be driven upon the world, without house or home.

The general spirit of the speech is to the point; however, even making allowances for eighteenth-century highfalutinism, the account which says that the old man kicked Mr. Smith down the stairs is more true to his character.

3

ALL temptation, then, to think of Kerry as a colourful place has to be resisted. It was a hard place for hard men. They saw nothing colourful in it, though their natural *pietas* did, of course, see much that was grand and inspiriting in it. Even then it took a good deal of mental enlargement, of national spirit, and, what was more important, of freedom from economic pressure, from fear, from hunger, to be able to idealize the cruel sod and rock. Never, to make the point where it can be made easiest, did any O'Connell see colour or romance in the smuggling business. The word business, a proper word, explodes such sentimentalities. Those three O'Connells, Morgan, Maurice, and Count Daniel, were all smugglers—the one running rum, silks, lace, wines, tea, brandy, sugar; the second ostensibly exporting hides, butter, and beef, but sharing in his brother's schemes, inevitably involved in their illegality by his knowledge of them; the third smuggling recruits into France. For all three it was a simple matter of life and death, for, if caught, they would have had to face jail and transportation. It was all not a whit more glamorous than emigration to America a hundred years later, and it was dangerous, as that was not. Even for the Protestants who liked their wine cheap, or their wives who liked French silks, there was always the sting of justifiable suspicion that more than dry goods came stealing out of the hold of those foreign vessels—a friar, or a priest, for example, in from St. Omer or Douai.

The O'Connells were honestly realistic about their world. "Graziers," Dan called his people, long after—"graziers, or gentlemen farmers," with no more than the exaggeration of understatement; he omitted the smuggling. We may keep Darrynane on the same quiet key. Its reality is wild enough, and interesting and vital enough, and heart-breaking enough when one thinks of the awful wretchedness of the mud-wall cabins, the bare-footed peasants, the whole cruel struggle for life, without trying to add picturesqueness. That rain-swept, hungry peninsula, jagging out into the Atlantic, can never be thought of as lovely as long as we remember that it was—even on its brightest days—as hard as the welts on the hands of the women and the men; as lonely as a cock-crow; and as utterly lost to the world—lost, apart from its rent-roll, even to Dublin, with its sham Parliament—as some slave plantation in the Carolinas. It is all very well for us to go down into Kerry now, and rejoice in it—though even now it cuts the grease of our romancings to meet an old woman in bare feet who shamefacedly cadges the leavings of a lunch-basket. What was it like, then, when it was but one corner of the vast slave-plantation of Ireland? The pictures of that hard life have been gathered over and over again, but I refuse to regather their misery. One picture alone, and that a happy one, is enough to make the heart pause, and the conscience reject romance; it is from that Darrynane district in the year 1845, and from one of the most intelligent of all observers, that fine old American lady, Asenath Nicholson, and it is intended to underline what she had so often been delighted to find among the filth and dirt, the "benevolence," "kindness," "patience," even "content"—recurring words in her diaries—of the people among whom O'Connell was reared as a herd's foster-child:

Next morning [she writes] the tempest was still high, and, venturing upon the strand, I saw there, as at Valentia, crowds of females busied. Speaking to one, she replied:

"These stawrmy nights, ma'am, blow good luck to the poor. They wash up the say-weed, and that's why you see so many of us now at work."

The company increased until I counted more than sixty, and busy, merry work they made of it, running with heavy loads upon their heads, dripping with wet, exultingly throwing them down, and bounding away in glee. Truly, a merry heart doth like a medicine.

"And are you not cold?"

"Oh no, ma'am, the salt say keeps us warm. The salt say never lets us take cold."

"And how many days must you work in this way before you get a supply?"

"Aw! Sometimes not forty, but scores of days."

"And all you have for your labour is the potato?"

"That's all, ma'am, that's all. And many of us can't get the sup of milk with 'em—nor the salt. But we can't help it. We must be content with what the good God sends us."

She hitched her basket over her shoulder, and in company with one older than herself, skipped upon the sand made wet with rain, and turning suddenly about, gave me a pretty specimen of Kerry dancing as practised by the peasantry.

"The sand is too wet, ma'am, to dance right well on."

And, again shouldering her basket with a "God speed ye on your journey," leaped away.

I looked after them among the rocks, more with admiration for the moment than with pity; for what hearts, amid splendour and ease, lighter than these? And what heads and stomachs, faring sumptuously every day, freer from aches than theirs with the potato and the sup of milk? This woman who danced before me was more than fifty, and I do not believe that the daughter of Herodias herself was more graceful in her movements, more beautiful in complexion or symmetry, than was this dark-haired matron of the mountains of Kerry.

So the smuggling and the rest of it was not romantic, but it was very important. Had it not been for the patronage of the old Count and the old smuggler-farmer, Dan O'Connell might have spent his life there among those rocks, or behind the counter in Cahirciveen. Lying abed at Carhen, or Darrynane, faintly aware of the to-and-fro of the milkers, or hearing the ritual dawn-cry, under the gate, from another of his uncles:

> "*Cuir amac Seainín O'Chonaill agus an cú!*
> (Send out Johnny O'Connell and the greyhound!)*"

he might have dreamed his fill of greatness (as, on his own re-peated admissions, he did dream over and over again), and never have got much farther than the town of Tralee. It was the money-bags that sent him to the hedge-schoolmasters, O'Ma-hony, Lenihan, and Burke, sent him away to Long Island, near Cork, to a Father Harrington, and then to Liége, Louvain, and the English college of St. Omer, along with his little brother, Moss; even as it was the influence of Hunting Cap that kept him on the safe and solid road to success, and the influence and drive of his mother, Mrs. Morgan O'Connell, the cheerful, cock-nosed woman whose merry face he inherited, but which (in his por-traits) so many painters softened and flattered out of existence. It was a great combination, and it has become a tradition—pa-rental drive behind filial ambition. It is the drive of history be-hind the individual.

4

The visit to St. Omer was in January 1791, Dan being a lad of sixteen, and Moss a year or two younger. It was a tremendous adventure for the two lads, for they had to be smuggled abroad. Had they waited one more year it would not have been quite so exciting, for by the Catholic Relief Bill of 1792 the people were at last permitted to send their children abroad for education, and more important to the future Liberator, they might even practise as barristers.

That bill had been introduced by Sir Hercules Langrishe, a cynic who told the Marquess of Townshend the real reason why the Phœnix Park was swampy. "Because we are so busy draining the rest of the kingdom." It did not clarify the future for the people, but it helped. It was a great deal when added to the other minor relief bills that had begun since 1771, with the decline of all fears of a Stuart invasion. For after 1771 an Irishman might lease a bog for a brief period, if it was a mile from a town (though towns are still rare enough in Ireland and far enough, as a rule, from peat), and if the lessee guaranteed to reclaim at least half of his bogland within twenty-one years. He was allowed to take a perpetual lease after 1778. Not until 1782 were the worst provisions of the code repealed—O'Connell then being seven years old. Then a man could, if he had the money, buy a bit of land, and own a decent horse, and the clergy were given complete freedom of movement; a man might, for the first time, reside in the city of Dublin or Cork, and not, like a camp-follower, have to squat in the surrounding "Irishtown," like the Paris beggars around the *zone*. In short, a Catholic, i.e., one of the people, was suddenly acknowledged as a species of citizen, if a very inferior species of citizen; so inferior that our historians of Dublin under the Georges have been unable to find a single detail about the people, and all we can gather about them is to be inferred from the contemporary theatre in which they begin to appear as the faithful, if rather foolish servant—usually a footman or a runner behind a coach. As to who read such earlier appeals to their spirit as Swift's *Drapier's Letters* nobody knows, though many Catholic Irish must have lived, precariously, in the cities before the law permitted it—the parents of Tom Moore, for instance, since he was born in 1779 in the city of Dublin. All one picks up is broken shards of that underground life, such as a Gaelic

Catechism, or a broadsheet ballad. It is naturally so, since every
office was closed to the native—unless he apostatized—the army,
the law, and the civil service, though he could become a doctor
in private practice, or open an apothecary's shop. Not until
1793, two years after Dan O'Connell went abroad, could a native Irishman enter the army, and then under definite restrictions;
he was allowed to own a gun, on certain strict conditions; and
he could take a university degree (in the Protestant university).
But he could take neither hand, act, nor part in the government
of his country, for he could not enter Parliament, or hope for
any representation therein on this side of charity. He walked
with the word Pariah branded on his forehead.

By that Relief Bill of 1792, then, which allowed the Kerry boy
to train for the bar, we might cynically add Sir Hercules Langrishe to the list of Dan O'Connell's patrons—fitting addition,
since Langrishe had also laid it down that the best *History of
Ireland* is "*the continuation of Rapin.*"

So the two boys vanish from Darrynane with their great trunk
that would not fit into their room in St. Omer, taking eleven
days to get to Dover, by diligence from Ostend to Louvain,
handed on carefully from town to town by the Ireland that had
fled overseas—exiled Franciscans, Dominicans, and Jesuits. At
last, the big childish handwriting begins to travel back from St.
Omer, at six shillings a time for postage, *To Darrinane, near
Tralee*—"near" because only forty miles of familiar mountain-
road separate their beloved home from the market-town.

In these letters, preserved by Hunting Cap—it is the kindly
side of him—young Dan tells how they are studying Latin,
Greek, French, and English, and in their recreation hours may
study also music, dancing, fencing, and drawing. With a reasonable pride in his hedge-schoolmasters, he tells that he has
already got second in Latin, Greek, and English, and eleventh
in French. He lists the authors, Cicero, Xenophon, Cæsar, Demosthenes, Homer, Mignot, Dagaso.

Always in his letters he tries to be most careful over money matters. He always "submits to your superior judgment," or adds to a suggestion, "but this as you please," answers within not more than a fortnight, and apologizes for the delay. It is clear from these letters that his Uncle Daniel, the Count, always proposes, and that his Uncle Maurice, the smuggler, always disposes—and takes his time about it; one January, for example, they wish to study mathematics at a guinea a month, but by April Hunting Cap is still hesitating about that guinea. Always, too, to these little suggestions is added some such peroration as:

We hope, my dear uncle, that our conduct will merit a continuation of your unparalleled friendship toward us. You may be convinced that we do our utmost endeavours for that purpose, and as we know that you require no more, we hope, with God's assistance, to be able to succeed.

A letter from the principal at St. Omer to Uncle Maurice has a double interest. One can, for one thing, see the cautious old patron asking for "a candid opinion" about the boys, "and no nonsense about it."

You desire [said the priest] to have my candid opinion respecting your nephews. And you very properly remark that no habit can be worse than that of the instructors of youth who seek to gratify the parents of those under their care by ascribing to them talents and qualities which they do not really possess.

You add that, being *only the uncle* of these young men, you can afford to hear the real truth respecting their abilities and deficiencies. It is not my habit to disguise the precise truth in reply to such inquiries as yours. You shall therefore have my opinion with perfect candour.

Having thus cleared the air, he analyses the two boys with great astuteness:

I begin with the younger, Maurice; his manner and demeanour are quite satisfactory. He is gentlemanly in his conduct and much loved by his fellow-students. He is not deficient in abilities, but he is idle and fond of amusement. I do not think he will answer for any la-

borious profession. But I will answer for it, he will never be guilty
of anything discreditable. At least, such is my firm belief.

With respect to the elder, Daniel, I have but one sentence to write
about *him*, and that is, that I never was so much mistaken in my life
as I shall be unless he be destined to make a remarkable figure in
society.

Thus encouraged, Uncle Maurice continued his patronage,
and now that the law had opened the Law to the Irish, he made
up his mind that the boys should learn it. That they might study
rhetoric and philosophy he shifted them to Douai. There the two
boys came in August 1792, and from there we have one letter
which mentions, rather touchingly, the important matter of two
boyish appetites. Writes Dan:

The pension here is 25 guineas a year. We get very small portions
at dinner. Most of the lads get what they call seconds, that is, a second
portion every day, and for them they pay £3 or £4 a year extraordinary. We would be much obliged to you for leave to get them—
but this as you please. You may be convinced that it is only the desire of satisfying you, and in letting you know in what way your
money is spent, that makes me do so.

Things were by now getting so hot on the continent that
these quiet studies had to be stopped abruptly. The boys had to
fly, and leave Douai to be looted and sacked behind them by the
revolutionaries. All the English and Irish colleges on the continent suffered. St. Omer also was looted. The English college
at Rome was seized, and the students disbanded by Berthier in
'98. Various convents in the Netherlands were likewise scattered. (It was out of this destruction that Stonyhurst rose, established in '94 by the ex-Jesuits of Liége; so, too, Oscott, Crook
Hall [later Ushaw], Ampleford under the Benedictines, and Ac-
ton Burnell, which removed to Downside just before Waterloo.
The Irish Clongowes did not come until 1814, but Carlow Ecclesiastical College had had a lay school ever since the Relief
Bills made it possible.)

That flight from France left a nasty taste in the mouth. They had already been frightened by the passage of Dumouriez, when a trooper shouted at *les jeunes Jésuites, les Capucins, les Récollets*, and laughed to see the boys flying helter-skelter for the safety of the college. When they left Douai for Calais, all wearing tricolours for safety, it was January 21, 1793—the king had been executed in Paris that morning—and the soldiers hammered their carriage roof with muskets, and on the way they were howled at for young aristos and little priests. By way of revenge they hummed the anti-Revolution song:

> *Marat est mort,*
> *Marat est mort.*
> *La France encore respire.*
>   *Satan!*
> *Prends garde à toi,*
> *Car aujourd'hui,*
> *S'il entre votre empire,*
>   *Demain,*
> *Tu ne seras plus roi. . . .*

To the voyage home belongs the story of the two travellers who broke in on a frightened conversation in the cabin, and horrified Dan and Maurice by showing a handkerchief browned with the throat-blood of Louis XVI. These men were the brothers Sheares, who, when their own time came, broke down, poor devils, and begged in vain for mercy.

5

"As we walked down the Haymarket together," Dan writes later in his diary, speaking of one Darby Mahony, of, probably, Castlequin, and doubtless a relative, for all Kerry was "related," "I showed him some caricatures." It is only the slightest glimpse we get of the two O'Connells after their arrival safe and sound in London. Dan went to school to Fagan's academy—another relative, and his last schoolmaster. Presently the war sent up prices in London, and Fagan found himself with only two boarders; between these discouragements he shut up shop. Where exactly Maurice was, in London, is not clear; all we know is that he is already in hot water with Hunting Cap, and the Count keeps on pleading for him, hoping the honest, honourable, good-hearted, but lightheaded boy (the adjectives are his uncle's) "will conform to your commands and merit your goodness." He did not: he had been given his chance—three years of it—and the old patron was not a man to throw good money after bad, so back he goes to Kerry; then away from Kerry again, to satisfy his heart's desire and become a soldier; ultimately to die in the swamps of Santo Domingo of fever.

It was March 12, 1794, when Dan saw his brother off on the coach for Milford Haven, and returned to his lodgings near the Temple, his name already on the rolls at Lincoln's Inn. So the Irish peasant, as in our day the Indian, the Egyptian, or the African, begins to see and examine for himself the polite centre of Empire, and to learn there many lessons, some of which it has taken him a long time to forget, some of which have, through him, become part and parcel of the political education of his people.

That summer he had one holiday in Kerry, his first visit since leaving it for St. Omer. It was an unfortunate holiday; to it refers the sarcastic letter of Hunting Cap which we have already read—the one in which he speaks of the vacuum left in his purse, and the ineradicable impression left on his mind by Dan's weakness for hares, otters, foxes, and wedding parties. After it Dan pulls in his belt, and takes himself to task. He opens a diary which reveals the veritable adult O'Connell in embryo, though the interest of these pages is not so much what they overtly admit as what they unconsciously disclose. One of the first touches, for instance, seems to confess prudence, but it discloses something more tough, more hardy, less endearing far than the open, and gallant, and expansive ways of his brother Moss. Lodging in a Coventry Street "digs," the nineteen-year-old Kerry lad joins a club called The Ancient Society of Codgers. He was a good member for such a club himself—to use the word in its relic sense —a *codger*, i.e., a cogitating fellow, precocious beyond his age. He liked the club, for it was both convivial and intellectual, but down in his diary suddenly goes the entry:

I have entirely lost this day owing to my being in town. I believe it will be better for me to attend the Society no longer. It is true I acquire there a great fluency of speech, but the loss of time and money makes me conceive it preferable to go there no more.

It is the note of self-protection that jars, the peasant caution to be translated into some such form as:

What a fool I'd be now to be wasting my time and money with these fellows! I have no more to get out of them.

He protected himself still more thoroughly by leaving town altogether. He went to lodge in Chiswick, at that time well out in the country, and not, as now, a Thames-side cluttered with gasworks, furniture stores, cranes, and factories. Walpole House, where he lodged—it is still there, pointed out as the "Miss Pinkerton's" of *Vanity Fair*, where Becky Sharp taught—was a lovely eighteenth-century house, if not eighteenth century by the Irish calendar. Fronting the river and an island covered in by reeds, it faced Barnes on the one side, and (as Dan adds with a touch of that snobbery that never left him) "the Marquis of Ansbach's house and improvements" on the other. From this safe retreat he wrote one letter to his uncle that, for a youth of twenty, is a marvel of soothering Kerry tact. It was clearly intended to rehabilitate himself in the eyes of his uncle, and it makes it clear that the old man kept a tight rein on his nephew, even to the point of dictating where he should lodge:

Chiswick, near London.
December 10th, 1795.

MY DEAR UNCLE,
    I delayed answering your letter until I should have it in my power to inform you that I had changed my place of residence in conformity to your desire.

On calculating the expenses of retiring to a cheaper spot, and returning to keep my term on January 1st, I found it would not answer, so I dropped the scheme. I am now only four miles from town, yet perfectly retired. I pay the same price for board and lodgings as I should in London; but I enjoy many advantages here besides air and retirement. The society in this house is mixed, I mean composed of men and women, all of whom are people of rank and knowledge of the world, so that their conversation and manners are well adapted to rub off the rust of scholastic education, nor is there any danger of riot or dissipation, as they are all advanced in life, another student of law and I being the only other young persons in the house. This young man is my most intimate acquaintance, and the only friend I have found amongst my acquaintances. His name is Bennett. He is an Irish young man of good family connections and fortune. He has good sense, ability, and application. So that, on the whole, I spend my time here not only pleasantly but, I hope, usefully. . . .

I have now two objects to pursue, the one the attainment of knowledge, the other the acquisition of all those qualities that constitute the polite gentleman. I am convinced that the former, besides the immediate pleasure that it yields, is calculated to raise me to honours, rank, and fortune. And I know that the latter serves as a first passport or general recommendation. And as for the motives of ambition you suggest, I assure you that no man possesses more of it than I do. I have indeed a glowing, and—if I may use the expression—an enthusiastic ambition, which converts every toil into a pleasure, and every study into amusement. . . .

If the old man over in Kerry may have grumbled a little at the start—with an "I hope so," or "I hope the young fellow puts it into practice"—he must surely have been won over by this time. But Dan persists:

Though nature may have given me subordinate talents, I never will be satisfied with a subordinate position in my profession. . . .

("That's the way to talk!")

No man is able, I am aware, to supply the total deficiency of abilities; but everybody is capable of improving and enlarging a stock, however small, and in its beginning, contemptible.

("Rubbish. My Dan has plenty of abilities. Must tell him so. All the O'Connells have plenty of brains.")

It is this reflection that affords me most consolation. It is not because I assert these things now that I should call on you to believe them. I refer that conviction that I wish to inspire to your experience. I hope, may I flatter myself, that when we meet again the success of my efforts to correct those bad habits that you pointed out to me will be apparent. Indeed, as for my knowledge in the professional line, that cannot be discovered for some years to come, but I have time in the interim to prepare myself with greater *éclat* on the grand theatre of the world. . . .

I am, dear Uncle,

Your affectionate and dutiful nephew,

DANIEL O'CONNELL.

And if that did not soften the heart of Hunting Cap, what could? No wonder, years after, that O'Connell called his Dublin meeting-house Conciliation Hall. Did Dan wink to himself as he signed that letter?

6

THE young man's remarks on the company at Walpole House are revealing. For one thing he sketches them well enough to have interested any social novelist in their doings; for another, he sketches them deliberately, for—as with everything he did—stated reasons—major, minor, and the conclusion: (*a*) because they may at some future period be amusing; (*b*) the drawing, or attempt thereat, must be "of present utility"; and (*c*) "These arguments justify in my mind the enterprise."

The landlady, Mrs. Rigby, is an education in herself. She had tried, like Becky Sharp, to teach school; she is (notes Dan) about forty-five years of age, of an aspect as ugly as sin, strong of mind, clear of comprehension, tenacious of memory. Speaking French and Italian, knowing Latin, some history, and an enormous amount about the stage, her mind is, in addition, a register of the English peerage, and she has learned heraldry from her father—a coach-painter. A democrat and a Deist (both through peevishness, notes Dan), she pleases her young Irish lodger, who is, by now, rather deistical and radical himself. In fact, while she is under notice from her landlord, she and young O'Connell waste each other's time talking about plays, or Tom Paine's *Age of Reason*, or they argue politics in the drawing-room, and she fondles her tribe of pet cats, while the servants (notes the diarist brutally) are plundering her in the kitchen. She has a refuge in her sorrows, and her peevishness, however, and O'Connell notes it down like a police detective: "She gets drunk sometimes. . . . She is at all times familiar, but when heated with drinking, she is rude in her familiarities."

That dossier measures the softness of the young man. He is as hard as a nail. In the whole five years of the diary there is not a trace of unselfish interest in others. It is a wholly egotistical document, and when it breaks out in a cry of misery, here and there, it evokes pity only because we realize that he is human underneath his armour.

There is, for instance, the American lodger, a widow, with her blind daughter, to whom he so kindly reads novels, or passages from the topical *Manual of Liberty*, which was a compilation from such rationalists as Godwin, Rousseau, Voltaire, Machiavelli, Bacon, and Burke in his more enthusiastic mood, in short, a handbook for the nineteenth-century democrat. The youth does not fail to observe the weaknesses of Mrs. Hunter, such as her foible for boasting of her rank in American society. He also observes that she seems to be attached to another lodger, a Mr. Brady. Still, in general, he approves. "She is tall, and well made; her eyes retain a youthful lustre; when young, her beauty must have been uncommonly striking; her manners are agreeable and genteel; she possesses a fund of good sense, knowledge of the world, and politeness."

There are visitors, such as old Arthur Murphy, the intimate and biographer of Dr. Johnson; people met at parties; a shark who tries to gull the inexperienced young Irishman. This shark, named Hobson, proposed that O'Connell, himself, and a youth named Fullarton, aged seventeen, should go security in a *post obit* bond for £1200, to be paid by Fullarton when he inherits £30,000 from a rich uncle. O'Connell toys with this proposal for twelve days, but Kerry shrewdness wins in the end—*rather than Kerry honesty*, observe. In his usual old-fashioned way he argues it out:

- (*a*) My uncle might find it out.
- (*b*) Supposing Fullarton died before he was twenty-one!!
- (*c*) Supposing Hobson went bankrupt, in the meantime, and left me with the debt?
- (*d*) Fullarton could refuse to pay on a plea of nonage if his rich uncle died too soon.

Conclusion: "Hobson has neither information nor worth to induce me to continue his acquaintance; the line of conduct which this fact bids me follow is obvious." [He also adds that Felix McCarthy, a cousin, is living with Hobson.] "An intimacy with this man may be dangerous. I must therefore shun him."

We hope he means *shun Hobson*, not McCarthy; but we feel that he is quite capable of shunning his cousin if it were advisable.

There were, we are relieved to notice, some escapades to add a touch of normal humanity to this slightly priggish and overcautious young man. The escapades were doubtless part of the "polite gentleman" business. At a General Morrison's in Hammersmith, a Miss King took his hand in the seclusion of the drawing-room, whereupon Douglas Thompson, a local brewer's son, suddenly entered the room, took her other hand, and led her out. The word "rascal" was used. Dan had to interview the brewer's son in the morning, received three smacks of a cane, did not return the blows, sent his "friend" with the usual message, and ended by having to give securities to keep the peace.

Not a particularly glorious first affair of honour, but Dan rea-
soned it out all right:

(a) I did not strike the man, because I might have killed him.
(b) For I was, and know it well, stronger than he is.
(c) Besides, I was afraid of the law, "having no witnesses."

Of early temptations there is mention of one woman:

I dined with X on Friday and spent the night with him. The lady
of the house is a fine young woman. She seemed to be partial to me,
and I endeavoured to improve that partiality. She is a most debauched
woman. She pretended before we parted to have taken a great liking
for me. Nay, she acted the part of the inamorata. My vanity has *not*
infrequently suggested the idea that it may in reality be so. But when
I recollect the side of her character which her conversation showed
me, I must imagine that she is only an artful woman who meant to
take me in. However, I have little chance of ever being able to profit
by her good graces, did I possess them, for want of an opportunity.

That may be interpreted as pleases. It must be. Perhaps it was
intended to be? There is, in any case, an unpleasant note of self-
deception, even self-contradiction about it—the old mixture of
Kerry shrewdness, hardness, ambiguity, and self-protection, so
different from the frank, open note of the diaries of Wolfe Tone,
the Protestant Anglo-Irishman, when *he* writes about his amours.
But we must, in justice, add that there is common-sense, too, and
what we resent may well be no more than this constant application of common-sense without any corresponding sensibility.
That would be a natural failing in an uncultivated man.

It is a genuine relief to find this Caution, Child of Precaution,
in a really riotous scrape. Having made up his quarrel with
Thompson, he invites him, Dick Bennett, his fellow-lodger and
student, and a fourth, de Vignier, to drink at the Packhorse in
Turnham Green—it is still there, now among the tram-lines, not
far from Chiswick Mall. They get drunk, and they get bucki-
fied, and they rap at the doors of private houses along the way;
they frighten a woman, knock up Mrs. Rigby's landlord, de

Faria, a Portuguese, and are met by his servant, George Middleton, a mere boy. De Vignier, like a "polite gentleman," kicks the boy in the belly; the boy bangs Bennett on the jaw; Bennett thrashes him; out come the Misses de Faria and spiritedly pommel Mr. Bennett, whereupon the four brave bucks fly, are met by the watch, who take Bennett, grossly cursing de Faria all the way and followed by half the village, to the watchhouse. Dan sticks by his friend, and the two spend the night in the bridewell consoling each other. This affair dragged on for nine months, and the effort to hush it up cost a nice lump of Dan's time. In the end the Bennett *v.* Middleton case came before the courts, but we do not know its conclusion.

This is not, however, *The Diary of a Churl,* and I have deliberately emphasized here the less attractive side of O'Connell's character, partly to get some of it over and done with, partly because it is a permanent side of his character. There is a great deal more in him than that; there are hours that torment his heart, hours when he is vulnerable, soft, combustible, explosive. And here we must make a distinction.

We get a hint of it in the trite observations that open and close so many of his entries in this private diary: "*Sed dum loquimur fugit invida aetas*"; or, "The day stole away, so true it is that Procrastination is the Thief of Time"; or, "The year closes, how fleet has it been in its progress, how rapid in its close." Or we get the same hint in his remark on the execution of two highwaymen: "O Justice, what horrors are committed in thy name." We observe, in short, that this is all as much part of the century as the man. O'Connell was, in every respect, true to his first period of his life *in the eighteenth century,* to its hardness, its slight cynicism, its spirit of sentiment, even of romance, early or late, baroque, or highflying, rather than to the century in which he did most of his work; although it is true that a good deal of the heavy sentimentality of the Victorians comes to sink him towards the end. That reflection of his times, that assimilation is natural to the opportunist O'Connell; and it is natural to every Irishman, who is always spoken of as adaptable when he is, so often, merely elastic. Caoutchouc, not malleable.

So when Dan hears that Darby Mahony of Castlequin has died in '96 in the West Indies, he cries, in the convention and language of '96, though he undoubtedly feels the loss deeply:

O Darby, O my friend, accept this tribute from him who loved thee. But already are the particles that composed his frame dissolved in their union; already have they been absorbed by the elements to which they belonged. How soon will this be the case with me? And who will then strew a tear of sorrow over my grave? O, that I were remembered by some soft sympathetic heart; that the gay and thoughtless may sigh over my tomb; that the sedate and grave may bend mournfully over the spot that contains my ashes.

Reading which, one turns to the list of books that he read, disappointed at not finding Young's *Night Thoughts*, but reassured by finding Macpherson's *Ossian*. Nor are we surprised that the man who had read *The Man of Feeling* should write to a lady whom he loved at this time, '97 (for a whole fortnight):

Sweet Eliza, let my love for thee mingle in the cup of my sorrows. Perhaps the time is near when the infusion of so many ingredients may make it strong enough to overpower my reason. There must, there assuredly must be an exquisite pleasure in madness. Would I was mad! Then, Eliza, I would rave of thee. Then should I forget my uncle's tyranny, the coldness and unfeelingness in his heart, my own aberrations. What more can I write, on what other subject can I speculate? Wherever I should endeavour to lead off my thoughts, hither they would continually return.

That is a fine example of emotional rococo, as different from Wolfe Tone as the difference in dates would suggest, who could also write in a highfalutin way, and also weep easily, but who could never be quite so solemn because he had the greater cynicism of the earlier time. It helps us, also, to understand a certain amount of O'Connell's later flamboyance and we may dismiss the apparent hollowness behind it by remembering the convention.

After all, just about the same time we find another great man writing in this strain:

Wander in the country; take shelter in the lowly hut of the shepherd; spend the night stretched on skins, the fire at your feet. What a situation! The clock is heard striking twelve. All the cattle of the neighbourhood come out to graze; their lowing mingles with the voice of the herdsman. Remember it is midnight. What a moment to retire within yourself, and meditate on the origin of nature while tasting the most exquisite delights!

That was written by a sentimental young man named Napoleon Buonaparte. Again, however, a qualification, to be found in a comparison between that and the somewhat more relevant application of Nature to man, in O'Connell's letter to Landor:

Perhaps if I could show you the calm and exquisite beauty of these capacious bays and mountain promontories [of Kerry], softened in the pale moonlight which shines this lovely evening, till all which during the day was grand and terrific has become calm and serene in the silent tranquillity of the clear night—perhaps you would readily admit that [I am] in truth a gentle lover of nature, and an enthusiast of all her beauties, "fond of each gentle and each dreary scene"; and catching from the loveliness, as well as from the dreariness of the ocean, and the Alpine scene with which it is surrounded, a greater ardour to promote the good of man in my overwhelming admiration of the mighty works of God.

That is rather more nineteenth century. This entry, truly comical, about ghosts is neither one century nor the other. It is just Dan O'Connell at the top of his form:

I have often said that I would wish to see a ghost.

But he admits that he therein did not tell the truth. For, although:

If there were ghosts it would be *extremely useful* for me to see one [the italics being his own]. There are none. Philosophy teaches me there can be none.

Nevertheless, though there are none, he resolves to go by night to the abbey by the sea below Darrynane, because, he says:

I can by doing it give a practical proof of my disbelief in ghosts.

What a magnificent example that is of the complex Irish mind, leaving half a dozen loop-holes for eventualities, as compared with the simple and direct Anglo-Irish Grattan, who used to go every night to a graveyard to rid himself of an admitted terror of ghosts—learned from his Irish nurse.

Yet, in truth, that ambiguity is a form of wisdom; and with it he has something that keeps a check on all the early-romanticism of his youth in the nineties, on the glooms of "I know not why I should not shoot myself, what is the advantage of living?"— twice in his diaries he mentions suicide; on the early intimations of mortality, often mentioned; on the contemporary sensibility of "Tears blind me," or (in a letter to his wife) "Sweet Mary, I rave of you, I sigh for you, I weep for you, I almost pray to you." He is, as against all that, extraordinarily solid at bottom. He meets a new acquaintance, one Marshall, and with arrogance, secretiveness, and proper self-opinion he writes down:

I like Marshall very much. He *knows* me not; yet he wishes to be acquainted with my heart, my disposition.

I will not hurry his knowledge of it. Let time unfold by degrees that which it would not be easy to show at once. A man, I believe, meets with many difficulties in playing even his own character.

Surely this is the control of a mind, fundamentally objective. "Others studied books," remarks Lecky. "O'Connell studied men."

The core of worldly wisdom is always there, whether in observing the follies of others or his own. He envies his colleague Dick Bennett on the occasion of his marriage, and looks forward to his own felicity. On the spot he pulls himself up. This cannot be allowed.

"When I have done this or that I will be happy." Such is the usual language of men. But, lo, the period of the completion of our wishes is arrived. The once-desired object enjoyed, happiness again removes and is again sought in vain.

He recalls Goldsmith's lines:

> Impelled by steps unceasing to pursue
> Some fleeting good that mocks me with the view:
> That, like the circle bounding earth and skies,
> Allures from far, yet, as I follow, flies. . . .

and thereupon closes his mind and his journal on the matter with:

Read two chapters of the Bible.

The picture such extracts from the diaries gives us may not be as clear as a line; but its complexity is not more confusing than a landscape of many features, and as from that chequer of virgin fields and forests may rise anything in time—"chariots and purples and splendours"—so from that mind, which became a type of the Irish mind, there might come also a real greatness. But, with such a complexity of national genius—using the word as Arnold used it, meaning national character—there was great need for firm guidance. Tremendous honesty, or a tremendous purpose could be that guide.

In such a confusion of politics it is doubtful if any man could have relied on honesty alone—with the ends so undefined and the implements so inadequate and so unmeasured. O'Connell had the purpose. In everything he does and says there is the active liver, fed on practical ambition, driven on by an interior force that defies the currents and whirlpools of his own complexities. But there is more, much more, an external force that keeps that very ambition steady and sane. Prig, snob, careerist, egoist—the Kerry boy is all these things; but he is also, and always, and most violently a patriot. One of the greatest of the whirlpools that caught him was his own pride and his own intelligence, and these and the times turned him for many years—of this there is no possible doubt—into something very near to an atheist, so near that it is doubtful if he cast off his Rationalism until the very end; yet, even there, one can see the old religious instinct giving and withholding, however vaguely, its moral sanction. Because of these three things: Ambition, Ireland—with all its harsh realities and its incessant appeal—and Religion, he managed in the end to possess himself, and to guide himself to ends that by their own greatness made him greater even than he was by nature.

7

To the last we have had to leave the consideration of the intellectual ideas he formed in London. It is true they crop up all the time, but in the chronology of his development they come last; though they are, indeed, no more than the definition or articulation of his instinctive ideas, again born of the growing mental association in his mind between his own problems and the needs of his people. There we are back at Balzac: "Four men have had an immense life, Napoleon, Cuvier, and O'Connell, and—I mean to be the fourth. O'Connell was great because he incarnated a whole people." These ideas are properly left to this point not because their interest is personal to him, or relative to the place where he first clarified his mind about them, but because at the time he did clarify them his mind was already turned definitely towards the idea of a life devoted to Ireland.

In brief, a Tory in France—frightened by the Revolution—he was not long out of it before he became a Radical. He toppled on the brink of Atheism. He recovered as a Deist. He ended not quite as a Catholic, but as an Irish Catholic, which among Irish intellectuals is so often little more than two words for one. I doubt if there were more than one or two Irish patriots who did not run a similar course in relation to religion—Tone, Emmet, Lord Edward, Davis, Mitchel, Parnell, Stephens and most of the Fenians, Collins, Clarke, Connolly, almost all wavering in a typically ambiguous way, barely stopping short on the edge of complete revolt from orthodoxy. For O'Connell all one can say, with certainty, is that he *behaved* from the year 1800 on, in public, as a Catholic, even to the point of magnificently defending Catholic doctrines from Protestant attacks, and not only associating himself with clerical interests but, though political opportunism must have entered there, identifying his cause with them; and that he died a Catholic in his blood and bones.

Yet it is impossible for anybody who makes a serious study of his life to take him at his face-value. He is consistently ultramontane, in the eighteenth-century sense, in his attitude to Rome, but defying it openly when it interfered with him in politics, rejecting with insult, and organizing the clergy behind him in that, the explicit instructions of the Sacred Congregatio de Propaganda Fide. He maintained, in a characteristic Irish way, that sins against faith were worse than sins against morals, and all his political behaviour is that of a man for whom morality is the elastic law. As late as the trial of Magee, in 1813, he could say: "Every religion is good, every religion is true to him who in due caution and conscience sincerely believes it. There is only one bad religion: that of a man who professes a faith in which he does not believe."

As to his own private morals it would be unfair to drag them in here, and however saintly or however lecherous he may have been, they can hardly be of first relevance to the opinions of a man who held that they were matters of secondary importance. But here, I recognize, we are treading on very delicate ground, as well as entering an extremely interesting psychological region; and it is as well to state the premisses at the start.

The Catholic metaphysic is based, as is the metaphysic of every religion which purports to be more than a mere code of morals, on a supernatural idea acknowledged by faith; and faith, being thus at the root, is of pre-eminent importance in the Catholic cosmology. Therefore, for O'Connell to say that sins against faith are more dangerous than sins against morals is philosophically sound. Actually, I do not think he was speaking of it in this sense, not speaking of the philosophy of the Christian faith where a false metaphysic may emerge as a heresy, dangerous to Christianity; or dangerously in a preliminary way to a man's certainty, but, more simply, and personally, of the danger of hell-fire in sins of wilful doubt. So, in Christopher Manus O'Keeffe's account of one occasion when O'Connell spoke of sins against faith, and sins against morals, he quotes verbatim that such sins are grievous because the sinner is "deprived of those ordinary channels of grace and modes of reconciliation with God of which all stand in need. Even though a Catholic should have sinned more grievously than a person outside the pale of the Church, yet the position of the former"—i.e., the sinner against the moral law—"is in one respect better, namely, that he stands a better chance of obtaining the grace of repentance." This is not at all a reference to the pre-eminence of faith in the cosmology of Christian doctrine, and to the danger to the Christian religion in the denial of faith as (to quote St. John Chrysostom) the only "Source of justice, the head of sanctity, the foundation of religion, without which no one ever deserved the enjoyment of God—no one ever ascended to the summit of perfection." It is a reference to the risk, in the sin against faith, to a man's ultimate salvation.

When O'Connell talked about sins against faith as being worse than sins against morals he was probably thinking, also, of his own case, in retrospect—remembering his early unhappy Deism, in which the words "honest conviction" replaced "faith"; and where the honesty of his mind justified to his soul its rejection of formal religion, but brought it no content. He is indicating that he has meanwhile realized that simple acceptance, not rational conviction, is what is required to hold on to any religious belief. And as he had never ceased to believe in the Deity, had always preserved some religious instinct, the transition for him from "conviction" to "acceptance," i.e., faith announced by the will, was easier than for most agnostics.

In such a matter, the Reformation mind—with which, if I am to be understood, I must confess some, but very little, sympathy on the point—is not intimidated by the idea of faith as the basis of religion; but it is liable to be a little shocked by the lesser stress laid on morality. It does, indeed, often envy the warm and intelligent humanity of what we sometimes loosely call "continental Catholicism," which, to the more unsophisticated churches, seems to succeed in enjoying the "best of both worlds." But while this Reformation mind envies this sophistication and humanity of the liberal-minded Catholic, it rejects it for a humanity of its own: the colder, often nobler, but much more simple-minded humanity of the Renaissance humanists. It tests the supernatural idea in terms of natural action. It takes for its text, "By their fruits ye shall know them," and the more unsophisticated its exponents are, the more rigidly does it seek to cultivate the human virtues rather than cherish supernatural faith. Until, dropping "lower" and "lower" in the hierarchy of the Christian churches, we come, via Puritanism, Quakerism, the curious Jansenist condition of modern Catholic Ireland, Calvinism, the very Low-Church Church of Ireland, down to the (very) Primitive—and, it may be added, stern and good-living—Baptists of the American backwoods. We need not be surprised if, in this declension, there is an ascension of morality. (Thus, to interpolate into a serious discussion a lighter note, I venture, for the sake of illustration, to mention the experience of an Irish Inspector of Taxes who found that the best people to pay their lawful debts to Cæsar were the Quakers, and the worst were the Catholics. It is a light but effective test of the reader's attitude to the general problem to ask whether he has not, in secret, the fullest sympathy with the Catholics here.)

All that concerns us in this digression is that, in terms of biography, we can find no way of testing the sincerity of O'Connell's faith other than this inadequate human test of his behaviour; and the inadequacy of such a test, for so complicated a man, and a

member of so sophisticated a Church as the Catholic Church, is
patent. The only option open to a biographer is the simple alternative of not discussing the matter at all, and though that—
with a man who was, in his period, the personification of Catholicism—is hard to face, it is, more or less, the alternative I
choose. We can look at him only from the outside, state the
problem, and utter an opinion—which has the bare worth of an
opinion and not a shred more—as to his religious sincerity.

It is absolutely beyond question that for a period of years in
London, as a young man, in his formative stage, he was not a
Catholic. In fact, he rejected Christianity, coldly and deliberately. This was first observed by Dr. Arthur Houston in his edition of the Journals. They cover the years between 1795 and
1802, and show that the progress of O'Connell's youthful mind
was from Liberalism to Rationalism; and that it was complete.

Before his reading began to affect him he had already been
turned from a Tory to a Radical by attending the "disgustingly"
iniquitous trials of the Radical English leaders, Hardy, Thelwall,
and Tooke, in '94—that year in which his brother left him alone
in London as a boy of nineteen. The event, records his son, converted him to "popular opinions" and increased his detestation
of "tyranny"; later on he wrote things in his journal that he later
tore out, and the presumption is that they were too violent to
be kept in his possession during the scare year of 1798. Nothing,
however, remains of these pages but the word *Liberty*, and the
syllables, *Revo—*. Thereafter the young man who used to spend
hours discussing Tom Paine with his landlady devoured the popular Radical literature of the day. His reading is informative.
It includes Rousseau's *Confessions*, Godwin's *Political Justice*,
which almost anarchically hoped for a day when men would act
freely and morally without external restraint, and advocated the
abolition of monarchy, punishment, property, and marriage; he
read *The Rights of Women* by Mary Wollstonecraft, who married the Godwin who wanted to abolish marriage; he read

Hume's *Essays;* Voltaire's *Works;* Tom Paine's *Age of Reason,* a Deist essay affirming God, denying the divinity of Christ, and asserting the absolute equality of man; he read the *Recueil Nécessaire,* which is a collection of pieces by various "freethinkers"; and the *Zapata's Questions* of Voltaire, which is directed towards the difficulties presented by the Old and New Testaments, ending with that marvellous piece of cynicism:

Zapata, not having got any answer to his problems, proceeded to teach God simply. He proclaimed to men the Father of men, who rewards, punishes, and pardons. . . . He was gentle, kind, and modest, and he was roasted at Valladolid in the year of grace 1631.

He read all these books, and he read them in delight.

These books are the pertinent items. He read much more: novels, portions of encyclopædias, poetry, sentimental and otherwise, outside his ordinary legal interests; indeed he was both voracious and catholic, and he must have been a very quiet lodger for Mrs. Rigby in Walpole House. In one day and night he read 85 pages of *Ossian,* 108 of Godwin, and 234 of Pindar's *Odes!*

That he read all these tendentious works with approval is beyond question. Far from disagreeing, for instance, with the *Age of Reason,* which denied the divinity of Christ, he says:

In treating of the Christian system he is clear and concise. He has presented many things to my sight in a point of view in which I never beheld them before. . . . It has put the foundation of the religious question of the Christians in a point of view in which a judgment is easily formed on its solidity. I have now no doubts on this head. I may be mistaken. But I am not wilfully mistaken if the expression has any meaning. My mistakes I refer to the wisdom of that Being who is wise by excellence. To the God of Nature do I turn my heart; to the meditation of His works do I turn my thoughts. In Him do I find my soul saturated. He will not, Justice tells me, punish me for a darkness, if such it be, that cannot be removed; He will not punish for the unbiased conviction of the soul. To affirm the contrary would, in my opinion, be to calumniate.

That might conceivably be read as an affirmation of beliefs contrary to Godwin's, if we did not recognize the characteristic jargon of the eighteenth-century Deists—"Justice tells me," "God of Nature," and below, "First Cause," "Great Spirit"—and have other unmistakable admissions. Having finished Paine, and still devouring Godwin and Gibbon, he continues to examine his soul; not at all happy about it, he almost forces himself to keep his ground as a Deist:

The prejudices of childhood and youth at times frighten and shake the firmness of my soul. These fears, these doubts, perhaps imply a libel on the First Cause, the Great Spirit who created the planetary systems that roll around. It is impossible that He, whose justice is perfect, should punish with eternal torments the belief that is founded on conviction. It appears impossible because the conviction of the mind does not depend on us. We cannot prevent, we cannot change, the beliefs that our souls form on the perception of the senses. Again, those perceptions are not in our power. We receive impressions from the surrounding objects notwithstanding all our efforts to the contrary. It would in fact be as absurd and criminal to say that the Great Spirit would punish me for saying that it is now noon, as to affirm that He would inflict tortures for not believing another proposition, the belief of which is equally impossible.

It is evident that when he said, so long after, nearly twenty years after, that sins against faith were worse than sins against morals, he was not speaking of sins against the Catholic faith, but against any faith formed on personal conviction, whatever faith that might be. It was a position which made it easy for him, in his political career, to attract many non-Catholics by the liberality of his thought, as when he rejected the intransigent and even bellicose zealot Catholic, Dr. Drumgoole, who wanted a warfare against Protestantism, by saying, in 1813, that "any man who worships the Deity in the form which his unbiased conscience prescribes is worthy of respect."

So he cries when he has left London and is living in Dublin:

O Eternal Being, Thou seest the purity of my heart, the sincerity of my promises. Should I appear before Your august tribunal after having performed them, shall I not be entitled to call for my reward? Will the omission of a superstitious action, will the disbelief in an unreasonable dogma, that day rise in judgment against me?

There can be no reasonable interpretation of these comments on such books other than that he agreed entirely with them. "This work has given me a great deal of pleasure," he says of Tom Paine. Of Godwin, "I admire this work more, beyond comparison more, than any I ever met with." He began to translate *Zapata*, surely not from aversion? He makes up his mind about the rights of women (and *The Rights of Women*) by saying that Godwin has proved that government to be best which laid fewest restraints on private judgment. His general remarks on Christianity are not complimentary.

Whether he attended carefully, even when in Ireland, at this time to his own religious duties we cannot say, but I doubt it. The phrase "omission of a superstitious action" is suggestive. Once only he mentions going to Mass, never while in England; he gets up at an easy hour on at least some Sundays; twice he is drunk on Sundays—once, and that in Dublin, where one might expect him to be more restrained, to the point of a nauseating debauch (his own words); his Sunday reading is as secular as on any week-day. One sincerely hopes he did *not* conform outwardly, there is enough of involution in his conscience as it is. And once more, when one thinks, in disgust, of the whole compulsion towards outward conformity, in those years of the Penal Code—such as when O'Connell's father is married in a Protestant church, or when Tom Moore is entered at Trinity College as a Protestant—one feels this later outward conformity on the other side, so often just as hypocritical, was, of all things, the worst inheritance of an uncivilized and uncivilizing government.

Ultimately O'Connell found some kind of *modus vivendi* as between his private and his public conscience. When political and religious beliefs began to go hand in hand, he became in practice piously Catholic, vociferously Catholic, while evidently retaining at bottom a powerful reservation of independence, some smothered scepticism, the widest tolerance of other re-ligions, and great elasticity in action. That has become (surely under his influence?) the normal condition of most Irishmen, and a condition utterly exasperating to all foreign observers. Yet some such technique of living in a state of repressed scep-ticism under a shell of apparent acquiescence was inevitable to a race that had learned from brutal experience that frankness was best prefaced by a snail's feeler for danger? Crude as it was, it took a hundred years to perfect that technique, and it will take a hundred years more before it disappears entirely; indeed, even yet, frankness is in most Irishmen no more than that wavering tentacle, swiftly retractile beneath the defensive hide of outer conformity. It is part of the greatness of O'Connell that he dis-carded that method, not wholly, but to an astonishing degree; he was one of the first Irishmen who refused to cower. If it was inevitable that the duality should still persist, in him it at least persisted shamelessly and openly—in the *double entendre,* the mental reservation, the limiting clause, the disingenuous qualifi-cation and proviso, all as explicit to everybody but a fool as the suave and evasive clichés of the British diplomat. All that is pat-ent in his political behaviour. I find it impossible to credit that the same mind would not employ the same methods in matters religious. However complex a man may be, he has only one brain to hold his complexities, and that brain infects itself.

The man is, early on, only too well aware of the power of mass opinion, and the danger of running counter to it openly. Of organized religions, including Christianity, he says:

Oh, Religion, how much has mankind suffered from thee. It was thou who wouldst have caused the banishment, if not the death, of Anaxagoras, because he believed in one intelligent Supreme Being. But what shalt thou return for the life of Socrates, of the first of philosophers? Christianity has had her millions of victims. . . . Could not men be moral without such assistance? We are not permitted to inquire. . . .

Those who do not pay the tribute of coincidence to our decisions become our most hated foes. We would tear them, we would devour them. Of all the animals that infest this wretched planet of ours, that species of monkey called man is certainly the most absurd and unaccountable.

On top of all that, scores of Rousseauistic sentiments might be culled, here and from his later speeches and writings, to prove him in complete agreement with the revolutionary ideas of Wolfe Tone—also a Deist, a Democrat, a Radical, and a lover of the Catholic Irish. While Tone, in France and Holland, was putting those ideas into practice, O'Connell, the young lawyer, differed with him only as to the method; it is the difference between the daring soldier and the far-seeing lawyer, between the man of swift action and the man of wider, more involved and inclusive thought.

We need not, therefore, be too impressed by O'Connell's later orthodoxy. He may have deceived himself; he certainly impressed others. Underneath it all was the effect of these decisions of his formative years, the only years in which his mind was free of the persuasion of opportunism. We need not, for all that, call him a hypocrite. It is enough to say that he was, all his life long, as open as a shellfish, that he twisted and dodged, canted and recanted, endlessly, and that he always kept to one guiding idea —the creation of some kind of condition or image that would liberate his people from such a necessity. But who trusted him completely trusted a chameleon. We need not. He was a Tammany lawyer and a great patriot. Any man who would dare emulate him must also have some mighty image to keep him from being lost in his own labyrinth.

8

So far the matter is fairly straightforward; but if we should come to ask how soon, precisely, O'Connell recovered his lost faith, what we then try to do, really, is to tie down the hovering ghost of a secret human conscience without any evidence—for the diary, which could alone convince us, has ceased at 1802. The thing is not less hazardous and complicated and delicate.

Outwardly, indeed, we see him becoming more and more closely associated with the cause of political Catholicism, and we must certainly feel it impossible to conceive that anybody but a double-dealing scoundrel could, inwardly, have persisted in his Deism after becoming the personification of militant Catholicism in Europe. Its triumph in Ireland came in 1829, so that we may, without risk, put the date *ad quem*, in this matter of his conversion, at 1820. Somewhere, then, between 1802, when he was twenty-seven, and 1820, when he was forty-five, he reverts to his original position with whatever residue from the conflict adhering to him. I do not think it possible to be much more precise.

For while he may not, once involved in politics, have dared to admit his earlier doubts, even to himself, until he could reject them, that is a very different thing from ceasing to be influenced by them. All it really means is that he *was* influenced by them until he definitely, and overtly, and explicitly faced and foundered them; and we have, unfortunately, not a shred of evidence, at the moment, as to his ever having had such a stand-up fight with himself. All we know is that he weaned himself gradually from his Deism. The speed and method of the process we do not know.

The heart of man is not a simple machine in these matters; and this man was the least simply constructed of all Irishmen known to history. The conscience is not a bell that rings the true answer to even the most earnest questionings (we do well to remember, rather, that lovely comparison of Newman's between the conscience and a ghost that comes and goes); and less likely was this man's ghost to answer the half-questionings that his busy and hard-worked mind would have scarcely had the time, let alone the wish, to formulate for many years after 1802. For he was not now an idle, dispersed reader as he was in his more leisurely student days. The years 1797 and 1798 were "misspent"; a glance at his fee-book and diary shows how hard he worked after that; his very last entry in the diary, June 1802, says that he was in bed at half-ten, up at seven, and in court the greater part of the day. By 1804 he has doubled his income of 1802, and by 1809 it is eight times what it was seven years before.

We all know, on the contrary, how men can, and do, live for years in the most equivocal condition of mind about the most vital subjects, the most personal subjects, whether it be an unhappy marriage, a disappointing son, an unfaithful friend, or a gnawing unease about religion. On that last, the proud of heart can crush down the final act of submission for years; the meek can remain palpitating so timidly that emergent decision can be shattered by the lightest footfall. We do not have to pretend to any particular wisdom to know this; all we have to do is to look into our own hearts to see the truth of it. O'Connell was both proud and disingenuous. The last word to apply to him is "candid"; and we must admit that few men possessed and controlled a more tortuous mind. If we hesitate over this, all we have to do is to recall the words of John Mitchel, a man who was no prig, but who knew his O'Connell—"Mean old man . . . lying tongue . . . smile of treachery . . . heart of unfathomable fraud . . ."—and (while making every allowance for a political opponent's personal dislikes) acknowledge that O'Connell was a man capable, at least, of many mental reservations about everything, including religion.

Side by side with this we may recall the candid confessions of men like Mauriac, the Catholic novelist, for years obedient in word, but not in will; or re-read the life of Racine; or the life of even Augustine, Catholic after his conversion, in word and in will, but for a long time Platonist in mind. Such lives reveal to us that there is in the human heart a terrifying power to resist an inevitable conclusion; and more, the power to deceive itself into thinking it has made a decision when, in truth, it has again escaped with a simulacrum.

It may be said that there is a tradition that O'Connell was a fervent believer long before 1820. There is also a tradition that he was sexually promiscuous; yet we have no reason (as I will show) to believe that bit of folk-lore. Why should we be so simple as to conclude, either, that this serpentining Kerryman, full of self-pride, arrogant as the devil in his intellect, founded in his most impressionable years on a Rationalist position, gave ample proof of a wholehearted conversion merely by making statements in public about the rights of his people to practise their religion? Indeed, that was the correct position for a Rationalist to take up, and he consistently and emphatically adopted it all his life long in relation to every religion that came his way. His *forte* was tolerance.

As a matter of fact, the student of his public career will read many pages of his collected speeches before coming on anything which, though all is in defence of the Catholics, confesses him as personally a Catholic. While his diary goes on into 1802, without any rejection in its later pages of the opinions in the earlier, he is apologizing in January 1800 for "the necessity of meeting as Catholics." But always, after that, he refers to "the" Catholics. It is never "we" Catholics. "The Catholics had been insulted. . . . The administration were personal enemies of the Catholic cause." In 1811 he does say, amid many such impersonal references, that "ignorance of our situation" is what prevents the emancipation of the Catholics. In 1812, under the influence of his objection to the Veto on the appointment of ecclesiastics (a wholly political objection), he speaks of his own motives.

They are disinterested and pure—I trust they are more. My object in the attainment of emancipation is in nothing personal, save in the feelings which parental love inspires and gratifies. I am, I trust, actuated by that sense of Christianity which teaches us that the first duty of our religion is benevolence and universal charity; I am, I know, actuated by the determination to rescue our common country from the weakness, the insecurity, which dissension and religious animosity produce and tend to perpetuate, etc.

The quality of these speeches, hitherto generalized, from 1800 to 1812, in relation to Catholicism, becomes more particular as we proceed with the Veto controversy, and by the end of 1813 we find him, for the first time, as far as I have observed, declaring himself a Catholic. That may be read in his passionate reply to Richard Lalor Sheil in the first volume of his *Collected Speeches* (page 349). It is the first, even of his public speeches, which is pertinent enough to be of interest. He is then two years short of forty. It is the earliest date for which there is any evidence as to his private opinions after the period of the diary.

O'Connell's public utterances, then, with regard to religion need not be taken too ingenuously for, certainly, eleven years, perhaps more, after 1802. They are not evidence, in so far as evidence is merely a series of minor facts from which we induce a major fact; and the public utterances of politicians are hardly facts. Even this public association with Catholicism was dangerous to his private conscience, since it was essential to his fight for his people that he should at all times be warmly tolerant, reassuringly pliant; and both of these he always took care to appear, and both of them, as a matter of history, he always was. On the other hand, supposing he did, in excess of a mere public identification with Catholicism, revert quickly and completely to Catholicism in his heart and conscience, he was—it is only

fair to say—in an even stronger position. Provided he was
grounded with sufficient subtlety in the theological distinctions
of his faith he could make as many apparently "broad-minded"
speeches as he liked.

O'Keeffe's way of referring to O'Connell around 1813 is in-
terestingly suggestive of what he was up to then. He says, writing (in 1866) while men were alive who knew O'Connell well:

> The selection of O'Connell by the bishops, in 1813, to present
> their lordships' address to the Catholic Board, proves that his conduct
> had merited their confidence, and evinces that they appreciated the
> sincerity of his religious professions. At that time the paschal duty
> was generally neglected by the Irish gentry. "You did not see more,"
> said O'Connell, "than perhaps twenty male communicants in the
> year." Owing to this general negligence, he himself was negligent;
> but his staunch sincerity, his firm devotedness to the faith was be-
> yond the shadow of doubt. The religious opinions of O'Connell *at
> this time* were entirely at variance with those of Pope, who says:
>
> > "For modes of faith let graceless zealots fight—
> > His can't be wrong whose life is in the right."

(Which, incidentally, tends to jerk us back to that controversial
problem of how far faith can be a kind of charitable umbrella
for morals; a general matter outside our immediate concern.)

Public utterance and tradition alike are thus of not more than
a qualified use. Of the two, tradition is the more fallible; for it is
impure, filtered by partisans on both sides. Unless he were un-
characteristically indiscreet in his private conversation his private beliefs need not, in any case, have become the property of
his acquaintances. There can, in the same way, be nobody of any
percipience today who cannot readily think of a dozen acquaintances whose religious opinions must seem in every way conventional to those whose acquaintances they are not; but their religious opinions, to us their acquaintances, are a closed book.
Give such men place, fame, their memories the protection of
national admiration, and how absolutely positive this so-called

"tradition" would be about their religious ideas fifty years after their death! In O'Connell's case we know so little about his intimate circle that it is extremely doubtful if he had any such thing. As I have said, at the very beginning of this book, he was a sufficiently lonely child; and he was an unusually lonely man.

So, if we wish to pursue the subject further, we come back to the point where no test is left but our own reactions to this lonely man's general code of behaviour, and what we can image for ourselves of his mentality. These two things are of so debatable and equivocal a nature, that the more we think about them the more absurd does it become to try to close further that gap of years between the time when he was a blatant Deist and the time when he cannot be thought of as other than a Catholic.

As to code and mentality, the notion we may form depends, as it always does, on an accumulation of detail—which may, or may not, emerge from the *full* course of this biography; for, with his mentality once fixed, any one part of his life will throw its illumination on any other. On the one hand, it all filters down to his persistent duplicity, whether as lawyer, politician, or committee-man, ranging from clever casuistry to plain fraud; as when he gets jobs by the score for his associates—altogether commendable in a country where such things were the mark of political triumph or political slavery—but tells Sharman Crawford that he never did get a single job for anyone (page 311); or as when he tells Fitzpatrick how to take what any normal man would call a false oath without incurring the guilt of perjury (page 284). On the other hand, both code and mentality are governed by the conditions that created them, and they have to be thought of in relation to the horrible circumstances in which he worked. For, ultimately, such things become entirely a matter of conscience, which is not a thing that moves in a vacuum.

I should not be surprised if O'Connell had a subtle conscience. O'Keeffe, recording that conversation with a Protestant friend

who said that sins against morals were worse than sins against
faith, quotes O'Connell as saying, in the course of the discussion:

Nothing short of a thorough and perfect sincerity, and moreover
a cautious sincerity, can acquit the holder of erroneous faith from
the guilt of heresy. Of course (added O'Connell) every person thus
thoroughly and cautiously sincere is free from heretical guilt.

When I first read this I jumped to the conclusion, apparently
rashly, that he was giving himself away, again, as a Deist; that he
was speaking on the same plane as the frankly Deist entry in the
diary, which reads:

It is impossible that He, whose justice is perfect, should punish
with eternal torments the belief that is founded on conviction. . . .

But a Catholic friend, more versed in the distinctions of theology, pointed out to me that the first statement was perfectly
sound Catholic doctrine. Any man, he explained, might main-
tain, through error, a *formal* heresy without incurring the *guilt*
of heresy; he might even proclaim heresy without being a here-
tic. If this is so, we may be dealing with an O'Connell as subtly
founded in the dialectic of Catholicism as we could expect from
a man of his resilient intellect and Jesuit education. And in all
that may hereafter emerge to suggest mere hypocrisy or ambiguity, we may see rather the keenness of a highly trained dialec-
tician. Another of O'Keeffe's stories gives us a hint that O'Connell had something of this type of mind. He says:

The conversation then turned on the utter incompetence of private judgment to retain a man in the path of faith—to preserve a
Christian's belief in the doctrine of the Trinity.
"The Socinians," observed his friend, "allege that if the Trinitar-
ian doctrine be true, it is very strange that the word *Trinity* does
not once occur in the whole Bible."
"Oh, as to that," said O'Connell, "if the word Trinity were found
in every page of the Bible, Socinian Protestants would not believe in
the doctrine one whit more than they do at the present moment.
They might get rid of it on the ordinary Protestant principles of

interpretation. They might deal with it as they do with the real presence in the Eucharist. They might say that the word Trinity did not really mean a Trinity at all—that it only meant something that was figuratively called a Trinity!"

This method of interpretation was exactly the method O'Connell himself employed in dealing with the law.

To sum up: what position have we arrived at? Probably as many positions as there are types of readers. The one, sarcastic and frigidly moral, will say that faith covered more than a multitude of sins for O'Connell, that it was quite a large and comfortable moral umbrella. Another, even more strict and stern, rather like our modern Irish Catholic with his curiously untraditional Puritanism about morality—too ascetic and humourless for the Irish nature—may dismiss him, at all periods, and certainly at this, for a bad Catholic, or even as a man who was not a Catholic at all. That is the common judgment passed by such folk today on anybody who shows any unusual shades or variations or complexities in character or thought. Or a third reader, blunt and straightforward as that type of Englishman who prizes "character" above everything else, will call him a hypocrite and have done with it. But surely the sensible thing to do is to say that it is all no concern of ours; to take up a more human, a more Irish, a more O'Connellish, and indeed a more normal Catholic position, and be content not to be too literal-minded? We can then say that he adopted the title of Catholic even before he had discarded the title of Deist—that he interpreted that title according to his conscience at all times—that he gradually, however slowly, or swiftly, came into line with what the term means to those whose more simple, artless, and economical spiritual lives render explicit obedience easy in all things.

Must we have a moral judgment? With so little to go on? Is it not enough that the Catholic religion is one of fine distinctions, sensitive to the complexity of human nature, charitable to human frailty, so that the most sophisticated and the most ingenuous find room within it, and that O'Connell would not have been human if he did not avail himself of this sophistication to the limit, stretching it like an elastic band until its fineness becomes a wonder—just as does every politician, statesman, and business man under the sun with his particular creed? It was, at any rate, the saving grace of O'Connell that he did it all in times so dreadful, for so good a cause, that one not only forgives him a great deal more that one might to lesser men in other times, but wonders at his restraint; besides, he did it all with such a comical, winking, nudging, rascally good-humour that—to steal the famous phrase—what rascality he allowed himself loses half its harm by losing all its grossness.

That is the O'Connell to whom a righteous colleague said furiously, after an acquittal in the courts: "Do you realize you have freed a wretch unfit to live?" Dan swept up his papers with a merry laugh and cried: "The poor wretch was more unfit to die!" That was the O'Connell who was adored by his wife, who adored his children, who had not an intimate in the world, but was loved by the crowds in the street as if he were the son of each individual one of them.

There is one last thing on which every cultivated person may side with O'Connell. He did a great thing for the emergent Ireland if he established, at whatever cost, his right to his own conscience. Nor does it matter here in what way he established it, or in what way he lived by it—whether it was a life of recompense by subterfuge defended in casuistry, or a life of recompense by evasion defended in subtlety, or a life of strict continence which needed no defence. In whatever way he brought tolerance into Irish life, he kept the religion of the simple democracy he was fashioning from consolidating, for forty years, into any form of bitter Low-Churchism. It was one of the tragedies of his career, and of the history of Irish democracy, that in the end he had to yield a good deal of his ground—beaten down by obscurantists like Archbishop MacHale, whose nationalism and fervour were unsweetened by any form of liberality, whose attitude to the "private lives" of his flock would probably have been that they had no right to such a luxury, at the same time that, to the day of his death, he would not permit a National School in his diocese where they might have educated themselves into the right to possess consciences of their own. In the end—or, no! in our time—it is the obscurantist type that has won out. "Morality" has won. *What*, it is not for me to say. I suspect —a pinch of incense.

9

WHATEVER about his religious difficulties, the one guiding idea of Irish liberty harmonizes all his lesser contradictions. He wrote in his diary:

I believe it was Johnson who said that he did not love the man who was jealous for nothing.

The sentiment is quite in unison with my own opinion. Give me the man whose generous mind is now inflamed with an ardent enthusiasm, now is chilled with causeless apprehensions. I mean not the apprehension for self, which degrades man, but the apprehension that arises from excess of desire and anxiety for success. The man who conceives strongly is the man of genius. He is the friend and the patriot.

That powerful conception is always in O'Connell. He has an accurate idea of his own force and power, and he constantly directs it, in these diaries, towards his fated purpose in life. "I would pursue the good of my country" is the theme of several entries. Penniless, and twenty-two, and at a time long before any Catholic could dream of entering Parliament—thirty years before—he writes, with amazing arrogance:

I have been thinking this day of the plan to be pursued when I come into Parliament. If to distinguish myself was to be the object of my exertions, that would be best done by becoming a violent oppositionist. But as it will be my chief study to serve my country, moderation will be a proper instrument for that purpose. Moderation is the character of genuine patriotism, that patriotism which seeks for the happiness of mankind.

To him liberty was "less a principle than a passion." To him, also, "patriotism . . . is a principle." Principle and passion drove him on like a storm through life.

A young man's fight with himself is never simple. So O'Connell found, and he turned on himself in hardness and discipline. All through his diaries (1795–1802) he keeps nagging at himself for lying abed late. By the end of that period he is getting up at seven. Later on, he might be seen of mornings through the fog on his windows in Merrion Square, standing at his desk at 5 a.m. The drunkenness stopped, too, firmly and finally. When his journals end he is edging into the ring, for the first time really alone with himself, facing the obstacles that are to disclose his real self.

In every sense he is alone. His brother Moss is dead; his grandmother Máire Duv is dead; his father dies a few years after; his brothers and sisters are engaged in their own struggles; only old Hunting Cap remains to watch his bantam fight his way to fame. It is that lonely fight that is most interesting, and all the feints and misses of that fight. He passes through Lincoln's Inn, and Gray's Inn, London, and the King's Inn, Dublin—but that thousands have done. He carouses a little when there is money up from Kerry, reads widely, spending the live-long day in the library at Eustace Street, converses with his betters—but these again are the commonplace habits of every law student. It is the contradictions that bring him home to us; as when he joins the Lawyers' Artillery Corps as a Volunteer of 1782, in the year 1798, vain as a boy in his new uniform, after he had been for a space a United Irishman, and was reported by the Sham Squire, Higgins, a government spy, as "the most abominable and bloodthirsty Republican I ever heard"; or as when he wishes, one day, that he could "get entirely rid of all propensity to falsehood," and resolves the next to "avoid disclosing my political opinions as frequently as I do"; or as when he admits to vanity and longs for virtue, and continues vain and is not virtuous. But were there no such oppositions there would be no combustion; there would be no wisdom without that fight between his inner self and his outer self, no life-cleverness to teach him how to live and conquer in a country where all such as he were treated naturally as beggars.

In time it is all put under control, all except, perhaps, the vanity which made him a leader with many agents but no colleagues, and left him to the end at the mercy of himself, having to fight to the very end for his Unity of Being with the complexities of character he inherited from the conditions that made them.

That May of 1798, when he was called to the Bar—it was the day they arrested Lord Edward Fitzgerald—he had, finally, a powerful and healthy body. He was handsome and eager. He had curly hair and a merry eye. He might, to all appearances, have been just any young lawyer starting his career when, on the day after, he took his first guinea. Yet within ten years he was earning thousands; within twenty he was known all over Europe and he led millions. He did it by hardening his young idealism in one of the filthiest cock-pits known to man—the Irish Bar before and after the Union.

III : THE BAR AND POLITICS

1798–1813

I

IT was a stirring summer for Dublin. The Government agents, after dogging Lord Edward for months, had suddenly run him to earth in Thomas Street, helped by a spy—a young Catholic lawyer whom O'Connell must have often seen and perhaps talked with about politics. Five days later, when O'Connell was drawing up a declaration on a promissory note, and adding another cipher to his fee-book, he would have heard the news that fighting had broken out in Enniscorthy, down in Wexford. Oulart and Three Rocks followed, and men knew by then that the '98 Rising had begun. Next came news of Wexford and New Ross; Kildare was up; there was fighting, across the mountains, in Carlow; that horrible business of the burning of hundreds of Protestants in the barn of Scullabogue would have spread like a smoke in wind. The carts came trundling into Dublin piled with rebel dead, to be emptied out in heaps in the Castle yard. Every night the lamps in the city went out, at midnight, one by one.

General Lake readily suppressed the flicker in the north, but Dublin was nervous, forced everyone indoors from 9 p.m. to 5 a.m., and called out its reserves. As a member of the Lawyers' Yeomanry Corps, O'Connell found himself under arms on one of the Canal bridges to enforce that curfew order. He was fortunate to be in Dublin, with a kind of Black-and-Tan atmosphere spreading over the countryside, where, in the words of Abercrombie, the English Commander-in-Chief, "every crime, every cruelty, that could be committed by Cossacks or Calmucks" was being perpetrated by the "licentious" military—the adjective being, again, Abercrombie's. This sense of fear, of personal danger, grew so great that O'Connell—though he could not know that his name was, thanks to Higgins, in the secret files of the Castle—made himself scarce.

With eighteen others he went aboard a potato-boat at the Dublin quays—the only means of transport since the Rebellion had broken out—and sailed for Cork, thence by road to the quiet sands of Kerry. The same week Wolfe Tone, hearing what was going on in Ireland, was tearing to Paris to take part in whatever should be planning there.

Dan squandered the summer at Darrynane. Of the year before he had written down, "I misspent my time"; now again, "It is a year which has been wretchedly misspent." He was ill; he caught a chill while hunting hares and nearly died of it that autumn, and when he came back to town in the winter he returned to the dirty dregs of the excitement. He heard tell of the trials and executions; three hundred men in jail; eighty banished by Act of Parliament; about three hundred gone to serve the King of Prussia—yet another foreign Brigade, Limerick repeating itself on a small scale; another two hundred and fifty gone as convicts to Botany Bay—a poor end to the first flicker of spirit out of Ireland since 1691. He was in town in time to hear of Tone's death, John Philpot Curran fighting for him to the last; to taste the dishwater of politics when the implacable Earl of Clare set Duigenan to fling mud at Grattan; to hear and be appalled at the damage done by the Rebellion, some said up to a million pounds, and to pick up in a far more lively way than we can imagine all the street-corner and club-fire tales that alone can make an event like '98 seem real and immediate—personal notes still personal in Carlow, and Kildare, and Wexford, or dramatic news-snippets that linger in the memory, like the rumour that Irish bacon would not sell in the Dublin shops, because people said the pigs had fed on dead men. Finally, he began to hear again the old talk about a projected legislative Union between Ireland and Great Britain. The Dublin Parliament may not mean as much to us as it did to him (and still does to many of the fine old school of Irish patriots); but that even the Dublin Parliament should be abolished was the last blow to his country.

Sick at heart had been his words for himself that January; sick at heart are his words as the year closes, that misspent first year of his career. He records it on 31st December, with a sore head and a sick belly from a drunk the night before, full of youthful melancholy, thinking of poor dead Moss, and then, two days later, he is confessing again that all his good resolves are in vain, that he is losing all delicacy of feeling; two days more pass and he writes that he cannot correct his sluggish habits. . . .

Fortunately he has to earn his living. And as it lifted us somewhat out of the awful squalor of the cabin-life to enter Darrynane with him, it lifts us from the despair and ruck of the Rebellion to go with him on circuit. Here, fifteen years or so before Dickens saw the tail-end of it vanish before the effects of Industrialism, is the life of the inns and coaches, duellists and highwaymen, of carousing and gambling, in full swing. Twenty years afterwards, O'Connell, and O'Connell's contemporaries—such as O'Neill Daunt—used to talk fondly about that life, and romantic writers like Gerald Griffin "wrote it up" colourfully. It had a real colour, however, as its raconteurs often endowed it with a false one. For if the inns were often dirty, and the roads always foul, and highwaymen no more pleasant than smash-and-grab raiders of today, there were two actualities that packed a certain electricity into the air. One was that the general happy-go-lucky light-heartedness of the times encouraged an expansive way of living—and of dying; personality had room, room even to swell into monstrous idiosyncrasies; the "character" made his appearance and learned how to exploit his own drama. The other actuality of the times was that lawlessness and danger and insecurity extroverted men. There was a premium on action and the active life. The old adventurous world of the eighteenth century, that world which was at the centre of the universe, was passing away in England, but it was not yet gone in Ireland; for if it is evident from the slightly sardonic comments of Miss Austen and Dr. Sterne that the mind was being jerked into awareness elsewhere, there was no Austen or Sterne in Ireland, and no need for them. The drama of life was protected. Between Anglo-Irish playboyism, then, and Anglo-Irish zest for life, one had something like a play where actors and audience were one. But the whole thing was nevertheless real—its desperate reality constantly emphasized by the misery of the nation. It would have been a thoughtless and utterly decadent period if that rabble of beggars were not all the time whipping it into an *Irish* awareness by their groaning and growling in the distance.

That groaning and growling cuts across all temptations to dally with the duellists and boozers. Things like those vast competitions in drinking, with the shoes removed and the empty bottles carefully strewn in bits on the hall and up the stairs, the decanters made specially with rounded bottoms so that they could never be set down, and the wine-glasses with broken stems, the tables upholstered underneath to protect the heads of the stupefied, and the doors locked until the last man, perhaps after two days' sousing, rising to open it, would survey the battlefield behind him—all that seems to belong to a world that has little to do with O'Connell or with Ireland, as long as our ears are open to that distant murmur from the massing helots. The duelling—which was as much part of any lawyer's training as his *Coke on Littleton*, so that a man had two prices for his briefs,

a "fighting price" and an ordinary barrister's price—sounds like
play-acting with death when a whole race is dying. Yet it is all
there, with the seductions and the abductions, and the wild gambling and the rest of the irresponsible life of the upper classes,
and we must take note of it. The only sensible note to take of it,
however, is to consider it all—duelling, gambling, seductions and
abductions and carousals, men making sudden fortunes and men
losing them, peers living like paupers and peers living like swin-
dlers, the wealthy battening on the poor and the poor being
hanged for trivial offences—as the sign of the insecurity of life
natural to a country that had never been integrated by wise
government, refusing to be wisely aware (like Miss Austen or
Dr. Sterne) because it had always—*as a country*—been denied
responsibility. For a country it was not: it was a shambles of exploitation.

O'Connell was conscious of that sense of insecurity. He wrote
in his diary that, as things were, it seemed as if he never might
proceed with his work at the bar. With the filthy business of
Union-mongering in everybody's mind it became a period of
scramble for the upper classes—but let us never forget the honourable exceptions—and fresh fear among the lower. There is
barter on every side, and nobody knows what to expect in the
way of political change. All personal relationships are disturbed
by the disclosure of traitors and the knowledge of the presence
of spies. In that confused atmosphere of suspicion Grattan could
not walk the streets after '98. In confusion of mind some of the
Catholic archbishops and bishops, craven from the period of the
Penal Laws, conspired with Castlereagh in '99 to sell the Irish
Parliament and accept a Government Veto on their own appointment. Many Catholics, like O'Connell's own uncle, were
supporting the Union in public or in private. All of them were
gambling in futures.

Clearly a good time for a young man to work hard and forget

it all. The hardness of the life gritted him—the roads, the distances. His first circuit in '99 illustrates how he settled to it. He left Carhen, in Kerry, at dawn; by the afternoon he was up on the Shannon at Tarbert, resting his horse. Outside Listowel he had met a kinsman who said, when he heard O'Connell was bound for Tarbert: "Why so late?" thinking he had started from Tralee, which is forty miles on the Tarbert side of Carhen. On hearing that the gallop had begun away down in the Kerry wilds, all he could say was: "You'll do, young man, you'll do." Yet Dan went to a ball at Tarbert that evening, stayed up till 2.30 a.m., rose at 8.30 a.m., and was in the Limerick courts that afternoon.

He got his first cross-examination behind him on his return to Tralee. It was in every way a type of his future methods. "I did not," he said, "as I have seen fifty young counsel do, yield the examination to my senior." Which was the etiquette of the bar. "I thought it due to myself to make the attempt, hit or miss and"—the unfailing self-esteem—"I cross-examined him right well." The cross-examination was in Irish, a language capable of useful ambiguity to astute witnesses; this one said he was not drunk, he had merely taken his share of a pint of whisky. "*Mo chuid*," was doubtless the word, as used loosely in Irish. "I suppose," teased Dan, "your 'share' means all except the pewter?"— and the witness had to smile and admit it. After the assizes, Jerry Keller, the "Father of the Munster Bar," also said: "You'll do, young man, you'll do." Keller had the wit to see that a young lawyer who was astute enough to get inside a witness's mind in a small thing would do it also in a big thing, and the easy manner that could please even a discomfited witness would go far to please a judge and jury. Even the touch of boldness in "grabbing" the cross-examination spoke for the spirit of the young man.

2

THAT astuteness, ingratiating manner, and boldness O'Connell developed to the limit. The boldness increased until it pervaded his entire being. *Mobiliate viget* became Sheil's word for him— the man thrives by activity. It was soon activity of the most violent kind. In fact his manners and his methods achieved a magnificence from the ardour of almost brute spirit with which he forced them both on the courts. But the courts themselves were of a piece, filled by time-servers who regarded him and his like as, in the words of the Earl of Clare, "the scum of the earth." Violence was thrust on him. Baron McClelland once publicly rebuked him for interfering in a case where he held no brief. "It was not in this way I behaved," said the Baron, "when I was at the bar." "No," flung back the young man, "but when you were at the bar I never took you for a model, and now that you are on the bench I am not going to submit to your dictation." Another day, in Cork, he was prevented by the bench from entering certain evidence; in the morning the court relented. Impatiently O'Connell burst out with: "Had your lordship known as much law yesterday as you do today you would have spared me a vast amount of time and trouble, and my client a considerable amount of injury. Crier! Call up the witnesses!" It took time before he arrived at that degree of assertiveness. It was always in his nature; self-confidence, necessity, and success were all that was required to bring it out.

He cannot have had any idea, however, when he was studying law in London and Dublin as to the kind of legal Bedlam he would have to face, and he presumably did no more than adapt himself to it as he found it. It was one of the basest periods of the Irish bar, from the point of view of corruption, for the bench was filled with inefficient men who had, as often as not, bought their way to preferment. O'Neill Daunt listed nine judges who had risen to the bench by political double-dealing.

O'Connell mentions several more. It was a bad time above all for Catholic barristers, who were excluded from the inner bar until 1829 and suffered from the common opinion as to the inferior talents of all Roman Catholics. The result was a court that was always unpredictable and often not far removed from a bear-garden.

There was old Judge Daly who had never in his life held a dozen briefs but became prime-serjeant for his services at the time of the Union; the very juniors used to twit his ignorance to his face. "Are you a judge in the value of land?" he asked a witness. "Have you any experience of it?" "Why, my lord," interposed the defending attorney, staring hard at the ink-pot, "did you ever know a judge without experience?"

There was old Day, who to the age of ninety-eight, as O'Connell said, "preserved his intellect unimpaired—(such as it is)." At a Cork assizes he told O'Connell there could not be another speech, "because the fact is, Mr. O'Connell, I am always of opinion with the last speaker." The method of elevation to the bench was well put by Keller to the fat, pompous Mayne on the first day of his arrival in the courts. "Congratulations," said Keller. "Some are floated into port by their gravity, and some, like myself, are sunk by their levity."

The cream of these curious creatures who administered the law must have been John Toler—Lord Norbury—the Hanging Judge whom the gravediggers honoured by a grave of twice the normal depth, "so that he should have rope enough." This cruel buffoon, pitiless to the law-breaker, indifferent to such considertions as provocation (which in such a time should have been primary considerations), would mingle with his remarks constant jokes, original or borrowed from the penny jest-books. He would become more and more quotatory as he warmed to a case, standing up and puffing aside his robes, maybe flinging off his wig, pouring out the most outlandish jumble of disconnected material, anecdotes of his early life, snatches from Milton and

Shakespeare, more or less to the point but always finely delivered, sarcasm against the defence, urging opposing counsel to a battle-royal of sophistries, assertions, and contradictions, until the consequent noise would swell Norbury's roars to bellowings, the court become a perfect din, and the order of the case collapse into inextricable confusion at which the jury would stare gob-open. It was only then that his lordship would really begin to enjoy himself. His charge to the jury was said to be invariably in the nature of a direction against his chosen victim—generally the defendant, for Norbury, for some reason, tended to lean towards all plaintiffs.

As he rolled and gestured and chuckled, and hurried on from what could be called a point to what could only by courtesy be called a point, and thence to what by no stretch of courtesy could possibly be called a point, his brother judges would become more and more bilious—some like Fletcher or the heavy Mayne were even known to groan in disgust—and the climax would come when, in his grotesque vehemence, the old man would fall over one of his colleagues, and pull himself up, blowing but gleeful, amid the laughter of the spectators.

A genial soul, one might think! Yet, when he sentenced some wretch to be flogged from College Green to the quays, and the man said: "Thank you, my lord, you have done your worst," he spat out: ". . . and back again!" He sentenced a man to death for stealing a watch with "Ha-ha! You made a grab at time, egad, but you caught eternity." One relishes the retort of Curran at the bar dinner where there was question about the beef being a bit too fresh. "You try it," suggested Curran, "and then it'll be sure to be properly hung." An unhappy creature named Sterne, a general, or to give his full name, Henry William Godfrey Baker Sterne, came before him on a charge of *crim. con.* He was to spend thirty years in the Marshalsea owing to the enormous damages allotted. "There you have him, gentlemen of the jury," cackled Norbury, "from stem to stern, and if Mr. H. W. G. B.

Sterne had as many Christian virtues as he has Christian names he wouldn't be here today, gentlemen of the jury, to answer a charge of *crim. con.*" (No wonder he once told a witness who said he kept a racket-court: "So do I!") "All these gentlemen," he proceeds with his charge, "have argued the case most cleverly, and I have the greatest pleasure, yes, the greatest pleasure in bearing witness to the delight, yes, the delight, and I will add the assistance, yes, I will add the assistance, yes, the able assistance we have had from their masterly, yes, masterly views. I can't say which was best. Gentlemen, they were all best. They all quoted from Fearne *On Remainders*, but I declare, gentlemen, the arguments were so knotty they were like a hare in Tipperary, all to be found in fern. . . ."

One thinks of the unhappy ragged creatures who for stealing a hen or a sheep came before such courts for sentence—badly defended, perhaps not defended at all—to stand shivering in the dock while being dispatched with a joke from a buffoon.

O'Connell once walked into his "racket-court" to find him giving a younger barrister than himself, named Martley, a bad time. He spoke to some of his seniors and begged them to interfere; they were too timid or too cautious, so he stood up himself.

"My lords," he said, "I respectfully submit that Mr. Martley has a perfect right to a full hearing. He is not personally known to me, but I cannot sit silent while a brother barrister is being treated discourteously."

"Oh, we have heard Mr. Martley," said Norbury. "And we can't have the time of the court wasted further."

"Pardon me," insisted O'Connell, "but you have not heard him——"

"Are you engaged in this case," asked Judge Johnson heavily, "that you presume to interfere?"

"My lord, I am not, I merely rise to defend the privileges of the bar, and I will not permit them to be violated either in my own person or the person of any other member of my profession."

While the court waited for the thunderbolt, Norbury yielded with a: "Well, well, well, well, we'll hear him. Sit down. Sit down."

That kind of thing must have come out of O'Connell only on finding that he had entered a profession subject to a degradation unforeseen in his ingenuous student days. To serve his country and make a name for himself had been his ambition. Here was the sordid material with which he had to work, a stage where there was no glamour, little decency, small romance. The times themselves, so coarse and crude, were a challenge to his hide; times when drinking meant sottishness, duelling thuggery, property involved no responsibility, place meant only security, and honour was most common among thieves. Sweet words were few. The licence with which even the London *Times* spoke of its opponents was such as would in our time be thought shocking in the mouth of a pimp. In a leading article it called the priests "surpliced ruffians"; O'Connell "an unredeemed and unredeemable scoundrel," a "miscreant"; his Catholic Association "a system of organized ruffianism." It screamed: "How long shall such a wretch as this be tolerated among civilized men?"; and it saved itself from apoplexy when it published the well-known verses on him beginning:

> Scum condensed of Irish bog,
> Ruffian, coward, demagogue,
> Boundless liar, base detractor,
> Nurse of murders, treason's factor. . . .
> Spout thy filth, effuse thy slime, etc.

When Sheil, the poetic and romantic, could speak of Lord Eldon as "the procrastinating, canting, whining, griping, weeping, ejaculating, protesting, money-getting, money-keeping Eldon," it was mild for O'Connell to call Lord Alvanley "a bloated buffoon," or when referring openly to the Duke of York's mistress, Mary Ann Clarke, a Hoxton street-woman, to speak of her only as "his amen-echoing clerk." When Plunket could in the Irish Parliament gibe at the "green and sapless twig shivering on the floor," and the "hag grinning in the gallery"—the impotent Castlereagh and his wife—it was almost jovial for O'Connell to talk about cabinet ministers as "Booby Bexley, Doodle Dudley, Squeaky Wynne, Maw-worm Grant." But one sickens of it—there is no defending O'Connell when he calls Wellington "a stunted corporal"; if it is real satire to say "Peel's smile was like a silver plate on a coffin," it is merely vulgar to say that "he was squeezed out of the workings of some English factory," or to call somebody else "a chance child of fortune and of war." The best one can say is that if it was not genteel, neither were the Penal Laws; these had, at one time, for instance, suggested the castration of priests. The best one can say is that Dan O'Connell spoke for five million [1] slaves, and spoke well for them. There had always been a little too much of the gentleman about Englishmen exploiting the miserable creatures of the world.

But how far it all was from his young idealism! And how necessary (again and again one has to say this) that he should have had that guiding purpose always before him! Time and again, without it, we would otherwise turn from him in distaste, or in confusion, like to his own frequent confusion when the strain becomes so great that he is like a great whale lashing around madly on all sides. He would pretend, then, that he had lashed out, not in anger but in calculation. That was only his vanity. His quarrel with Cobbett is enough to show him in a rage so blind that he could in public speak of his ally as

comical only when he tries to be serious, truly doleful when he tries to be jocose, but, serious or jocose, at all times a miscreant. . . . I

---

[1] In 1800 the population of Ireland had risen from a million and a quarter in 1700 to four and a half millions. By 1841 it was over eight millions. After the Famines culminating in Black Forty-Seven it was down to six and a half millions.

will call him in future a vile vagabond. . . . He is malignant, he is treacherous, he is false. He has outlived his intellect.

It cannot be said of him that his wine of life is on the lees, but his gin of existence is on the dregs, and that fluid . . . is now but a muddy residuum, productive of sickness and nausea, and incapable of giving one exhilarating sensation.

Yet, a little later, and he is talking of the "unpurchasable Cobbett, their gifted advocate," with his "manly and transcendent intellect."

What a world to crush the gentleness out of a young man! It leaves us without hope for that gentleness when that same Keller, the Father of the Munster Bar, said in public that he did not mind being called anything under the sun so long as he was not called a son of a whore.

All that was left of gentleness in O'Connell was what his chivalry preserved, and that was a great deal, for he was chivalrous to the point of sentimentality, and what (later) his domestic life sheltered from the world. He also extracted a good deal of charm, suavity, blandness, good humour, and other such ingratiating qualities from the caverns his heart formed within itself by way of shelter from its own gall. "Ah, Dan," said his lawyer friend, Harry Grady, "I foresee you'll go through the world fair and easy"—when Dan, by flattery, had got some ammunition from a soldier who had just before refused Grady's blunt request. Fair and easy he never could or did go through anything, however. His ambitions drove him into constant combat.

3

THAT winter of 1800 he chose to come out in the open on the great political question of the day—the Union. He had, in spite of tremendous exertion, made in that year a bare £200, and was at the start of his career, but he could not be silent while the debates raged in Dublin.

I was travelling [he said] through the mountains from Killarney to Kenmare. My heart was heavy, and the day was wild and gloomy. The deserted district was congenial to solemnity and sadness. There was not a human habitation to be seen for miles. Black clouds sailed slowly across the sky, and rested on the tops of the mountains. My soul felt dreary at the loss Ireland had sustained, and I had many wild and Ossianic inspirations as I traversed the wild solitudes.

He came to Dublin in time for the passing of the Act which ended the Irish Parliament, and heard the bells of St. Patrick's peal out joyfully—the bells of Swift's cathedral—and saw the new flag go up over the Castle, the harp crushed away into its little corner. "My blood boiled," he goes on, "and I vowed that morning that the foul dishonour should not last if I could put an end to it."

He spoke against the Act at a public meeting of Catholics which, if his son is correct, he was mainly responsible for organizing, and it is remarkable that he was already well known enough to be asked to move the main resolution. The meeting was first raided by the notorious Major Sirr, who had taken Lord Edward, and as the tramp of his soldiers was heard outside it is said that the whole meeting held its breath. Only when the major had read the resolutions and flung them back contemptuously on the table did they dare breathe again. To measure the folly, or the pluck, of young O'Connell's action, at such a time, when every man was being thus watched so carefully by the Government, is impossible. Any of his colleagues could have told him that he had taken the short-cut to failure in his career. True, a month before, some of the leading advocates, Bushe, Plunket, Smith, Saurin, and others, had denounced the Union in the freest terms—but for a young Catholic to do the same was another thing. Sirr, we note, had not dared interfere with his Protestant colleagues.

What he said is a summary of what he advocated all his life after, even to his caution in toning down Curran's draft resolutions in order to keep inside the law, as well as his astuteness in quoting freely from speeches already made in the defunct Commons.

He first said that he regretted that they must speak as Catholics rather than simply as Irishmen; but they had been calumniated as having, as Catholics, acquiesced in the Union, and "that we must first deny." The real reason why they had, in spite of themselves, to speak as a sect, was that they were said to have sold—worse still, abandoned—their country in the hope of gaining religious toleration. "And that," cried O'Connell, "is a lie!"

Let every man who feels with me proclaim that if the alternative were offered him of the Union, or the re-enactment of the Penal Code in all its pristine horrors—he would prefer without hesitation the latter as the more sufferable evil: that he would rather confide in the justice of the Protestants of Ireland than lay his country at the feet of foreigners.

The meeting cheered that to the echo.

Yes [he proclaimed], I know that the Catholics of Ireland still remember they have a country, and that they would never accept any advantages as a sect that would destroy them as a people.

There is vision behind that declaration. It is so fine, so early, so bold, generous, and statesmanlike. It cut across sectarianism to nationality. It was the kind of thing Tone and the United Irishmen had sought for far and wide, and found nowhere except among enlightened Protestants. Here was a man of the people accepting the oneness of Ireland, inside the historical fact of conquest and invasion, because to his realistic and pragmatical mind the mingled strain in Irish life was something that, accepted, could create a new nation. It was the appeal of the first national leader, since the fall of the Gaelic State, to the remnants of its fall, to build Freedom on Conquest.

The political and social ideas implicit in that appeal held Irish loyalties up to and through the founding of Sinn Fein, and were the policy of Sinn Fein. It implied government by the King, Lords, and Commons of Ireland, and, so far from defining, hardly foresaw the gradual social changes that would have been inevitable under it. The alternative was the subterranean Separatist idea, with its natural corollary of Republicanism, social revolution, and social antagonisms even after the revolution. That O'Connell abhorred, for, though he said he was a Radical, he was not a Radical as we now understand the word. He was an eighteenth-century Whig, more accurately still, an eighteenth-century Irish Whig, or still more to the precise point, an eighteenth-century native Irish Whig, one of the first, and so *sui generis*. To that add the fact that he was a man seeking a political revolution, and we get the measure of his proclaimed radicalism. The English Whigs—once the Great Revolution was over, and the new great Houses, business Houses, began to raise their stony faces against the stony faces of the other kind of great House—were eager to preserve that new position, and expand as imperialists and industrialists; they were men amazed and delighted at the dropsical vegetation of colonial and backyard wealth which, if those accursed Tories did not interfere, promised to shoot up and up like a magical beanstalk. Not until well into the nineteenth century does the Whig become a Liberal, with ideals, and deserve (for a brief space) to be called a Radical in the modern sense. The same is true of O'Connell—radical only in relation to his times; never a Republican, far from it; never a social reformer, except in so far as Irish Freedom was one gigantic social reform. And even that aspect of his work (as we shall see) never seemed to him as more than incidental and problematical. There is no reason to blame him for that. His day is not ours; the social problem was not acute; the whole social alteration was something hardly envisaged, not yet a realistic problem at all, and, if somebody even dreamed of it, it could have been imagined at most as an unpredictable, undefinable evolutionary process in the lap of the gods.

In so far, therefore, as he was not a Radical he was Irish, and inclusive. The Separatists, by being Radical, were less Irish and exclusive. He would have embraced all elements in Irish life, on terms, and it is not his fault, but the fault of the old Protestant vested interests, that his policy had to give way in the end to Radicalism. It is equally not the merit of the Separatists that they replaced him, but the folly and selfishness of the vested interests which refused to move before anything but an absolutist revolution. In that way, with Tone, Protestantism invented Republicanism; and, with Carson, Protestantism consolidated it. So, too, Republicanism is untraditional in Ireland in the sense that for the first one hundred years or so of the modern Irish democracy—1800 to 1916, when the Irish Republican Brotherhood stole Sinn Fein—the sole expressed and supported idea of the vast mass of the Irish people was for a hierarchical form of society, based on the *status quo;* for the fullest freedom of action and opinion; and for a native government of that order in peaceful union with Great Britain under the symbol of the Crown.

Implicit in that change-over from O'Connellism is the modern appeal to the sanction of the Gaelic past; for that is merely Republicanism (thus untraditional in Irish thought) faking a tradition for itself independent of, and even contemptuous of, O'Connell's acceptance of the mingled strain of Anglo-Ireland. O'Connell, like Tone, admitted the upper classes were Irish; the upper classes refused to admit the Irish were any class. O'Connell would (certainly at this stage) have moulded all into one new national entity, had the vested interests been ready to nationalize their own traditions, and share and share alike with the people of their adopted country. With outstanding exceptions—one thinks of Berkeley, Davis, Parnell, Yeats—they held aloof, futile as men and contemptible as Irishmen, hugging their aristocratic origins and ideas, and despising the folk. It was only natural that, sooner or later, the folk, thus despised, should, in isolating themselves politically (as Separatists or Republicans), also isolate themselves culturally, exaggerate the antiquity of what traditions they had in order to inflate their importance, and base themselves, for pride's sake, on a history previous to Anglo-Ireland. It was only natural—but it is a sardonic twist of history that the Irish people should thereby ask for the sanction of a native aristocratic tradition that had equally despised them, which abandoned them on its fall, and which had never contributed to their rise.

There is no doubt that O'Connell overdid the surgery which cut away that effete past; but the truth remains that if the modern Irish democracy, which he created, ever looks at itself in the looking-glass of its actual history, it will see there, not the lineaments of antique heroes, but the faces of poor men, glowing in the presence of a man who accepted them for what they were, who needed no illusion to pride in them in their rags, who loved them for the simple humanity he found in them, and who taught them how to depend on themselves alone, in their own times, in their own conditions, in their own self-respect, for their rehabilitation as Irish democrats.

4

CAUTIOUS and conservative old Uncle Maurice did not approve of Dan's appearance at that January meeting in the Royal Exchange. He would have been less than pleased if he knew of some of Dan's goings-on in the two years following, 1801 and 1802; for Dan was still partial to a jovial carouse; so drunk on claret one night that he nearly tore up a whole street with a pick-axe, and just escaped being run through by a soldier's bayonet. He had also quietly become a Freemason. And in June 1802 he secretly got married.

He was very eighteenth-centuryish about that, very sententious, and insistent on feeling the proper emotions. He once told Tom Steele, his satellite of later years, how to propose to a lady.

Now, take so-and-so [he explained]. He was so injudicious as to propose to that widow at an early stage in his courtship. That was very precipitate. Of course, he might have been tender and assiduous. But he shouldn't have declared himself until she was desperately curious to know whether he was going to propose to her at all. Then take the way he proposed—he showed such want of tact, such ignorance of human nature. He actually held it out as a lure to her that she would share his honours to the full. What he should have said was this:

"I am starting on an ambitious career. I may over-rate my prospects. But there is one thing which would essentially contribute to it, and that is . . . *domestic felicity*."

And even then he should have spoken tenderly, and earnestly, and only let her guess his meaning. But instead of that, he blurts out his trashy bag of fame and his offer of marriage all at once. Pooh! The fellow had a grand opportunity and he didn't know how to make use of it.

Still, when it came to his own turn, however delicately he may have felt his way, he was fairly direct at the end.

I said, "Miss O'Connell" [she also was an O'Connell], "are you engaged?" She replied, "I am not!" I said, "Then will you engage yourself to me?" "I will," was her reply; and I said I would devote my life to make her happy. She deserved that I should. She gave me thirty-four years of the purest happiness that man ever enjoyed.

Their married life was one of the most sincere comradeship. He spoke constantly, in tenderness and gratitude, of her person and her helpfulness, saying such things as "She had the sweetest, the most heavenly temper, and the sweetest breath"; and even when she was dead he could not refrain from speaking of her in his public speeches. She well recompensed him for the fury of Hunting Cap, who wrote several letters trying to dissuade him, even threatening to disinherit him, offering as an alternative a wealthy spinster in Cork, whose nose, unhappily, was as long as her purse. One letter will do to show the depth of his content in that first year of youthful passion.

DARLING,

I can write but a few lines as it is grown late and my time is small. I was finishing some law-business which I had solemnly promised to dispose of this night.

You well know, my heart's dearest treasure, that whether I write few or many words, there certainly is not in this world a man who more fondly dotes on, or who so anxiously longs for the arms of his wife. Day and night you are continually present to my fond thoughts, and you always increase my happiness or lessen my cares. With you I could live with pleasure in a prison or a desert. You are my all of company, and if I can but preserve your love I shall have in it more of true delight than can be imagined by any but he who sincerely loves. Sweet Mary, I rave of you! I think only of you! I sigh for you, I weep for you, I almost pray to you.

Darling, I do not—indeed I do not exaggerate. If there be more of vehemence in my expressions, believe me that vehemence has its justification in my heart—a heart that is devoted to the most enticing of her sex. Indeed, you are a dear, charming, little woman.

Your last letter I have read again and again. It is in every respect a most pleasing letter to me; not only from the heart-flowing strain of tenderness in which it is written, but the saucy gaiety of some of the passages show me how much recovered my love is . . . Mary, how fondly I shall cherish the little stranger coming. I hope it may be a daughter and as like you as possible. O God, how I then will love her! How sincerely will I express my affection to the mother in the caress I bestow on the child. Dearest, sweetest wife, I can thus hope to be able to prove to you the ardour and the purity of the pleasing affection—to me at least the most pleasing affection—with which my whole soul dotes on you.

Dearest, I am writing with great rapidity but still my thoughts run much faster than my pen. I could praise you a thousand times faster than I write, as I love you a thousand times more than I can tell.

I shall see you soon, dearest darling. Love to dear mother.

Ever your devoted husband,

DANIEL O'CONNELL.

P.S. In a week we shall be able to fix the time of our departure. Happy, happy moment that gives me my sweet wife again.

The "little stranger" was Maurice, his first son, born in 1803.
Marriage held up politics. Somebody once asked Lord Chief
Justice Kenyon how to get on at the bar. "That is easy. Spend
your fortune. Then spend your wife's fortune. Then you'll have
to work." Dan had no fortune, and neither had Mary, and Hunting Cap had cut him off without a shilling. So he did have to
work. If then, in 1803, we find him (after that fine speech against
the Union) still in the Lawyers' Corps, the year of Robert Emmet's rising, and for three nights under arms, we may be gentle
with him; though it is odd to hear him in after years point out
the dusty red-brick Grand Canal Hotel in James Street (the
canal docks are near by) with "I searched every room in that
house one July night in 1803." "For what?" "For Croppies."
(That is, Catholic rebels.) Besides—what with Emmet's rebellion, fear of foreign invasion, apathy among the Catholic upper
classes, who were the only people vocal at the time, and the suspension of the Habeas Corpus Act, with the consequent restraint
on public meetings—Catholic agitation was hardly thought of in
Dublin, let alone outside it. An occasional mild petition, privately fostered by a few Catholic peers and a few commoners
like the business man John Keogh, was the only sign that the
Catholics were not wholly beaten.

Even that much took a great deal of organizing. Pitt was back
in power in 1804, and since he had led many people to believe
that the Union would purchase religious toleration, and further
encouraged them, in 1801, by resigning on that question, the few
vocal Catholics there were abstained from "embarrassing" him.
When they met in February 1805, in a private house, it took all
the persuasive powers of O'Connell to induce them to forward
a petition for relief under the care of Lord Fingall, Sir Thomas
Ffrench, Sir Edward Bellew, and two business men, Scully and
Ryan. Pitt refused to hand that first humble plea of the Catholics
to the Imperial Parliament—and Fox had to present it in his stead

to the House of Commons. A hundred Catholics, noblemen and gentleman commoners, signed it; a wholly unrepresentative body, self-elected, self-authorized, privately gathered, and inevitably ineffectual.

Yet, weak as that only voice from Ireland was, these generous and too-confiding men refused to petition once again when Fox succeeded Pitt in 1806. And when in 1807 the Habeas Corpus Act was restored even O'Connell agreed not to petition. The situation changed, however, with the death of Fox. The Whigs were now hesitating about giving some minor sops to the Catholics; the half-idiot king was bullying his ministers; the ministry became rebellious; and the Irish Government actually began to parley with the Catholic aristocrats.

Here begins O'Connell's life-long connexion with the Whigs —a connexion fatal to himself and to Ireland, but an unavoidable part of constitutional agitation. He declared manfully for an immediate petition. In spite of all his efforts they met and re-met, hesitated, argued, and pondered for four months—a foretaste of that endlessness of meetings and re-meetings, committees and councils and speeches, that were to test his physical endurance and his mental resistance during forty years of agitation. By the time they were approaching a decision the Whigs were out and the Tories were in, and then when there seemed to be no reason now to avoid embarrassing the Government, O'Connell at once moved that they *do not* petition; this rather than it be said they abandoned their friends, the Whigs, when they were no longer of use to them. He was promptly dubbed "the changeable and ever-changing barrister"—not without reason and not for the last time. It was as typical of his compliancy as of his pliancy to change over again the following January and insist that the petition be now presented, as it was by Grattan, in May, with results of the least expected kind.

For the moment the thing has no importance or interest except for the light it throws on the cumbersome machinery of

what can hardly be called agitation at this date, and its revelation
of the involutions of O'Connell's mind. He had, for one thing,
not imbibed his early education from the Benthamites for nothing: he never could see any great merit in consistency. For another he was already sufficiently a student of human nature to see
great merit in playing to the gallery. It became almost a rule
with him to hold onto his opinion to the very last, no matter
what the opposition, but to change over at the first sign that the
opposition was too powerful. He would then, after pleading for
a thing from forty angles, after justifying them all, after trying
every possible appeal, if he failed, put his hand on his heart, ab-
jectly admit he was wrong—though usually explain that it was
for good reasons—say that he wished to do nothing but serve
Ireland, raise a laugh or wring a tear, and amid the cheers of the
delighted mob gently repeat his original resolution in a new form.

This persistence was one of the first things he discovered as a
sine qua non in politics; dogged, terrier-like persistence on the
main issue, however combined with pliancy as to the details.
One of the shrewdest observations ever made by a political agitator is thus put by him, after many years of experience:

That which is once or twice advanced may possibly strike for a
moment, but will then pass away from the public recollection. You
must repeat the same lesson over and over again, if you hope to
make a permanent impression—if in fact you hope to impress it on
your pupil's memory. Such has always been my practice. Men, by
always hearing the same things, insensibly associate them with received truisms. They find the facts at last quietly reposing in a corner of their minds, and no more think of doubting them than if they
formed part of their religious belief.

Nobody who has not had some little experience of political
agitation can realize what demands that method makes on the agitator: but, above all other necessities—beyond persistence which
might become obstinacy, and pliancy which might become weakness—the method required a guiding vision outside himself, and

that he had in the image of his people. His love for them enlarged him in his strength and renewed him in his weakness.

5

HIS work at the bar goes on side by side with these political distractions. His carefully kept fee-book measures the tempo.

1798	2 fees	£2	5	6
1799	16 fees	£27	3	6
1800	77 fees	£205	0	0
1801	109 fees	£255	18	9

The fees are numerous enough, the payment small. That was the price he had to pay for being a Catholic, with the prospect of always drudging in the same way in the other bar, and never—of course—hoping to sit in ease on the bench. Instead he will live to see his Protestant colleagues pass him by, one by one, while he clutches angrily at his stuff-gown, and flings on his shoulder a bag full of cheap briefs.

Yet, as his reputation rises, he begins to demand better payment, even as he can extract proper deference from the bench. Glance at his fee-book again.

1802	£346	18	0
1803	£465	4	9
1804	£715	9	9
1805	£840	12	0

That is the gratifying result of hard work, three, four, or five cases every day: and still the sum mounts.

1809	£2736
1812	£3028
1814	£3808

If we put beside it his day's routine as given by his daughter we may see why it mounts: he worked a twelve-hour day.

4 a.m.   Rise. Prayers. Light fire.
5 a.m.   Sit to work.
8.30.   Breakfast.
10.30.   Walk to the Four Courts—two miles in 25 minutes.
11 to 3. In Court.
3.30.   Call to the offices of the Catholic Association.
4.   Dinner.
4 to 6.30 Sit with family.
6.30.   Sit to work.
10.   Bed.

Out of his income he had the expenses of constant travel all over the Munster Circuit, comfort coming slowly, and his family coming fast. Up to 1811 he was living at No. 4 (now 33) Westland Row, by no means a fashionable quarter even then. When he moved, in 1811, to No. 30 (now 58) Merrion Square, the address must have cost him every pound of his income.

He made his reputation almost wholly as a relentless and astute examiner of difficult witnesses. He would nag away at them tirelessly, worming his way into their minds, until he got some sudden clue that put them at his mercy. It was his own absolute knowledge of the Irish mind that enabled him to do it. So with some old woman he once began with "How did you come by this calf, my good woman?" and had to put the question in a dozen ways before she would admit that she "bought it": she knew as well as he what must follow on that admission. "And where did you get the money, my good woman?" would begin another long series of questions before she was driven to disclose that. Only then was he really able to begin. For an hour he worried her, teasing her, joking her, involving her temper in the bargaining transaction that he was trying to clarify, until she burst out, in a rage, with one of the best judgments passed on him by any of his victims: "Aha! You knows all about the roguei of it, but you don't know at all about the honesty of it!" At whicn even he had to laugh.

Cut off from the higher advocacy as he was, this game of hare and hound became in his hands the art of a specialist. He has to defend a man charged with stealing a dead cow, and, failing at every other defence, he succeeds by pointing out that the charge is for the larceny of a cow whereas it should be for the larceny of beef. Once a perjuring witness, in a will case, kept on swearing that the testator was alive when his hand signed the will; but O'Connell noticed that the witness used the same phrase every time: "*Bhí beatha ann*"; literally, "There was life in him." After battering at the man for an hour O'Connell suddenly challenged him to deny, by his God who would judge him, that there was a live fly in the dead man's mouth when his hand was put to the will. In terror the witness admitted the conspiracy.

"Oh! Mr. O'Connell!" cried a highwayman to him, "what would happen to me if anything happened to you? The Lord spare you to me!" This man O'Connell had defended in Dublin for burglary, gone down to Cork and found him before the court for assault and burglary, got him off a second time, came back to Dublin only to find him there again, charged with stealing a collier, selling the cargo, buying arms, and pirating along the coast. Again O'Connell freed him by arguing that the case should have come before the Admiralty because the crime had been committed on the high seas.

He accepted a case and found to his dismay that his client had, without telling him, also employed another barrister of senior rank but little merit; that meant, by the etiquette of the bar, that the chief witness must be examined by this senior counsel. Quickly glancing around the court he saw a vacant face among the loungers present; calling up this foolish fellow he had him put into the box, from which he was ejected within five minutes as incapable of giving a pertinent answer. The material witness succeeded him; the senior sat down; and Dan calmly rose to begin the case.

An example of even more light-hearted and unscrupulous inventiveness was his constant treatment of Judge Day, the man who always "agreed with the last speaker."

Aye, poor Day! [said O'Connell] most innocent of law was my poor friend Day! I remember once I was counsel before him for a man who had stolen some goats. The fact was proved; whereupon I produced to old Day an old Act of Parliament, empowering the owners of cornfields, gardens, or plantations to kill and destroy all goats trespassing thereon. I contended that this legal power of destruction clearly demonstrated that *goats were not property;* and I thence inferred that the stealer of goats was not legally a thief, nor punishable as such. Poor Day charged the jury accordingly, and the prisoner was acquitted.

His biographer, Fagan, records an occasion when he was counsel in a certain case with some of the most eminent men on his circuit. He was in another court, pleading for another client's life, when an urgent message was sent to him to come and see if he could save what had become a desperate situation. He continued with his pleading, and although he received another and yet another message, he finished his speech before he went off to the next court. He entered casually, gaily jesting with some friends as he passed on his way, pulled out his brief, and after giving it a glance or two rose just in time to stop a verdict from being given. "In a few brief sentences he cleared away the difficulty that had embarrassed his colleagues; in a few more turned the tables on the enemy; and then, in one of the shortest speeches ever known for so important a case, banished all idea of a nonsuit from the mind of the bench. Then closing his bag, and informing the judge that the remainder of the argument would be carried on by one of his colleagues, he returned calmly to the death-trial from which he had been summoned." By a hundred such incidents, an accumulation too great to permit of any talk of "good luck," or "happy chances," he gradually created a legend that has become part and parcel of the history of the Irish Bar.

There was no secret to his success. He had all the gifts: good presence, memory, concentration, order, industry, bodily vigour. He had gifts beyond necessity, such as courage by the ton, invention quick as a knife, so much mental freshness that the formulæ and traditions of the law were always pliable, open to new interpretations, in his hands. He had a superflux above and beyond these in his sense of the drama of the courts, his terrific zest for the triumphs of that stage where utter ruin, even death, can be signified by no more than a little murmur about the barristers' table. In a word he got fun out of the thing—it is the only word to indicate his positive happiness as a lawyer. He used to acknowledge it, with that simple boastfulness that is one of his most endearing weaknesses: "As for myself, to my last hour at the bar I kept the court alternately in tears and in roars of laughter." To all that add the thing John Mitchel said of him: "He took all Ireland for his client," and we are back at the enlargement of the man by the symbol, and for that there is no measure but his life's work.

6

THE year 1808 brought him to the brink of his real career. It closed in storm, with Napoleon threatening to engulf Spain, and the Peninsular War unfolding its seemingly endless coils. In England Grattan had finally presented the much discussed Irish petition in a splendid speech on the folly of disunion between two islands "matched against all mankind." "Will you," he asked the Commons, "in such a crisis depend on political opinions and religious schisms to prop a falling world?"

But he then went on to say something that was to divide the powerless minority in England, and the powerless majority in Ireland for a full twenty years. To prove the loyalty of the Irish he declared that the Irish bishops would, if the king desired it, give the British Government the right to annul any high ecclesiastical appointment that might seem obnoxious for political reasons. By saying so he began the famous Controversy on the Veto, and opened for Ireland the whole question of the limits of the powers of Church and State.

7

THAT question had long been fought over in Europe. For Ireland it had never arisen, for the simple reason that the only legal Church was the Church of the Reformation, and its problems were not Irish problems. Elsewhere, however, the Catholic Church had found itself being driven more and more to the wall before the attacks of the new Liberalism which, in Lecky's words, had "rendered the union of politics and theology an anachronism by pronouncing their divorce." It was only natural that, at this date, Rome should, for Ireland, rest rigidly on the principle of authority, oppose everything in the nature of Gallicanism among Catholics, reject the old teaching of the Jesuits with regard to the lawfulness of disobedience to a tyrant, and lean towards the form of government which was most likely to foster those habits of absolute obedience to authority, whose rejection, in France and elsewhere, had brought her to bay; even as among Irish Protestants she was not likely to heed the Low-Church Presbyterians who, like the Low-Church English Puritans, instinctively stood for liberty as against despotism. She was, that is to say, more likely to heed Grattan than to heed Wolfe Tone; as subsequently she preferred to heed the English aristocrats, although they insulted her by calling themselves Protesting Catholic Dissenters, than to lend a hand to the Irish poor who were fighting for their political liberty in the name of the Christian Faith.

It was well for Ireland, in this crisis, that O'Connell had imbibed something from the Europe of his youth. He opposed the idea of the Veto from the start, and he fought it tooth and nail to the end; for, if he did not contemplate the absolute secularization of politics, he had no intention of seeing politics become the chequer-board of the bishops. His fears were justifiable, although it was not discovered until two years later that the bishops on the board of Maynooth had already, in the year previous, agreed in secret to an identical proposal for government nomination, and for financial support of the clergy from government funds—the composite agreement being tantamount to a conspiracy between the Irish Church and the English State. It is hard to tell how much the poor folk in the country understood this, but, had they understood any of it, they could only have felt that they were being abandoned to slavery by their last friends—the priests.

The whole proposal showed one thing clearly to O'Connell —that the Irish aristocrats would sacrifice anything for religious toleration, even to the point of abandoning the political liberty of their country. He had, in his first public speech, repudiated that approach to emancipation, but he realized that it would always be tried by others, unless the agitation was based on the rights of the people as a whole, and fought for by the people as a whole. It delighted him when the majority of the hierarchy, at a national synod, declared against nomination or veto by the Crown, and he may have, even then, foreseen a time when priests and people could be organized into one vast army, autonomous but interdependent.

He had already, with hardly any thought of it, cut off the new politics from all connexion with the past. He was now to cut them off from the influence of the native aristocracy. Presently he would also cut them off from the Catholic aristocracy in England. The time was to come when he was to cut them off from the interference even of Rome. So that if, for the time being, he had to work on with the Irish peers, it was only because he found but few hopeful lieutenants among the more popular supporters of agitation.

They were indeed a mixed lot. A man like John Keogh was

priceless, and bushy-browed Dr. Drumgoole, whose name re-
sounded so harmoniously with his bellicose nature, was also useful—though he was too much given to theology, and often spoke
with the zeal of a bigot rather than a reformer. James Clinche,
the lawyer, was loyal but ponderous and boring. Jack Lawless
never could keep his mouth shut. Nicholas Purcell O'Gorman
was a good, whimsical, earnest fellow; but it was a commentary
on him that, having once heard that Earl Grey wore striped
stockings on state occasions, he therefore always wore striped
stockings when he wanted to make a speech. Denis Scully and
red-headed Peter Bodkin Hussey were better founded, if not
particularly brainy. Richard Lalor Sheil would be the best of
them; but he was yet to come, with his pyrotechnic oratory,
packed with the most involved, fuse-crackling images.

For all that, weak as such men were, it was to be O'Connell's
discovery, to which this Veto question pointed the way, that it
was such men, and not the aristocrats, who could alone fight
with any effect for the combined social and political rights of
the people. In making that discovery about the power of a popular movement, he was merely making Wolfe Tone's discovery
of many years before, that the men of no property are always
the best men in a stand-up fight. The propertied folk may, and
indeed must, begin such movements. It is the men who have least
to lose who are always most ready to pay for them with their
lives.

8

WHEN, accordingly, the genteel Catholic Committee hesitated
again, in 1809, over the Madeira and the biscuits about presenting another petition, young O'Connell rebelled. He proposed
that they should cast off their casual character, and re-form as a
permanent Catholic Committee. But, fifteen years before, in
1793, when Keogh and Tone had done something like this, the

Government had promptly passed the infamous Convention Act, which forbade *delegated* bodies to meet in future under pretence of drawing up petitions. Keogh acidly reminded his young friend of the existence of this Act. On the spot O'Connell drew up a special resolution to the effect that they

> were not representatives of the Catholic body nor any portion thereof; nor shall they assume or pretend to be representatives of the Catholic body or any portion thereof,

and handed it to Keogh. A quite simple solution! And, to be sure, every honest man will add: "Quite dishonest." And every honest Englishman: "How those Irish lie!"

While thus chafing at the endless patience of the Keogh-Fingall faction, O'Connell suddenly got his first opportunity to appeal over their heads to the people. It was the Protestants of the Dublin Corporation who gave him his chance. They had woken up to the losses caused by the Union, and one of them, the same Robert Hutton who was proposed thirty years after by Grattan as a man fit to fight the Dublin constituency beside O'Connell, moved resolutions in favour of Repeal; at the same time demanding of the sheriffs a public meeting of the freehold-ers and freemen of the city to emphasize the loss to the Irish revenue. He declared that the nation had already a debt of ninety million sterling; that absentees were spending upwards of two million pounds annually out of the country, every penny of it wrung from a struggling peasantry; and that as much and more went every year in interest on their debt, until bankruptcy, famine, and despair were becoming visible in every street of Dublin. It is, in literature, the Dublin dealt with in Lever's nov-els, with their amused satire of the tarnished and flea-bitten fin-ery of the abandoned Castle, and the once-grand town houses of the gentry falling into a dishevelment that was the prelude to a decline into a slum.

As if he foresaw the probable trend of this new move, Keogh at once proposed a resolution against further agitation in the

Catholic Committee. It was his last throw against his young successor. Not only was he defeated but he was ominously thanked for "long and faithful services to the cause." O'Connell went to Hutton's meeting and made a manly speech that was straightway printed in broadsheet and scattered, with his portrait, through the countryside. "I date my first great lift in popularity from that speech," he used to say afterwards. Keogh was on his doorstep once more to make a last effort, imploring him to go slow, flattering him and importuning him by turns, now clearly foreseeing—wise and experienced old man—where this must inevitably lead them; but unable to foresee, for he was also a worn and weary old man, what power resided in that headstrong lawyer, or what force he was to call up out of the sleeping masses that were about to hear his trumpet call. O'Connell heard him out, and rejected his pleas. Keogh left him in a rage, and they never met again.

Only a few sentences are needed now from that Repeal speech to show the effect of O'Connell's masculine mind on his unromantic oratory. It juts out from him like a fountain, a projection of his energetic brain. There is only one image in the whole speech, where a Sheil would have packed hundreds.

After quoting his "facts," from the highest legal authorities, to prove the Union a violation of national rights he said:

The Union was, therefore, a manifest injustice, and it continues to be unjust to this day. It was a crime, and it must be still criminal unless it shall be ludicrously pretended that crime, like wine, improves by old age, and that time mollifies injustice into innocence. . . .

If the Union continues it will make crime hereditary, and injustice perpetual. We have been robbed, my countrymen, most foully robbed, of our birthright, our independence. Alas, England that ought to have been to us a sister and a friend—England whom we had loved, and fought and bled for—England whom we have protected and do protect—England, at a period when out of 100,000 seamen in her service 70,000 were Irish—England stole upon us

like a thief in the night and robbed us of the precious gem of our
liberty. She stole from us that which naught enriched her but made
us poor indeed.

(Of which, no doubt, he "did not mean a word.") He then considers the methods by which the Union was achieved, the bribery and the corrupt practices, the sale of every kind of office,
sacred and profane, in return for a vote. Then he winds into his
interest as a leader of five million poor Catholics:

The real cause of the Union lay deeper, but it is quite obvious. It
is to be found at once in the religious dissensions which the enemies
of Ireland have created and continue, separating us into wretched
sections and miserable sub-divisions. They revived every antiquated
cause of domestic animosity and invented new pretexts for rancour.
But above all, my fellow-countrymen, they belied and calumniated
us to one another. They falsely declared that we hated each other.
And they continued to repeat the assertion until we came to believe
it. They succeeded in producing all the madness of party and religious dissension; and while we were lost in the stupor of insanity
they plundered us of our country.

There, again, as always after, is the appeal to an undivided
non-sectarian nationality. Its arrogance and its statesmanship lay
in this unruffled assumption, by a man of the five million who
had been conquered and dispossessed, that the nation was just
as much their possession as the minority's. He was building, as
always after, on the *status quo*—taking the facts as he found
them, and hammering their brutal reality into an ideal:

Learn discretion from your enemies. They have crushed your
country by fomenting religious discord—serve her by abandoning
it for ever. Let each man give up his share of the mischief. But I
say not this to barter with you, my countrymen. I trample under
foot the Catholic claims if they can interfere with the Repeal of the
Union. Nay, were Mr. Perceval to offer me the Repeal tomorrow,
upon the terms of re-enacting the entire Penal Code, I declare upon
my heart, and in the presence of my God, that I would cheerfully
accept the proposal.

9

Not content with a permanent Committee, O'Connell, as Chairman, now proposed that *permanent* local boards should be formed throughout the country similar to the central one in Dublin. He thereby challenged the law and the aristocrats. And both responded.

The Fingall faction were up in arms at once. They had so long felt themselves as "the natural leaders" of the Catholics, had indeed been so called, that they were both jealous and doubtful of these lawyers and merchants. They began to talk of their "vulgar violence"; they spoke for hours, in committee, in praise of the policy of "dignified silence," of "frowning on their enemies," of "muttering curses deep not loud"—but of doing very little else besides. "Their faces decked with smiles," mocked O'Connell, "they smooth their whiskers, and entreat with courtly air that we should not embarrass our friends of the administration."

They had some reason to be perturbed. O'Connell was definitely forcing the pace. At the beginning of 1811 he was literally going out into the highways and byways; he used to stand on Carlisle Bridge (in our time O'Connell Bridge) and accost Roman Catholic passers-by, inducing them to come to the meeting in the adjacent Exchange Rooms, which were then rented in his own name.

"For more than twenty years before Emancipation," he wrote afterwards to Lord Shrewsbury, when that gentleman taunted him with being the King of Beggars, "the burden of the cause was thrown upon me. I had to arrange the meetings, to prepare the resolutions, to furnish replies to the correspondence, to examine the case of each person complaining of a practical grievance. At a period when my minutes counted by the guinea, when my emoluments were limited only by the extent of my physical and waking powers, when my meals were shortened to the narrowest space, and my sleep restricted to the earliest hours before dawn, at that period and for more than twenty years there was not a day that I did not devote from one to two hours, often much more, to the working out of the Catholic cause—and that without receiving or allowing the offer of any remuneration, even for the personal expenditure incurred in the agitation of the cause itself."

That February of 1811 they had their first tussle with the law. "Honest Hay," as O'Connell sarcastically dubbed the secretary of the Catholic Committee, called a General Committee of Delegates, thereby—whether through folly or malice—making them all, at once, guilty of a seditious act. In the event Lord Ffrench was put under nominal arrest, but after some *pourparlers* with the Castle they managed to scrape out of that trouble.

The Committee fought over it among themselves. Ffrench said that the lawyers were "men who ought to be suspected as having more to expect than any other description of Catholic." Whereupon Peter Bodkin Hussey, the roughest-tongued man in the Four Courts, leaped at him, and the air was rancid for ten minutes. (Peter was the lawyer whom a colleague challenged to a duel of impertinence. "Pooh," said Peter, "you are only impertinent to people who won't knock you down. I'm impertinent to everybody.") Shouting at Ffrench across the room, he declared that he understood him as well as if he were inside his lordship's head. "He talks about barristers with personal objects to gain. I tell him there are Catholic bankers with personal objects to gain. I tell him, moreover, that although I chastise him verbally now I wouldn't hesitate to chastise him personally if he came here again, a second time, on a similar errand." O'Connell was patient and paternal with his unruly children. He simply reminded them how the great Duke of Ormonde vindicated himself in 1661 against the charge of having allowed Papishes to congregate in Dublin. "I know by experience," smiled the Duke, "that the Irish Papishes never meet without dividing and degrading themselves."

O'Connell pushed the Committee before him. Defying a proclamation by the Lord Lieutenant, they met again. In August six delegates were arrested, including Taaffe, of Ffrench's banking house, Kirwan, a merchant, and Dr. Sheridan. Still the Committee stuck to their guns. They met in October, with one hundred and fifty delegates from all parts of Ireland, and managed to get their business done just before the police arrived.

It was now touch and go for the O'Connellites. They had dragged the more cautious section outside the law, and the courts set out to show, in the persons of the arrested delegates, what these Catholics must expect who dared raise their voices in public in this way. At the trial of the arrested men the Crown quoted the Convention Act, which had laid down that delegates must not meet *under pretence of petitioning*. This obviously meant, said the defendants, "under false pretence." The Crown argued that the opposite was meant, i.e., "*even* for the purpose of petitioning." After a long combat the jury decided for the prisoner—Dr. Sheridan. The O'Connellites had won the first round.

10

THE thing was now a war of wits between lawyers—the Crown prosecutors on the one hand, the Catholic defenders on the other. A few days after the trial of Sheridan the Committee again met and were again invaded by the police.

Hare, the magistrate, walked up to Fingall, who was in the chair, and began to try by every means to wring from him an admission that this also was a delegated committee. In the hall the members clambered forward, listening in excitement, exclaiming as at a boxing-match, even threatening the officers. O'Connell stood on the other side of Fingall listening to every word. It was a long move from the day they held their breaths when Major Sirr's soldiers were heard tramping down the hall;

and a longer day since, as old John Keogh said, you could tell a Catholic in the street by the way he cowered as he walked.

"Lord Fingall," said Hare, "I come here by direction of the Lord Lieutenant. As a magistrate of the city of Dublin I ask you, as chairman of this meeting, what is your object?"

"Our purpose is perfectly legal and constitutional."

"That is not an answer to my question."

"What is your question?"

"Is this a meeting of the Catholic Committee?"

"We have met for the sole, legal, and constitutional purpose of petitioning."

"My lord, I ask you, as chairman, in what capacity are you met?"

Here the body of the hall began to growl.

"We are met to petition Parliament," said Fingall, and the hall cheered and the growl began to increase. It was that hitherto distant growl from the hillsides at last invading Dublin.

Hare was insistent. He rejected the growling.

"My lord, that is not an answer to my question." He glares at the hall. "I hope I have leave to speak?"

The growl breaks into shouts. O'Connell stems them. More shouts: "Hear him! Hear the magistrate!"

Hare resumes doggedly: "I beg leave to ask your lordship again, is this a meeting of the Catholic Committee, constituted by the Catholic peers, prelates, country gentlemen, and persons appointed in the several parishes of Dublin?"

Fingall refuses to reply.

Hare interprets: "Your answer is that you are a meeting of Catholics assembled for a legal and constitutional purpose?"

(It sounds innocent, but the unfortunate Catholics dare not admit even that, and O'Connell interposes.)

He protests against this kind of cross-examination. Still Hare keeps at it, an image of the virulent persecution of the people by the government he serves.

"My lord, do I understand you refuse to tell me fully what you are here for?"

"We are met for a legal and constitutional purpose."

"And you will give no other answer?"

Again the hall rises in clamour, some shouting for Hay the secretary, some shouting: "Read the Petition," some again shouting: "Hear him! Hear the magistrate!" Hare refusing to yield, O'Connell again intervenes to make the thing quite clear by insisting that an answer once given has to be taken in its literal signification.

"My lord," Hare keeps at it, "I consider your refusal to answer is an admission that this is the Catholic Committee."

"Your belief," cries O'Connell, "is of no consequence to us. We are not to be bound by your opinions."

Hare (angrily): "Does your lordship *deny* that this is the Catholic Committee?"

Twice again the Catholic lawyers intervened, and then, at last, Hare came to the issue:

"Your lordship's refusal to give me a direct answer is an admission that this is the Catholic Committee. As such I require it to disperse."

Pluckily, Fingall refused to yield even to that. He declared he would not leave until forced to leave, and then he would bring an action against whoever removed him. Hare removed him formally. Amid excitement Lord Netterville was moved to the chair, took it, and was arrested. A third chairman was moved, and was about to be arrested when Sir Edward Bellew moved the adjournment.

In the event, the Government yielded again. There was no prosecution. That, at any rate, was a win for the "gentlemen" among the Catholics.

Reader and biographer might be forgiven for feeling at this stage the weariness of a long prospect, since, if that is all that is

meant by Ireland Resurgent—a few men arguing in a room in
Dublin, unknown to the great inert masses down the country—
what a tedious journey lies ahead! Yet it is from such little meetings in back rooms that every revolution has sprung.

11

SHELLEY was in Dublin, that 1812, for one of the as yet unin-
terrupted series of Catholic meetings. What he said—his large
eyes glowing, his febrile hands gesturing—must have sounded in
the ears of O'Connell with a fond familiar note, reminding him
of days already far off when he argued with the Codgers, or
heard the speeches of the London Radicals, or talked about
Godwin with his erudite landlady at Chiswick. The old phrases
were all there. "Power and wealth do not benefit, but injure, the
cause of freedom."

Emancipation is the foreground of the picture in the dimness of
whose distance I behold the lion lie down with the lamb, and the in-
fant play with the basilisk. . . . For it supposes the extermination
of the eyeless Monster Bigotry whose throne has tottered for two
hundred years. . . . I hear the teeth of the palsied beldam, Super-
stition, chatter, and I see her descending to the grave. . . . Reason
points to the open gates of the temple of Religious Freedom. . . .
Philanthropy kneels at the altar of the common god.

It was the rationalism of the recluse Godwin, and the romanticism of Diderot, Rousseau (to come forward), Chateaubriand, stuck, as a child dibbles flowers in the sand to make a
garden, in the rank Irish midden to make a Bower of Freedom.
One wonders what O'Connell thought of it. He possibly did not
hear a word of it. As he would not have heard, either, the next
time Shelley came to Ireland, that he was gone to live as a hermit
on an island in the Lakes of Killarney.

He had other things on his mind; not the least of them was the
trial of the second of those arrested delegates. For, though Sheri-

dan had been acquitted, the Government relentlessly pursued Kirwan. Here the O'Connellites were defeated; for, on the same charge, and with the same defence, the Government got a verdict. That ended, for the time being, the existence of the Catholic Committee as a delegated body, and old Keogh could now nod his head bitterly and say: "*I* told you so!"

The dissensions became more and more bitter following this reverse. The English Whig organs, too, were already noting the new departure, and were flattering the Fingallians for being "judicious," "well-concerted," "able," "adept at slow and well-regulated movements," "moderate and prudent." But where, asked the Left Wing, was the use in all these virtues when they did nothing but issue a Petition which was regularly received back marked, as it were, *Return to Sender?* The June of that year, 1812, with Fingall in the chair: what a pitiful tale they had to hear about their last Petition! Peter Bodkin Hussey reported that the gentlemen entrusted with it had been bluntly refused an interview with the Prince, ordered to present their petition at a levee in the ordinary way there, were graciously permitted to state its purport and origin, and before passing into the long queue of visitors and supplicants, hand the plea of five million people to the glove of a lord-in-waiting—yet one more leaf to be added to the vast monument of unregarded paper that comes, year after year, from every corner of the Empire to the English Rome. The fledgeling Irish gentlemen agitators—they would have shuddered at the very word—would never have had the spirit to regard their petitions and their reception in that way. It would have taken the rage and power of a Carlyle, as it took the fury of an O'Connell, to make them see St. James's Palace and Whitehall as the Old Clothes Market of "stainless ghosts"—those pieces of paper from Africa, or India, or Ireland, fluttering there like pigeons hopeful of a grain. Like somnambulists the aristocrats would have walked for ever in and out of these tombs of blood become dust without relating their magnificence to the deaths recorded by their very size, and not even the harsh peasant cynicism of O'Connell could have made them guess that it was, as it still is, one of the exasperations of Royalty that its great homes should be cluttered up with the prayerful gifts of loyal subjects that often accompany these petitions—all received with a smile, retained with a frown, and for ever after spoken of in sarcastic boredom. The Dublin gentlemen would probably have gone on adding to that boredom and exasperation for ever, petition after petition, visit after visit, hope added to hope, becoming sour or tired, or dropping out of it all in the end, but never once feeling the blast of honest rage at the insult implicit in the contemptuous patience of their governors. Not so an O'Connell.

He must have known by now that if their petitions were unheard he could raise among the denizens of the Kerry rocks, and all the other Kerrys of Ireland, a storm that must be heard; he must have known that the devil would not hold those wild, heart-scalding ragged-pants once the fire was kindled in them by any man; and, when he read those flatteries of the *Edinburgh Review*, known that others knew it besides himself. He said so —and said it in the presence of Lord Fingall:

Our enemies object to the tone which the Catholics now use. Yes, my lord, they dislike the tone that men should use who are deeply anxious for the good of their country. We assume the tone that may terrify the invader. We use the tone of men who appreciate the value of civil liberty and who would die sooner than exchange it for the iron sway of military rule. We talk as men should who dread slavery and disgrace, but laugh to scorn the idea of danger.

Then, with his now growing fondness for *double entendre* (he might be as easily referring to the English oppressor as to the Napoleonic danger), he quoted in his bull-throated voice:

Shall it be asked if an invader arrived:

    And was there none, no Irish arm
    In whose veins the native blood runs warm,

And was there no heart in the trampled land
Who spurned the oppressors' proud command?
Could the wronged realm no arm supply
But the abject tear and the slavish sigh?

Yes, my lord, we are told that, had we been servile and base in our language, and silent in our suppression, we should, in proving that we deserve to be slaves . . . ensure liberty!!

That kind of thing was the stuff that would waken Kerry. Spoken, as it was to Fingall, it was also the stuff that must disrupt the Dublin councils. It was the cry of a whole people against the cry of men who felt themselves wronged as individuals. Against the individual O'Connell was being driven to stand for the nation that was stirring in the womb of the century; he was being driven by that most powerful of all emotional pistons known to man, a blazing love of place and a fond memory for the lost generations of his tribe, the ineradicable *pietas* of all submerged peoples. With that momentum behind him there could be no holding O'Connell. Without it, or with but a weak form of it, these other Irishmen, all intellectually honest, all intellectually aware of the people, but not, as he was, suffering in their bowels for their children, were perforce left behind.[1]

How one wavers over O'Connell! He said he was a Radical, and intellectually it is clear that he was not a Radical. Yet you only had to scratch him, as you need only scratch any Irishman worth his salt, and you found you released an inferno of emotions that at the slightest excuse supported an utter Radicalism. When Perceval was assassinated that May of 1812, O'Connell had the spirit not to think like an Englishman because an Eng-

---

[1] Christopher Manus O'Keeffe sums up what O'Connell's generation thought on this. (His *Life and Times of O'Connell* was published in 1867.) "An insurmountable barrier separated the party which O'Connell guided and the faction which Fingall led. They could not be reconciled. While in Wicklow, Lord Fingall could see only two or three titled men, O'Connell in the same county saw one hundred and fifteen thousand inhabitants. In Westmeath Lord Fingall could only see the Marquess of Buckingham. O'Connell could see a perfect swarm of thousands."

lishman was dead. He chose, instead, to remember a poor Irish woman whose boy had been recently killed in an Orange clash.

Are all your feelings [he bellowed] to be exhausted by the great? Have you no pity for the widow who lost her son? Are her feelings to be despised and trampled on? Is the murder of her boy to go unpunished? Is there no vengeance for the blood of the widow's son? YES! *The head of the government which allowed the blood of that boy to flow unrequited may have vindicated the idea of a divine Providence!*

There again was the kind of talk that the country wanted to hear; and talk that made Fingall shudder in his chair and the *Edinburgh Review* froth at the mouth.

He tried to speak now as often as he could of the Union, and he found himself running counter, every time, to the gentleman of the party. Once Fingall could stand no more of it and held him up. For a second he stopped, and then he growled:

I submit. But I cannot stand over my country's grave without shedding a tear, and as I will never consent to the sale of my country, I despise the man who would accept any boon at its price. The man who would hug his chains for a day does not merit freedom. . . .

I 2

THE next year, 1813, ended the internal struggle. It was a year of schisms, opposition, state persecutions. The No Popery cry was on every lip in England. The signs of a revived spirit among the Catholics had provoked Orangeism into a series of daylight brutalities and fly-by-night Black-and-Tanism. The Lord Lieutenant, Richmond, had been told to play the game of conciliation, but the Orangemen would not listen to him. In Bandon they simply stood aghast when he dared to chide them, and then threw down their arms and left him looking at their backsides. There were scenes in the Commons. Irishmen like Colonel Hutchinson had already brought the House about their ears by their blunt denunciations, and Grattan was constantly trying to echo the feeble voice of his country by repeating and repeating the cry that "the naked Irishman has the right to approach his God without a licence from his king." Still government followed government and there was no change of policy. Liverpool followed Perceval, and the screw on the Irish remained just as tight as before. In Ireland Whitworth followed Richmond, and one of his first acts was to spend £10,000 in buying up the souls of the Dublin newspapers' proprietors in order to break this new Catholic Board.

Things were now at a gallop. In May 1812 the Castle had pounced on Fitzpatrick, a Dublin bookseller who was aiding the democrats by publishing a book on the Penal Laws; they combed it for sedition and found it in a footnote. The trial began in the autumn and was the first of O'Connell's open combats with the Crown. In the meantime there was a General Election and the Catholics fought it wherever they could. It was the first of O'Connell's open combats with his domestic enemies. It marks the position he had already attained, that, when they came to reckon up the results of the election in November and held a public meeting under the windy walls of Kilmainham, the cry that rose from every throat was "O'Connell, O'Connell!"—and the newspapers of the day described that cry as "a cry rising from all sides for *The Man of the People*."

He is now in his late thirties, not yet at his eminence, though rising to it—near enough to it to strike everybody as the picture of a popular leader. There he was in his element, under the open sky, where the slums still send their reek of turf-smoke up from the dumps and lanes on the fringe of Swift's ragged Dublin. With immediate vigour he drives to his subject, speaking with the voice of acknowledged authority.

I could not be an Irishman if I did not feel grateful, if I was not overpowered at the manner in which you have received me. Sorry, sunk, and degraded as my country is, I still glory in the title of Irishman. [Bursts of applause.] Even to contend for Ireland's liberties is a delightful duty to me. [Enthusiastic applause.] And if anything is wanting in addition to the evidence of such humble efforts as I have already been engaged in for the restoration of our freedom and independence to evince my devotion to the cause of my country, I swear now, by the kindness you have shown me, by any I have ever experienced at your hands, and by all that I hold valuable or worthy of desire, that my life is at her service. [Applause.] May the hand of adversity fall down upon me, and upon all that are dearest to me—the children of my heart—if I ever forsake the pure pursuit of the liberty of Ireland. [Cheering for several minutes.]

That is the note of every speech he ever gave from that day forward—the personal identification with Ireland, the easy acceptance of pre-eminence, the direct emotional appeal of the chosen leader. With it comes the growing note of defiance, expressed in sarcasm, direct abuse, or open contempt.

The period is highly important and calls for all the watchfulness, zeal, and assiduity of which we are capable. An administration (formed Heaven knows how) has promised that they shall not interpose their authority to interrupt the good intentions of any man. I will, however, give them little credit for sincerity. I believe they would not even pretend to claim *our* confidence. They have too much modesty to expect to be believed by us. [Laughter.] They are our national enemies. They hate liberty. They have an inherent abhorrence of freedom. And their hostility for us is particularly embittered by our contempt for them. [Loud applause.] Yes, gentlemen, such are the men whom you, in your resolutions, have justly termed "incompetent" and "profligate." Such are the men who now command the destinies of these realms, and probably the fortunes of Europe.

At this point he refers to the name of their greatest orator, John Philpot Curran, and is interrupted for several minutes by the cheers of the people. The reference shows us O'Connell building up a sense of native tradition.

I am not surprised that you should feel the most ecstatic emotions of the heart when I allude to the name of John Philpot Curran. The name has conducted you back involuntarily to that most awful era in our annals when we were metamorphosed into a colony of a people who were not and are not in the least worthy of being our masters. But, my friends, if we are true to ourselves, if Protestant and Catholics be alive to their commonest and most intimate interests, we may, profiting, among other aids, by the assistance of this very idol of ours, become a kingdom once more. [Thunders of applause.]

I advert to what my most venerated friend said at Newry. He said that Englishmen love the privilege of being governed by Englishmen. I say that Irishmen fully as highly value the privilege of being governed by Irishmen.

He then characteristically reviewed the result of the elections. "Johnny" Croker has been kicked out. "Jack" Gifford and "Billy" MacAuley, the police magistrates, could not get a man to oppose Mr. Shaw in Dublin. The "felonious rabble" of the Dublin Corporation had not the courage to present a man against Grattan, he "who watched Ireland's independence in its cradle, and followed it to its tomb." Then he uttered a sentence which the papers of the day describe as "received with shouts of applause that were taken up again and again for many minutes."

Such is the state of the elections. Such is the state of your cause. Is it not demonstrative that if you had a Protestant Parliament in Ireland they would emancipate you?

As an example of his early, entirely mild, and not very striking invective, to be compared with his later vitriol, there is a reference to Castlereagh, who had been returned in a Northern constituency.

In speaking of Lord Castlereagh I do not know how to select words adequately to express my feelings. I should become an old man in foaming out the torrent of hatred and indignation with which my bosom teems. He is not here, but I do not feel myself less authorized to speak as an honest and injured Irishman should speak. There is, in all probability, some spy lurking to apprise him of all that goes forward. Let the man who buried thousands of our brave troops in the marshes of Walcheren, and destroyed the springs of his country's liberty, know the feelings experienced by an Irishman when his name is mentioned.

Enough from that speech! There is nothing in it; there is everything in it—nothing to us because a hundred years of repetition have dulled the effect of what was then unheard of, novel in the directness of its attack and the width of its appeal—nothing to us, chiefly, because we have not the man. Add his bulk, his massive body, the magnificent head, handsome face, flash of eye, the roar and vigour of the lungs, and all his Irish passion and fire that made him acceptable as a symbol of what he spoke, and we may know how and why the people responded so wildly to him, as another people responded to the antique orator with —not *How well he speaks*, but *Let us march against Macedon!* It was said, likewise, of O'Connell, that when he once said, with a dash of his head and a flash of his eye: "*The Tories shall not prevail!*" he turned a whole vast mob inside out with excitement.

He could do that because, as says de Cormenin, "he handled the rough tools of the mechanics, went into their workshops and homes, grasped their hands, horned from toil; he put his heart to their hearts and felt the beatings." In body and soul, origin and life, in his ways and in his words, he was the epitome of all their pride, passion, surge, and hope—their very essence.

What would we not give to be able to come close up to even one such workshop or home, in any casual corner of the island, and see in their casual acts, hear in their casual words, let alone have revealed to us by some striking personal contact with him, what they really felt about O'Connell! And how they felt it, and exactly how expressed it, in what way it enlivened them! A novelist might intuitively imagine such incidents. None remain. The folk-memory is not helpful—it too readily seized on the symbol rather than the intimate detail, and has left us with a vague legendary O'Connell rather than a real one. All the folk-legends we have tell of his superhuman cleverness, his cunning ways, how he fooled a judge, saved a rogue, could be killed only by a wound in the heel, or was born with the sign of the cross on his back. I know only one story of a simple human nature, and that tells of his kindness to the son of an old tenant of his who had, unwisely, married above his class. This man had been a constable in Dublin, and his rich wife, her love cooling, began to despise him for his rough ways. In misery the man went to O'Connell. Characteristically the Counsellor's first question was: "Have you secured a dowry, or part of a dowry, for yourself?"

"No," sighed the unhappy husband.

"Then I can do nothing for you," said O'Connell, and was showing the poor fellow to the door when he took pity on him, and cast about for some way to help him. Finally he told him what to do. The following day (according to plan) O'Connell passed by the man's house, arm in arm with the Lord Mayor, and accompanied by several gentlemen, saw and "recognized" the ex-constable standing at his own door, and warmly greeted him. Then he sent in his card to the haughty wife, was asked to come in, and astonished and delighted her by the dignity and station of her husband's "friends." Thus, says the story, did the Liberator make a man of the constable, and from that day forward the lady and her relatives were proud of him.

If only we had a score of intimate stories of that kind. If only some peasant had kept a diary. If only there had been a few rural newspapers, however poor and ragged, in which we could read the crude letters of his admirers. If only . . . if only . . . ! And, again, how we curse those Gaelic songsters who might so easily have brought us by the hand and sat us down by the hearth of the people, and let us hear them on what most concerned them—instead of weaving their endless classical myths into hare-brained visions about the return of James Stuart.

Perhaps a dozen times, while writing this biography, I have come to some such point as this—a point where a formal account of the lives of the people seemed necessary; but having gathered and regathered the little, the terrible little, we know about the physical conditions under which our forefathers lived, I have thrown it aside each time as unrevealing and almost irrelevant, and I know, in the end, that to describe their daily lives is something I cannot do. All these details of outward debasement—the slatternliness, and the hunger, and the dirt, all the pitiable subterfuges by which starvation was barely evaded—seem to get us no nearer the reality of their lives, not merely because it is impossible to make these black pictures more vivid than Lecky, for example, has already made them, but because by the very fact of insisting on the physical degradation one suggests that the evil was itself physical, and so, easily remediable. It was neither. The horror of the eighteenth century, the hardly less searing horror of the nineteenth century, is the mental horror—the murder of the mind, the spiritual chloroform, the creeping paralysis of the soul that O'Connell checked.

There are the huts made of earthen sods, or of mud strengthened with straw; the rank reek of the wet turf on the hearth; the smoke that blinds the eyes as one creeps into the interior—often on hands and feet; there is the rain brown-dripping through the thatch; and there in the webbed murkiness are the huddled shapes of men and women, children and beasts. But if their eyes and our eyes seem to smart with the smoke and damp, is it not something more than the smoke and damp that makes them water? Come out into the air and visit another hut, and yet another hut, so alike that a dozen travellers have compared such clusters to an African kraal; and if, by good fortune, a better chance sends us to a cabin where there is, for some reason, a bright cloth, a clean table, or even a flower-pot, can the relief of it be unalloyed by the thought that this happy comparison only emphasizes the hateful norm? As late as 1845—when O'Connell's work was done—the American, Mrs. Nicholson, could find families burrowing in the sand, like rabbits, in the island of Omey; and she met a young man near Clifden who cursed the potato, the main sustenance of his people, because the landlords knew men could live and work hard on it, and kept their wages down accordingly. But that young man drove to the point, in his passionate fury crying out: "They keep us like slaves, and then they *despise* us!" That is the point to which one must come sooner or later. There *only* does the real search begin, with the thought that these poor wretches may have lived internally a life as wretched as they seemed. One comes, there, to broken pride. For that there is, naturally, no record but the absence of record: the emptiness of non-being!

The reader has a wide choice of authorities if he would get an elaborate picture of the externals of that Ireland—Lecky, Kohl, Nicholson, Caldwell, Carleton, Le Fanu, Barrington, Edgeworth, and a score else. Two books will give him all he wants, Michael Doheny's *The Felon's Track*, and *The Bible in Ireland* by Mrs. Nicholson; both the more impressive by being written late in the nineteenth century. It may be left to the imagination to decide what life was like before O'Connell.

I have already quoted from Mrs. Nicholson. I now give one description from *The Felon's Track*. Doheny was "on the run" down on the western peninsulas, in 1848. Near Glengarriff he took refuge in a mountain cabin, from near which he could see —as may still sometimes be seen—two British men-of-war in Bantry Bay. This cabin—it was only a mile from the hotel—was unusual; but the description is pertinent, since, even to this day, the traveller may find cabins hardly more tolerable in that hard region.

We had not [he writes], during our wanderings, met two such characters as this man and woman, nor had we taken shelter in so extraordinary an abode. They had a single child, a girl about four years of age, whose dark eyes and compressed lip already evidenced the presence of those terrible passions that had burned deep channels along the brow and cheeks of her mother. The cabin was ten feet square with no window and no chimney. The floor, except where the bed was propped in a corner, was composed of a sloping mountain rock, somewhat polished by human feet and the constant tread of sheep, which were always shut up with the inmates at night. The fire, which could be said to burn and smoke, but not to light, consisted of heath sods dug fresh from the mountain. A splinter of bogwood, lurid through the smoke, supplied us with light for our nightly meal. The tea was drawn in a broken pot and drunk from wooden vessels, while the sheep chewed the cud in calm and happy indifference. They were about twelve in number, and occupied the whole space of the cabin between the bed and the fireplace.

That is a typical *harsh* description of the poorer world that served O'Connell. (Mrs. Nicholson has them by the dozen.) But it is the humanity inside the shell that we want to get at; and Doheny goes far to let us enter into the hearts of these two poor souls. He goes on, and one cannot help seeing a symbol in the image of the woman he so finely describes:

In that singular picture, the figure of the woman stood out bold, prominent and alone, absorbing, in its originality, every character of the entire. Neither she nor her husband could be said to wear any dress. Neither wore shoes or stockings, or any covering whatever on the head; shreds of flannel, which might once have borne the shape of drawers, a tattered shirt of unbleached linen, with an old blanket drawn uncouthly about his waist and shoulders, completed the costume of the man. His wife's was equally scanty and rude, but so arranged as to present the idea that even in her breast the sense of fitness, the last feeling of froward womanhood, was not quite extinguished. The squalid rags and matted hair, by a single touch of the hand, a gesture, or a shake of the head, assumed such shape as she fancied would display to the greatest advantage what remained of a coarse and masculine beauty. The consciousness that she once possessed such beauty fired at once her heart and eye. Her foot and ankle, which had been rudely tested by flinty rocks and many a winter's frost, were faultless; her step was firm; her form erect and tall; her hair black as ebony, her features coarse but regular; her brow lofty but furrowed and wrinkled; and her terrible eyes dilated with pride, passion, and disdain.
Her lip's slight curl, or a shade of crimson suddenly diffusing her dark complexion, bespoke her feelings towards her husband. He was her drudge, her slave, her horror and her convenience. Her ruling

idea was to have it understood that the match was ill-assorted and compelled by necessity; though the last idea bespoke a youth of shame.

The child alone was dressed, and with some care, as if she wished to assert its claim to a superior paternity or better destiny. Among the predominant passions which swayed her, avarice was uppermost; and she scowled ominously on her stupid husband, whose rigid, impassive stolidity seemed impervious to all prospects and chances of pleasure and gain. . . . Both the people of the house slept on the hearthstone, without any bed, or, as far as I know, any covering but their rags.

The woman, so preserving in her shame some pride, some pitiable hope for her child, was called, locally, in derision of that saving speck of human dignity, by the name of *Finey*. That last touch, scorn of wretches by wretches, strikes me as being truly terrifying.

But "Poor naked wretches, wheresoe'er you are"—the poorest of them not far poorer than the mass of men and women who were called out by O'Connell to raise their country from its slime—what heart can read of them without such pity, and such rage, and such love for O'Connell, as blots out in the end every emotion but one of pride in them and him? That night, Doheny wrote a song as he lay awake—not a good song, not more than verse, in that spirit of love for his country, and sorrow—for it is 1848, with O'Connell dead and famine in the land—that her hour has not struck:

> 'Twas told of thee the world around,
> 'Twas hoped of thee by all,
> That with one gallant sunward bound
> Thou'd burst long ages' thrall. . . .

He knew the "thrall," outward and inward. The outward he has already summed up by his description. It may, even to this day, be summed up for any modern traveller by the sight of the remains of such huts as this one in which, thank Heaven, few now live; or by the sight of the ridges high upon the mountainside, now softened over with grass, detected only by the expiring sun, where no modern farmer would try to extract food from barren soil, but where such poorest folk as these climbed up into the desert places, and gladly sweated to get a potato or two for their wives and crying children. Below these ridges the economist-historian draws a line, and calls it the starvation-line. That century could not afford to make such a distinction. Or perhaps it is summed up in the total of over a million people who died of hunger in the two or three years of 1845–47 after O'Connell had closed his titanic struggle to lift them out of beggary. Or perhaps it is summed by Lecky's phrase for the eighteenth-century peasants, when he called them "torpid and degraded pariahs"; with, beside it for contrast, their sudden burst of hope and courage when O'Connell called them out as Moses called the children of Israel out of bondage; and then, for dreadful comment on the magnitude of his task, O'Connell's ultimate failure?

There are two stories that seem to me to define the inward "thrall" in human terms. The first tells of an old man whose son had, in some extraordinary way, managed to find himself a niche in Dublin and prospered, in whatever humble way, beyond all expectations. (The price paid for that one would dearly love to know—the price in terms of the young man's spirit, hurt pride, choked anger, bitter persistence.) Describing his son's career the old father was at a loss to find words for it, and he said, stumbling for some extravagant image of unprecedented success in society: "That boy . . . that boy . . . do you know what he might do yet? He might— What might he do? Glory be to God but that young boy might some day become a Protestant!"

The other story reminds us of the famous condition of rule by "deputies of deputies of deputies"—Chesterfield's phrase for the methods of absenteeism; further defined by Barrington's classification of the local petits-lords into Gentlemen to the Backbone, who lived in London, or Bath, or Dublin on rack-rents; Gentlemen Every Inch of Them, who may have lived on their estates, though rarely attending to their own affairs; Half-Mounted Gentlemen, or Squireens, who would come directly between the absentee and the peasant. We have to remember further, however, that even these had other, lesser, creatures to do the unpleasant work of bailiff, or agent, or rent-collector, often some poor peasant picked out from the mass to grind his fellows. Each one of these middle-men took his percentage or his salary, and the rents swelled and swelled so that the Gentlemen to the Backbone in Bath, London, or Dublin should not get too little from the land. It was this system that made revolt so futile. To dump a bailiff in a bog, to shoot a rent-collector, was like tearing down a fence that grew up again over-night. It makes one realize that "rack-renting" was a good name for the entire process. It suggests the turning of the screw.

In Kerry the local gentlemen, of whatever rank, were called "colonels." The story goes to prove that the local people knew well that these colonels were their real masters, and that Parliament, and even the law, was as nothing beside these local landlords or agents. It tells how a poor wretch was being condemned to death for cow-stealing; he paid so little heed to the sentence that the judge leaned forward and said: "Do you know what I am saying?" The condemned man looked up at him and said: "Yes, I do. But I don't heed you. For I am looking at Colonel Blennerhasset there, and he hasn't said anything yet."

That peasant was the realist of the court. He knew, roughly but truly, up to the Union, that the Dublin Parliament would do nothing for him. Many of the landlords were members; nobody in it but profited by the landlord system. No Catholic—none of about four millions—could be a member. He might vote after 1793, but for whom? He was not, for a long period, even permitted to listen to the debates, supposing he could have understood them. During the reign of George II, that Parliament had gone into conclave once every two years for thirty years without an election, so that there were members who were dead, members who were dying, members who were mad. And after 1800 that Parliament had gone to London, with all its faults thick upon it.

But the whole lesson of that story is that to talk of Parliament is absurd; not because it was rotten but because the people, until O'Connell came, knew nothing about it and cared less. How should they, when for a hundred years—up to 1782—there was not a school in Ireland, other than illegal hedge-schools, except, of course, for the minority? The people had no newspapers until O'Connell founded an organ, *The Pilot*, to support him, and then they would have had to get some literate person to read the English words to them. Up to 1782 there was not even that gathering at the church-doors which serves in country places for the dissemination of news. Indeed, before O'Connell, it is probably true that the people knew as much, if not more, about the affairs of France and Spain, to and from which their priests were smuggled, than they did about the affairs of Dublin or London. For such people the landlord—the Colonel Blennerhasset of each region—*was* the law. In his memoirs Sir Jonah Barrington records that, in his district, the Queen's County, the people firmly believed that the Lord of Cullenaghmore (the local Big House) had a feudal right to save a man's life at every assizes, and he adds:

It did frequently so happen that my father's intercession in favour of some poor deluded creature [he means some man who had the courage to rebel] was kindly attended to by the Government; and certainly, besides this number, many of his tenants owed their lives to similar interference. It was wise in the Government to accede to such representations, since their concession never failed to create such an influence in my father's person over the tenantry that he was enabled to preserve them in perfect tranquillity. . . .

Or, in accurate terms, in the perfect torpor of acquiescence.

It is when one realizes this acquiescence that the physical conditions dwindle into the background. They were the results of conquest, and they became the causes of torpor, it is true; but the torpor is the nightmare, for the torpor means the death of despair. We feel like throwing up our hands when, in Barrington, we come on that well-known description of how his tenants used to squat around the fires at night (and, of course, he compares them to Asiatics and Red Indians) to recount the traditional stories of how their landlord's ancestor escaped from the Jacobites. For, says Barrington, "the tenantry, though to a man Papists, and at that time nearly in a state of slavery, joined heart and hand in these rejoicings, and forgot the victory of the enemy while commemorating the rescue of the landlord." Not that one *blames* the tenants. The Barrington family seem to have been excellent landlords, for their time, and it was better that the people should serve and be protected, when there was no hope of better days, than not serve and die by the roadside. But it all marks the task of O'Connell, and the late hour of his arrival.

It means—and again one abandons hope of describing their lives—that when we try to realize their lives all we are left with is an image of a vast moving pall of human beings, stirring like a cloud of locusts that stirs with the first touch of the sun. We imagine their chaffering and murmuring, their myriad movement —like life being created at the beginning of the world. For all separate, secret, intimate, private life is lost to us unless we see its image in him—the die in whose shape he begins to emboss them as by the power of a hammer . . . one by one . . . a Vulcan manufacturing millions.

13

To think of him as already commanding power is, however, incorrect. Power he held; his power he always defended successfully; power he never "commanded." He ruled a "mutable Athens." They, who so cheered him on that fifth of November, were attacking him like dogs on the fourteenth of November. It is an incident not at all important; it is interesting only as a revelation of what the life of a democratic agitator is like from the inside.

It arose because that John Philpot Curran, so cheered at Kilmainham, had been defeated by two votes at Newry by a Catholic named Caulfeild. O'Connell wished to let the whole thing pass, but the mob was eager for Caulfeild's blood, and O'Connell's devoted slave and friend, Jack Lawless, was the most furious of all. "I beg you," besought O'Connell before the next meeting of the Catholic Board, "not to speak of this matter." Jack promised. He was even indignant when O'Connell reimpressed on him the necessity for not raising further dissension in a body already torn with dissensions. And then Jack went on the platform, and the first thing he did was to condemn the scoundrel who had dared oppose Curran at Newry. Long after, O'Connell knew how to handle the reckless fellow—"Cross him at the start," he found, "and he is off at a gallop; let him alone and he will bog himself." In his rage O'Connell could not contain himself; he not only "crossed him at the start," but he leaped on him and tore him to pieces. It was the wrong tactic. Jack was off at a gallop like a dog with a joint of meat. In vain O'Connell tried to side-track him. He pointed out the danger of these public condemnations; he told Lawless that his air-drawn dagger would soon be pointed at meritorious men; that he was letting justice dwindle into the petty, mischievous character of a tool for every ill-minded man to use in satisfaction of personal resentment; he as much as told him he was a coward to rob a man of his reputation in the dark; and finally he managed to get the discussion postponed.

It availed him nothing. His hot-heads were now uncontrollable, and Jack packed the next meeting. The very passages swarmed with his supporters. In dismay O'Connell fought him again, and tried another postponement, but the packed meeting voted him down. Outside the ballad-singers were baying the wretched Caulfeild with:

Then push about the glasses O,
Corruption, boys, we'll support,
While Caulfeild's whisky passes O.

The meeting paid no heed to the Man of the People, and
passed its factious resolution by a huge majority.

Doggedly O'Connell stuck to his point, fighting for his authority; he came back to it a week or so later, and he started the
wiliest of manoeuvrings to get the motion rescinded. He assured
his flock that he had *not* (!) already actively opposed Mr. Lawless because of a relationship with one of the people involved. He
did, in fact, disagree with Mr. Lawless's motion, but only because it was illegal.

My friends [he implored them, in effect], do you not realize what
you have done? You have gone outside the business of this Board,
which is here only to prepare petitions [!], and so played right into
the hands of the King's Bench. You are now at the mercy of the
Attorney-General. However, there is no need to get frightened,
because I am prepared to prove, on your behalf, if you so wish, that
you acted irregularly. This I do not say in any desire to diminish
the triumph of Mr. Lawless, but simply to show what a valid defence
we [!] have against the magistrates. I am sure they would have taken
legal action against you long before now but for one thing: that,
being our enemies, they feel that you are doing their work for them
by thus destroying us all by these dissensions.

Having thus terrified his unruly followers, he turns to the business of raising their spirits by attacking their enemies, and with
their nationalist fervour thus at fever-point, he opens his arms
wide to them in appeal:

Gentlemen, I conjure you in the name of that afflicted country,
which has so many ardent and affectionate votaries in this room, to
waive all matters of form. Let us now adopt a resolution of admitted
truth and necessary conciliation. Let us think that poor Ireland,
goaded and distressed, wants all our attention.

To which incident we may put the closure of an "Etc."
To which he could put no closure, since, when the meeting

is over, he goes back wearily to his routine of study, sleep, rise
in the dark morning—for it is now December (1812)—his walk
to the courts to labour, back from them to meet his disgruntled
followers, and that routine day in and day out. One must have
some slight experience of committees to know what it all means,
and to know that Ireland might thank God that his young back
was broad enough to carry her burdens. A week later and he is
at it all over again; another petition. And then comes the business of a contra-petition from the Protestants. It is amazing that
he could there show the rollings and gambollings of his mind,
mocking the patent forgeries in the signatures to the Protestant
contra-petition—a sample of his vivacious escape from the dull-
ness of routine, his power of rejoicing in all aspects of his work,
a sign of his real joy of life:

Forgery exhausted [he chuckles], mere fiction was resorted to,
but as there was danger in giving common names that might be dis-
avowed, the fabricators produced names that no man ever bore or
will bear. They united the nobles families of the Feddlies to the il-
lustrious race of the Fiddlies, they created the Johnnybones, and
added the Macoobens to the Muldongs. To the uncleanly Rottens is
annexed the musical name of Nasavora, the Sours and the Soars, the
Dandys and the Feakens, appearing with Fibgetts, Gent., five Ladds
and five Palks, Huzies, Hozies, Sparlings, Sporlings, the Hoffits and
the Phantons, the Chimnisks, and Rimnicks, and Clumnicks, and the
Rowings and Riotters. They threw in the vulgar Bawns, and they
concluded, after a multitude of fantastic denominations, with Zach-
ariah Diamond. [*Great laughter*, comments the Press.]

He enjoyed that. He would have enjoyed the ruffians who
took that short-cut to petition-making, because there was something racy and salty about that kind of rascality.

But, in his sleep, how he must have dreamed of resolutions!
Thousands of them! Every one of them to be proposed, seconded, spoken to, one by one. . . . An endlessness of resolutions! To be opposed, defended, lost, won. They would have
taken fleshly shape and gibbered at him in nightmare, and the

very words would have gone tramping barefooted, soft-padded, across his brain—as they do with the mind of every man who works with words on the minds of men. Ghostly gentlemen begging to propose, for who can possibly conceive, when, my lord, it has been said, contrary to the fact, of course, however, nevertheless, which I shall proceed to demonstrate. . . .

The curly head lies, meanwhile, on its pillow, half-hearing—for to such men there never comes a deep sleep—the far cry of the night-watchman, or the laughter of some dandified bucks echoing back from the lovely, staid Georgian fronts, the reckless contempt of the conqueror.

14

THAT Christmas over, we come to the three great events that thrust O'Connell into the throne of leadership . . . and left him there, with nothing between him and his enemies but the untrained masses of the Irish poor; as it left the Irish poor with nothing between them and their enemies but him. These three events were the trial of the bookseller Fitzpatrick, the trial of the journalist Magee, and the last straight fight with the aristocrats over the Veto.

From the outset it was patent that Fitzpatrick and Magee were only whipping-boys. The Government had, in the inconclusive trials of Sheridan, Kirwan, and Taaffe, arrested delegates of the Catholic Committee, fought two rounds with O'Connellism. When Saurin, the Attorney-General, began the prosecution of Fitzpatrick for his book on the Penal Laws, he made it quite clear that he was attacking the spirit of sedition through this one man. His words were without reserve. His methods of the most brutal. His intentions pitiless.

The offensive passages, he said, were without "regard to truth or decency," a "calumniation of justice under every Lord Lieutenant," "infamous as a libel," an "abomination," "full of jesuitical art," a "call to the people to break out into civil and religious war," while portions were "sufficient to inflame the Catholic mind to madness." It was, as may be seen, the old fight for the absolute authority not only of the State but of the Protestant State, not only for the imperial suppression of a people, but a piece of illiberal sectarianism ill contrasting with O'Connell's inclusive and tolerant liberality. It was a despotic argument as outdated as the Revocation of the Edict of Nantes. So that when O'Connell accepted the implicit challenge, ignored the innocence or guilt of Fitzpatrick as a man charged with libel, and concerned himself with the exposure in his case of the illiberality of English rule, and the intolerance it bred to thrive on, he lifted the whole case of that obscure bookseller to a plane on which it would have been intelligible and significant in any city in Europe. He extracted the principle of rational toleration, and of the separateness of Church and State, from a vulgar action for libel.

The main charge against Fitzpatrick was founded on a footnote which declared that a Catholic named Barry had been hanged in Kilkenny, in 1810, though "patently innocent." O'Connell called up the judge—it was Norbury—and coolly demanded that he be put in the witness-box. He did the same with Saurin, the Attorney-General. He did not get them, needless to say, but he got from the fury of Saurin, at the very idea, a definition of what they were really arrived at. "Were they," fumed Saurin, "to turn the Court of King's Bench into a Court of Parliament to try the King's Government?" *They were.*

O'Connell then called up Campbell, who had defended the unfortunate Catholic, Barry.

"Why didn't you proceed with the defence of Barry?"

"I applied for a postponement because the trial was suddenly transferred from Clonmel to Kilkenny, and the defendant could not procure his witnesses. The judge said he would not grant the motion and the trial must go on."

"Was there any opposition from the prosecuting counsel?"

"None whatever."

"Did any magistrate interfere?"

"Yes. Mr. Elliot was sitting in the bar-box. I asked him in open court if these witnesses resided at the distance stated. He said they did. I therefore drew up Barry's statement and asked for a postponement on it in order to procure his witnesses."

"What passed?"

"Some things," said Campbell, at this point, "that I do not want to repeat."

"However unpleasant, sir, it may be for you to answer, my duty compels me to request an answer."

"I told the judge I would not go through the mockery of a trial when the man had no witnesses. I told his lordship that he must defend the man himself. I threw up my brief and left the court."

"Anything more?"

"Yes. I received a mandate to attend the trial. I contemptuously rejected it."

"On what grounds did the judge refuse the application for postponement?"

"He said that if a trial was to be postponed on an affidavit so *complete* as mine, business could never be proceeded with, since prisoners would only have to employ counsel to draw up an affidavit when they wanted to postpone their trials. I asked his lordship what he would have said if the affidavit had been *defective?*"

"After the conviction did you make any effort to obtain mercy?"

"I wrote a respectful letter to Lord Norbury enclosing the voluntary statements of Barry's witnesses that he was in their company forty-five miles away when the robbery was committed. I received no answer."

"Did you mention the circumstance to any person?"

"I told it to everybody I met. I talked publicly of it in the hall of the Four Courts."

The judge interposed to ask in what manner he spoke of this affair.

"As a most shocking event."

"You had no doubt," insisted O'Connell, "it was a shocking circumstance?"

"It *was* a most shocking circumstance."

"Are you of the opinion that the conduct of the judge was a fit subject for Parliamentary inquiry?"

"I am. I repeatedly said so."

"Did you not by a letter to the Attorney-General offer to attend him and give every further explanation of this illegal transaction?"

"I did. But I never heard further from the Attorney-General."

The extract may halt there. It is enough to illustrate O'Connell's method which, in the case of Magee, was to become enlarged to its limit—far beyond its limit, indeed, as any other man would have conceived it. He pointed the moral in his final effort to set aside the verdict on Fitzpatrick that wherever a Catholic was on trial he was tried by men who had given a solemn and deliberate pledge of their hatred and dislike of all Catholics, i.e., of all the common folk of Ireland.

15

BLOODED by the carcass of Fitzpatrick, Saurin answered that charge of O'Connell's by bringing up John Magee, the proprietor of the popular evening paper, the *Dublin Post*, on the charge, again, of seditious libel. Magee was a Protestant. His crime was to have printed a nine-column libel on the Duke of Richmond. It had been written either by the Denis Scully who wrote the book Fitzpatrick published, or by Councillor James

Finlay, both of the democratic party in the Catholic Board. This trial became the most famous of all O'Connell's combats at the bar. He fought it with such wild courage that it not only marked him out definitely as the national leader, but defined the attitude of his party, smashed the aristocratic junta, and flung the entire movement into the balance between utter ruin and ultimate success.

The libel appeared while the Fitzpatrick case was still going on. By early July, Saurin had Magee in the dock and was already addressing a packed court and, it goes without saying, a packed jury. The atmosphere was similar to that of any one of the great State trials, less deservedly better known, of the Parnellite and Land League days. It was infinitely more tense; it began, from the start, to vibrate not only with the opposition of two personalities, Saurin and O'Connell, and was not only heavy with the political destinies of the individuals whom these combats between Castle lawyers and Catholic lawyers had involved, but it became a trial where the destiny of a people might easily be decided for years to come.

Peel, just appointed Chief Secretary, sat in the court. The Commander-in-Chief was just below the judges. Dignitaries of the Castle attended daily. The *Post* whipped up the excitement by persisting in its attacks on the Duke even while the trial continued. Saurin made the issue clear at the outset:

If the libel related only to the Duke it would have gone unprosecuted by me. But the imputation is made against the administration of justice by the Government of Ireland, and it forms only part of a system of calumny with which an association of factions and revolutionary men are in the habit of vilifying every constitutional authority in the land.

It marks the impression made by O'Connell's handling of this trial that it was hardly over before the Protestants in the Dublin Corporation declared that they were "frightened," and the Government printing presses began the business, which did not end till O'Connell's death (and not even then), of hammering out the words "ruffian . . . ruffian . . . ruffian . . ." whenever his name had to be mentioned.

Their abuse became meaningless; one of them called O'Connell a "bandy-legged dancing-master"; another printed a challenge from a bravo who wished to fight O'Connell "hilt to hilt." In cold truth the trial left the minority at a loss. Young Peel, the new Chief Secretary, wrote to Whitworth, Richmond's successor, in a tone of bewilderment, a summary of what he saw:

O'Connell spoke for four hours, taking the opportunity for uttering a libel even more atrocious than that he was proposing to defend, on the Government and the administration of justice in Ireland. His abuse of the Attorney-General was more scurrilous and more vulgar than was ever permitted within the walls of a court of justice. He insulted the jury, collectively and individually, accused the Chief Justice of corruption and prejudice against his client, and avowed himself a traitor, if not to Ireland, to the British Empire.

Yet O'Connell had only taken up the glove flung by Saurin and lashed it back into his face. He tried through two adjournments to defend Magee by law; spoke law and won it; mocked Saurin's law and forced the bench to support him; then he abandoned the case as an ordinary legal fight and launched himself bodily on the Attorney-General, on the Government, on the whole system which Magee had assailed, and while he did the court seems to have listened open-mouthed, aghast, silenced, unable to realize that a cowering Catholic, one of the "scum of the earth," had stalked into their courts and flung defiance in their teeth. To the people the thing was tremendous. To them, O'Connell's attack on Saurin, like Saurin's attack on Magee, became a combat between Nation and Empire.

The whole of that magnificent, battering, shamelessly irrelevant speech of O'Connell's in reply to the charge of Saurin should, however long, be read in its entirety; never forgetting that the thing was without precedent in Irish history: no man of the people had ever thus spoken before. It must be remembered that it became a legend as it passed from mouth to mouth, for it was, after the trial, printed as a pamphlet and scattered in its hundreds of thousands throughout the island. It was delivered on July 27, the second day of the thrice-postponed trial, and we may gather easily the nature of Saurin's charge from the course of this reply. The speaker was just thirty-eight. What follows is a truncated version.

O'Connell began in a breathlessly silent court:

Gentlemen of the jury, I consented to the adjournment yesterday, from that impulse of nature which compels us to postpone pain. It is, indeed, painful to me to address you; it is a cheerless, a hopeless task to address you—a task which would require all the animation and interest to be derived from the working of a mind fully fraught with the resentment and disgust created in mine, yesterday, by that farrago of helpless absurdity with which Mr. Attorney-General regaled you.

But I am now not sorry for the delay. Whatever I may have lost in vivacity, I trust I shall compensate for in discretion. That which yesterday excited my anger, now appears to me to be an object of pity, and that which then roused my indignation, now only moves to *contempt*. I can now address you with feelings softened, and I trust subdued; and I do, from my soul, declare, that I now cherish no other sensations than those which enable me to bestow on the Attorney-General, and on his discourse, pure and unmixed compassion.

It was a discourse in which you could not discover either order, or method, or eloquence; it contained very little logic, and no poetry at all. Violent and virulent, it was a confused and disjointed tissue of bigotry, amalgamated with congenial vulgarity. He accused my client of using Billingsgate, and he accused him of it in language suited exclusively for that meridian. He descended even to the calling of names: he called this young gentleman a "malefactor," a "Jacobin," and a "ruffian," gentlemen of the jury; he called him "abominable," and "seditious," and "revolutionary," and "infamous," and a "ruffian" again, gentlemen of the jury; he called him a "brothel-keeper," a "pander," "a kind of bawd in breeches," and a "ruffian" a third time, gentlemen of the jury.

I cannot repress my astonishment, how Mr. Attorney-General could have *preserved* this dialect in its native purity. He has been now for nearly thirty years in the class of polished society; he has for some years mixed amongst the highest orders in the State; he has had the honour to belong, for thirty-five years, to the first profession in the world—to the only profession, with the single exception, perhaps, of the military, to which a high-minded gentleman could condescend to belong—the Irish Bar—to that bar at which he has seen and heard a Burgh and a Duquery; at which he must have listened to a Burton, a Ponsonby, and a Curran; to a bar which still contains a Plunket, a Ball, and, despite of politics, I will add a Bushe. With this galaxy of glory flinging their light around him, how can he alone have remained in darkness? How has it happened that the twilight murkiness of his soul has not been illumined with a single ray shot from their lustre? Devoid of taste and of genius, how can he have had memory enough to preserve this original vulgarity? He is, indeed, an object of compassion, and, from my inmost soul, I bestow on him my forgiveness and my bounteous pity.

Such an opening, before such an audience, cannot but have cut Saurin to the bone. The topical description of its effect, in O'Keeffe's biography, reads already like legend. "It was to little purpose that the Commissioner of the Forces, who sat under the bench, Lord Kinnaird, Robert Peel, and the Chancellor of the Exchequer, endeavoured to console him with kind whispers and soothe him with looks of sympathy. The sweat trickled down his forehead, his lips were as white as ashes, his jaws elongated, and his mouth unconsciously open."

O'Connell drove on:

But not for him alone should compassion be felt. Recollect that upon his advice, that with him as the prime mover and instigator, those rash, and silly, and irritating measures of the last five years, which have afflicted and distracted this long-suffering country, have originated—with him they have all originated. Is there not, then, compassion due to the millions whose destinies are made to depend upon his counsel? Is there no pity due to those who, like me, must know that the liberties of the tenderest pledges of their affections, and of that which is dearer still, of their country, depend upon this man's advice?

Yet let not pity for us be unmixed; he has afforded the consolation of hope. His harangue has been heard; it will be reported—I trust faithfully reported; and if it be but read in England, we may venture to hope that there may remain just so much good sense in England as to induce the conviction of the folly and the danger of conducting the Government of a brave and long-enduring people by the counsels of so tasteless and talentless an adviser.

See what an imitative animal man is! The sound of ruffian—ruffian—ruffian had scarcely died on the Attorney-General's lips, when you find the word honoured with all the permanency of print, on one of his pensioned and well-paid, but ill-read, newspapers. Here is the first line in the *Dublin Journal* of this day: "The ruffian who writes for the *Freeman's Journal*." Here is an apt scholar; he profits well by the Attorney-General's tuition. The pupil is worthy of the master; the master is just suited to the pupil.

I now dismiss the style and measure of the Attorney-General's discourse, and I require your attention to its matter. That matter I must divide—although with him there was no division—into two unequal portions. The first, as it was by far the greater portion of his discourse, shall be that which was altogether inapplicable to the purposes of this prosecution. The second, and infinitely the smaller portion of his speech, is that which related to the subject-matter of the indictment which you are to try. He has touched upon and disfigured a great variety of topics. I shall follow him at my good leisure through them. He has invited me to a wide field of discussion. I accept his challenge with alacrity and with pleasure.

Here O'Connell commences his speech proper, seizing eagerly on the challenge so deliberately thrown out by Saurin:

My lord, upon this Catholic subject, I commenced with one assertion of the Attorney-General, which I trust I misunderstood. He talked, as I recollect him, of the Catholics' having imbibed principles of a seditious, treasonable, and revolutionary nature. He seemed to me most distinctly to charge us with treason. There is no relying on his words for his meaning—I know there is not. On a former occasion, I took down a repetition of this charge full seventeen times on my brief, and yet, afterwards, it turned out that he never intended to make any such charge; that he forgot he had ever used those words, and he disclaimed the idea they naturally convey. It is clear, therefore, that upon this subject he knows not what he says; and that these phrases are the mere flowers of his rhetoric, but quite innocent of any meaning!

It is impossible to refute such charges in the language of dignity or temper. But if any man dares to charge the Catholic body, or the Catholic Board, or any individuals of that Board, with sedition or treason, I do here, I shall always, in this court, in the city, in the field, brand him as an infamous and profligate *liar!*

Pardon the phrase, but there is no other suitable to the occasion. But he is a profligate liar who so asserts, because he must know that the whole tenor of our conduct confutes the assertion.

What is it we seek?

At this the court tries, in vain, to stem the irrelevant flow:

CHIEF JUSTICE. What, Mr. O'Connell, can this have to do with the question which the jury are to try?

O'CONNELL. *You heard the Attorney-General traduce and calumniate us; you heard him with patience and with temper; listen now to our vindication.*

I ask, what is it we seek? What is it we incessantly and, if you please, clamorously petition for? Why, to be allowed to partake of the benefits of the constitution. We look to the participation in the constitution as our greatest political blessing. If we desired to destroy it, would we seek to share it? If we wished to overturn it, would we exert ourselves, through calumny and in peril, to obtain a portion of its blessings? Strange inconsistent voice of calumny! You charge us with intemperance in our exertions for a participation in the constitution, and you charge us at the same time, almost in the same sentence, with a design to overturn that constitution. The dupes of your hypocrisy may believe you; but, base calumniators, you do both, you cannot believe yourselves.

The Attorney-General—this *"wisest and best of men,"* as his colleague, the Solicitor-General, called him in his presence—the Attorney-General next boasted of his triumph over Pope and Popery: "I put down the Catholic Committee; I will put down, at my own good time, the Catholic Board." This boast is partly historical, partly prophetical. He was wrong in his history; he is quite mistaken in his prophecy. He did not put down the Catholic Committee; we gave up that name the moment that it was confessedly avowed that this sapient Attorney-General's polemico-legal controversy dwindled into a mere dispute about words. He told us that in the English language "pretence" means "purpose." Had it been French, and not English, we might have been inclined to respect his judgment, but in point of English we venture to differ from him; we told him "purpose," good Mr. Attorney-General, is just the reverse of "pretence." The quarrel grew warm and animated; we appealed to common sense, to the grammar, and to the dictionary. Common sense, grammar, and the dictionary decided in our favour. He brought his appeal to this court; your lordship and your brethren unanimously decided that, in point of law—mark, mark, gentlemen of the jury, the sublime wisdom of law!—the court decided that, in point of law, "*pretence*" *does mean* "*purpose*"!

Fully contented with this very reasonable and more satisfactory decision, there still remained a matter of fact between us: the Attorney-General charged us with being representatives. We denied all representation. He had two witnesses to prove the fact for him; they swore to it one way at one trial, and directly the other way at the next. An honourable, intelligent, and enlightened jury disbelieved those witnesses at the first trial [*Sheridan's*]. Matters were better managed at the second trial [*Kirwan's*]; the jury were better *arranged*. I speak delicately, gentlemen; the jury were better arranged, as the witnesses were better informed, and, accordingly, there was one verdict for us on the representative question, and one verdict against us.

Next, he glorifies himself in his prospect of putting down the Catholic Board. For the present, he, indeed, tells you that, much as he hates the Papists, it is unnecessary for him to crush our Board, because we injure our own cause so much. He says that we are very criminal, but we are so foolish that our folly serves as a compensation for our wickedness.

He expresses the very idea of the Roman Domitian, of whom some of you possibly may have read: he amused his days in torturing men; his evenings he relaxed in the humble cruelty of impaling flies. A courtier caught a fly for his imperial amusement. "Fool!" said the emperor, "fool, to give thyself the trouble of torturing an animal that was about to burn itself to death in the candle!" Such is the spirit of the Attorney-General's commentary on our Board. Oh, rare Attorney-General! Oh, best and wisest of men!!!

I do not hesitate to contradict the Attorney-General on this point, and to proclaim to you and to the country that the Catholic Board is perfectly a legal assembly; that it not only does not violate the law, but that it is entitled to the protection of the law, and, in the very proudest tone of firmness, I hurl *defiance* at the Attorney-General.

I defy him to allege a law or a statute, or even a proclamation, that is violated by the Catholic Board. No, gentlemen, no; his religious prejudices—if the absence of every charity can be called anything religious—his religious prejudices really obscure his reason; his bigoted intolerance has totally darkened his understanding, and he mistakes the plainest facts, and misquotes the clearest law, in the ardour and vehemence of his rancour. I disdain his moderation; I scorn his forbearance; I tell him he knows not the law, if he thinks as he says; and if he thinks so, I tell him to his beard, that he is not *honest* in not having sooner prosecuted us—and I challenge him to that prosecution.

It is strange, it is melancholy, to reflect on the miserable and mistaken pride that must inflate him to talk as he does of the Catholic Board. The Catholic Board is composed of men—I include not myself; of course, I always except myself—every way his superiors, in birth, in fortune, in talents, in rank. What is he to talk of the Catholic Board lightly? At their head is the Earl of Fingall, a nobleman whose exalted rank stoops beneath the superior station of his virtues, whom even the venal minions of power must respect. We are engaged, patiently and perseveringly engaged, in a struggle through the open channels of the constitution, for our liberties. The son of the ancient earl whom I have mentioned cannot, in his native land, attain any of the honourable distinctions of the State; and yet Mr. Attorney-General knows that they are open to every son of every bigoted and intemperate stranger that may settle amongst us.

But this system cannot last; he may insult, he may calumniate, he may prosecute, but the Catholic cause is on its *majestic march;* its progress is rapid and obvious; it is cheered in its advance, and aided by all that is dignified and dispassionate, by everything that is patriotic, by all the honour, all the integrity of the Empire; and its success is just as certain as the return of tomorrow's sun and the close of tomorrow's eve.

We will, we must, soon be emancipated in despite of the Attorney-

General, aided as he is by his august allies, the aldermen of Skinner's Alley. In despite of the Attorney-General and the aldermen of Skinner's Alley, our emancipation is certain, and not distant.

He next turns on the jury.

I have no difficulty in perceiving the motive of the Attorney-General in devoting so much of his medley oration to the Catholic question, and to the expression of his bitter hatred to us, and of his determination to ruin our hopes.

You are all, of course, Protestants. See what a compliment he pays to your religion and his own when he endeavours thus to procure a verdict on your oaths; when he endeavours to seduce you to what, if you were so seduced, would be perjury, by indulging your prejudices, and flattering you by the coincidence of his sentiments and wishes. Will he succeed, gentlemen? Will you allow him to draw you into a perjury out of zeal for your religion? And will you violate the pledge you have given to your God to do justice, in order to gratify your anxiety for the ascendancy of what you believe to be His Church? Gentlemen, reflect on the strange and monstrous inconsistency of this conduct, and do not commit, if you can avoid it, the pious crime of violating your solemn oaths, in aid of the pious designs of the Attorney-General against Popery.

Oh, gentlemen, it is not in any lightness of heart I thus address you; it is rather in bitterness and sorrow. You did not expect flattery from me, and my client was little disposed to offer it to you. Besides, of what avail would it be to flatter, if you came here predetermined, and it is too plain that you are not selected for this jury from any notion of your impartiality?

Gentlemen, I sincerely respect and venerate your religion; *but* I despise, and I now apprehend, your prejudices, in the same proportion as the Attorney-General has cultivated them. In plain truth, every religion is good—every religion is true to him who, in his due caution and conscience, believes it. There is but one bad religion— that of a man who professes a faith which he does not believe; but the good religion may be, and often is, corrupted by the wretched and wicked prejudices which admit a difference of opinion as a cause of hatred.

The Attorney-General, defective in argument, weak in his cause, has artfully roused your prejudices at his side. I have, on the contrary, met your prejudices boldly. If your verdict shall be for me, you will be certain that it has been produced by nothing but unwilling conviction, resulting from sober and satisfied judgment. If you be men of conscience, then I call on you to listen to me, that your consciences may be safe, and your reason alone be the guardian of your oath, and the sole monitor of your decision.

At last O'Connell approaches the actual subject of the indictment, and the definition of the immediate issues involved:

Mr. Magee is charged with publishing a libel in his paper, called the *Dublin Evening Post*. Gentlemen, this is not a libel on Charles Lennox, Duke of Richmond, in his private or individual capacity. It does not interfere with the privacy of his domestic life. Towards the man there is not the least taint of malignity; nay, the thing is still stronger. Of Charles, Duke of Richmond, personally, and as disconnected with the administration of public affairs, it speaks in terms of civility, and even respect.

The publication does not involve any reproach against the Duke of Richmond in any other than in his public and official character. The word seditious is, indeed, used as a kind of make-weight in the introductory part of the indictment. But mark! and recollect that this is not an indictment for sedition.

In the third place, gentlemen, there is this singular feature in this case—namely, that this libel, as the prosecutor calls it, is not charged in this indictment to be "false." Attend to the case, and you will find you are not to try Mr. Magee for sedition, which may endanger the State; or for private defamation, which may press sorely upon the heart, and blast the prospects of a private family; and that the subject-matter for your decision is not characterized as false, or described as untrue. The case is with you. It belongs to you alone to say whether or not, upon the entire matter, you conceive it to be evidence of guilt and deserving of punishment. The Solicitor-General cannot now venture to promulgate the slavish doctrine which he addressed to Dr. Sheridan's jury, when he told them "not to *presume* to differ from the court in matter of law."

If the Solicitor-General's doctrine were established, see what oppressive consequences might result.

Here he adroitly introduces an acid portrait of Attorney-General Saurin.

At some future period, some man may attain the first place on the bench, by the reputation which is so easily acquired by a certain degree of church-wardening piety, added to a great gravity and maidenly decorum of manners. Such a man *may* reach the bench—for I am putting a mere imaginary case; he may be a man without passions, and therefore without vices; he may, my lord, be a man superfluously rich, and therefore not to be bribed with money, but rendered partial by his bigotry and corrupted by his prejudices, such a man, inflated by flattery and bloated in his dignity, may hereafter use that character for sanctity, which has served to promote him, as a sword to hew down the struggling liberties of his country; such a judge may interfere before trial! and at the trial be a partisan!

Gentlemen, should an honest jury, could an honest jury (if an honest jury were again found), listen with safety to the dictates of such a judge?

Having thus effectively alienated all the sympathy of judges, jury, and prosecutor, O'Connell deals with the law of libel. His ideas on that subject are wise and humane, though they might even in our day be thought radical. He declared that the law of libel, such as it is, originated in the time of the Star Chamber, when a free expression of public opinion would have been the terror of every oppressive force; that, when the Star Chamber was abolished, its powers descended, with too many of its traditions, to the courts of common law, where "servility at the bar and profligacy at the bench have not been wanting to aid every construction unfavourable to freedom, and at length it was taken as granted, and clear law, that truth or falsehood are immaterial, constituting no part either of guilt or innocence." He goes on:

This revolting doctrine has no other foundation than the oft-repeated assertion of lawyers and judges. Its authority depends on what are called the *dicta* of judges and writers, and not upon solemn or regular adjudications on the point. One servile lawyer has repeated the doctrine, from time to time, after another, and one overbearing judge has re-echoed the assertion of a time-serving predecessor, and the public have at length submitted.

I do therefore feel gratified in having the occasion to express my opinion upon the real law of the subject. I have no professional rank, station, or talents to give it importance, but it is an honest and conscientious opinion, and it is this—that in the discussion of public subjects, and in the administration of public men, truth is duty and not a crime.

We may, at this point, leave the court for about an hour, while, now well in his stride, O'Connell takes the libellous article, sentence by sentence, as it refers to the Duke and his predecessors, and with it takes the whole of Irish history for his province, thereby defending the article, not the author. Heaven knows what Magee thought of that part of his counsel's speech. One had but to read the life of any Irish Chief Justice—even of the first Catholic Lord Chief Justice of Ireland, Morris—to know accurately with what contemptuous Tory disgust it was heard by Lord Downes and his three fellow-judges. To them, the presumption, if not the folly, of O'Connell's reinterpretation of Irish history from a Nationalist angle must have sounded like Jacobinism let loose. We may return for one of O'Connell's most daring pieces of insinuation. The effect of it is hard to imagine; the boldness of it is beyond words. After quoting from Strafford's account of his iniquitous legal machinery as viceroy, he says:

Now, let me take any one of you; let me place him here, where Mr. Magee stands; let him have his property at stake; let it be of less value, I pray you, than a compensation for two years' imprisonment; it will, however, be of sufficient value to interest and rouse all your agony and anxiety. If you were so placed here, you would see before you the well-paid Attorney-General, perhaps malignantly delighted to pour his rancour upon you; on the bench would sit the corrupt and partisan judge, and before you, on that seat which you now occupy, would be placed the packed and predetermined jury.

I beg, sir, to know what would be your feelings, your honour [humour?], your rage. Would you not compare the Attorney-General to the gambler who played with a loaded die? And then you would hear him talk, in solemn and monotonous tones, of his conscience. Oh! his conscience, gentlemen of the jury!

But the times are altered. The press, the press, gentlemen, has effectuated a salutary revolution; a commission of defective titles would no longer be tolerated; the judges can no longer be bribed with money, and juries can no longer be—I must not say it. Yes, they can—you know, we all know—they can be still *inquired out*, and "packed," as the technical phrase is. But *you*, who are not packed —*you*, who have been *fairly* selected, will see that the language of the publication before us is mildness itself compared with that which the truth of history requires.

In the oratory of any time we may readily find better examples of stinging sarcasm than the attack on Westmorland that follows, but it may well stand alone for its passion, its occasion, and its image of a young Irish half-outlawed Catholic lawyer flinging his scorn at the jury that intends, as he well knows, to convict a man of their own class and creed because he holds different political opinions:

"*The profligate, unprincipled Westmorland.*" I throw down the paper and address myself in particular to some of you. There are, I see, amongst you some of our Bible distributors, and of our suppressors of vice. Distributors of Bibles, suppressors of vice, what call you profligacy? Suppose the peerage was exposed to sale—set up at open auction—it was at that time a judicial office; suppose that its price, the exact price of this judicial office, was accurately ascertained by daily experience—would you call that profligacy? If pensions were multiplied beyond bounds and beyond example; if places were augmented until invention was exhausted, and then were subdivided and split into halves, so that two might take the emoluments of each, and no person do the duty—if these acts were resorted to in order to corrupt your representatives, would you, gentle suppressors of vice, call that profligacy?

If the father of children selected in the open day his adulterous paramour; if the wedded mother of the children displayed her crime unblushingly; if the assent of the titled or untitled wittol to his own shame was purchased with the people's money—if this scene, if these were enacted in the open day, would you call that profligacy, sweet distributors of Bibles? The women of Ireland have all been beauteous to a proverb; they were, without an exception, chaste beyond the terseness of a proverb to express; they are still as chaste as in former days—but the depraved example of a depraved court has furnished some exceptions, and the action for criminal conversation—before the time of Westmorland unknown—has since become more familiar to our courts of justice.

Call you the sad example which produced those exceptions—call you *that* profligacy, suppressors of vice and Bible distributors? The vices of the poor are within the reach of control; to suppress them, you can call in aid the churchwarden and the constable; the justice of the peace will readily aid you, for he is a gentleman; the Court of Sessions will punish those vices for you by fine, by imprisonment, and, if you are urgent, by whipping. But, suppressors of vice, who shall aid you to suppress the vices of the great? Are you sincere, or are you, to use your own phraseology, whitewashed tombs—painted charnel-houses? Be ye hypocrites? If you are not, if you be sincere —and, oh, how I wish that you were!—if you be sincere, I will steadily require to know of you, what aid you expect to suppress the vices of the rich and great? Who will assist you to suppress those vices? The churchwarden? Why, he, I believe, handed *them* into the best pew in one of your cathedrals, that they might lovingly hear divine service together! The constable? Absurd! The justice of the peace? No, upon his honour! As to the Court of Sessions, you cannot expect it to interfere; and my lords the judges are really so busy at the Assizes in hurrying the grand-juries through the present-ments, that there is no leisure to look after the scandalous faults of the great. Who, then, sincere and candid suppressors of vice, can aid you? *The press;* the press alone talks of the profligacy of the great, and at least shames into decency those whom it may fail to correct. The press is your, but your only, only assistant. Go, then, men of conscience, men of religion, go, then, and convict John Magee, because he published that Westmorland was profligate and unprincipled as a Lord Lieutenant; do convict, and then return to your distribution of Bibles and to your attacks upon the recreations of the poor, under the name of vices!

With an expulsion of breath, a sigh composite of mingled emo-tions, the court leans back. But he is not done. He takes up the paper again:

"The cold-hearted and cruel Camden."

Here I have your prejudices all armed against me. In the administration of Camden your faction was cherished and triumphant. Will you prevent him from being called cold and cruel? Alas! today, why have I not men to address who would listen to me for the sake of impartial justice! But even with *you* the case is too powerful to allow me to despair.

Well, I *do* say, the cold and cruel Camden. Why, on *one circuit*, during his administration, there were *one hundred* individuals tried before *one judge*. Of these, *ninety-eight* were capitally convicted, and *ninety-seven hanged!* I understand *one* escaped; but he was a *soldier who murdered a peasant*, or something of that *trivial* nature. *Ninety-seven victims in one circuit!!*

There follows another palpable hit at Saurin (for his French origin):

Have you heard of Abercrombie, the valiant and the good—he who, mortally wounded, neglected his wound until victory was ascertained; he who taught *French* insolence, than which there is nothing so permanent—even transplanted, it exhibits itself to the third and fourth generation—he taught French insolence that the British and Irish soldier was as much his superior by land as the sailor was confessedly at sea; he, in short, who commenced that career which has since placed the Irish Wellington on the highest pinnacle of glory? Abercrombie and Moore were in Ireland under Camden. Moore, too, has since fallen in the hour of triumph—Moore, the best of sons, of brothers, of friends, of men; the soldier and the scholar; the soul of reason and the heart of pity—Moore has, in documents of which you may plead ignorance, left his opinions upon record with respect to the cruelty of Camden's administration. But you all have heard of Abercrombie's proclamation—for it amounted to that; he proclaimed that cruelty in terms the most unequivocal; he stated to the soldiery and to the nation that the conduct of the Camden administration had rendered "the soldiery formidable to all but the enemy."

Do, then, contradict Abercrombie, if you dare; but by doing so it is not my client alone you will convict. You will also convict yourselves of the foul crime of perjury.

I now come to the third branch of the sentence, and here I have an easy task. All, gentlemen, that is said of the artificer and superintendent of the Union is this: "the artful and treacherous Cornwallis."

He then proceeds, to the amused laughter of the court, to recall the days when Saurin had not been yet bought over by the Government:

The charge of being a Jacobin was at that time made against the present Attorney-General—him, plain William Saurin—in the very terms, and with just as much truth, as he now applies it to my client. His reply shall serve for that of Mr. Magee; I take it from the *Anti-Union* of the 22nd March 1800:

"To the charge of Jacobin, Mr. Saurin said he knew not what it meant, as applied to him, *except it was an opposition to the will of the British minister.*"

So says Mr. Magee. But, gentlemen, my eye lights upon another passage of Mr. Saurin's, in the same speech from which I have quoted the above; it was in these words:

"Mr. Saurin admitted that debates might sometimes produce *agitations*, but that was the PRICE *necessarily paid for liberty.*"

Oh, how I thank this good Jew for the word! Yes, agitation is, as Mr. Saurin well remarked, the price necessarily paid for liberty. We have paid the price, gentlemen, and the honest man refuses to give us the goods. [*Much laughing.*]

Now, gentlemen, of this Mr. Saurin, then an agitator, I beg leave to read the opinion upon this Union, the author of which we have only called artful and treacherous. From this speech of the 13th March 1800 I select these passages:

"Mr. Saurin said he felt it his duty to the Crown, to the country, and to his family, to warn the minister of the dreadful consequences of persevering in a measure which the people of Ireland *almost unanimously disliked.*"

And again:

"He, for one, would assert the principles of the glorious revolution, and boldly declare if a legislative union were forced on the country against the will of its inhabitants, it would be a *nullity*, and resistance to it would be a *struggle* against *usurpation*, and not a *resistance* against law."

May I be permitted just to observe how much more violent this agitator of the year 1800 than we poor and timid agitators of the year 1813!

But, gentlemen, is the Attorney-General at liberty to change the nature of things with his own official and professional prospects? I am ready to admit that he receives thousands of pounds by the year of the public moneys, in his office of Attorney-General—thousands from the Crown solicitor—thousands, for doing little work, from the Custom House; but does all this public booty with which he is loaded alter the nature of things, or prevent that from being a deceitful measure, brought about by artful and treacherous means, against which Mr. Saurin, in 1800, preached the holy doctrine of insurrection, sounded the tocsin of resistance, and summoned the people of the land to battle against it as against *usurpation?*

Gentlemen, pity the situation in which he has placed himself; and pray do not think of inflicting punishment upon my client for his extreme moderation.

A passage omitted from most summaries of the speech is of interest as a commentary on O'Connell's ideas about religion. Still referring to Saurin's former opinions, he goes on:

"This is," said he, "an exclusively Protestant government." Mr. Magee and he are agreed. Mr. Magee adds that a principle of exclusion, on account of religion, is founded on injustice. Gentlemen, if a Protestant were to be excluded from any temporal advantages on the score of his religion, would you not say that the principle on which he was excluded was unjust? For the principle which would exclude the Catholic in Ireland would exclude the Protestant in Spain and Portugal. And there you clearly admit the injustice. In this court, without the least danger of interruption or reproof, I proclaim the injustice of that principle.

Is it not then lawful to print what it is not unlawful to proclaim in a court of justice?

I begin to understand what the Attorney-General means by the Freedom of the Press. It means a prohibition of printing anything except praise, and of discussing any abstract principle of government. That, gentlemen, is the boasted liberty of the press—the liberty that exists in Constantinople—the liberty of applying the most fulsome and unfounded flattery, but not one word of reproof. He talked of the press being a protection to the people against government. Against what does it protect? Yet he calls for your verdict on the ground that no such things exist as that which he admitted, which the law recognizes, and he himself venerates.

We may also pass over a central portion of the speech, which is a digression to follow a digression of Saurin's into such topical affairs as the recent prosecutions of Fitzpatrick and Watty Cox, who had been jailed for not paying a fine obviously beyond his means. O'Connell might have ignored these side-issues if he had not determined to follow every cranny of the Attorney-General's mind, and at the price of lengthening his oration to four solid hours of invective, make the prosecution an example of dogged counter-attack by popular opinion on government methods.

That done, he brings up, on the head of another sentence in the libel, a procession of past Lord Lieutenants—Bedford, Hardwicke, Camden, Fitzwilliam, Westmorland—and scarifies them as men who, like the Duke of Richmond, last of their line, concluded their terms with a record of unfulfilled promises, hopes burnt to ash, delusions suddenly exposed. The transition back to the jury is easy, and it would almost seem as if he did have some slight hope of influencing them; for he now begins to play on their own dissatisfaction with Richmond, reminding them how His Grace had chided the Munster Orangemen, toasted Ireland with the Limerick Papists, checked the Mayor of Cork for proposing an Orange toast, come back to Dublin after he had most pleasingly impressed the Catholics in the country, and then taken a marked part with the Protestant minority. Reading the portion of the article which flatters Richmond, he throws down the paper and turns to them, mingles appeals to their manhood with taunts that they can have none, stirs their memories —their own Irish memories as Protestant anti-Jacobites—when he defends Magee for saying that Richmond was a frightful partisan of an English ministry "whose resentments he gratifies, and for whom he now canvasses."

Well, and did he not canvass? Was there a titled or untitled servant of the Castle who was not dispatched to the South to vote against the popular candidates? Such interference is unconstitutional and criminal. It is, in substance and effect, high treason against the people.

I will recall to your mind an instance of the violation of the constitution, which will illustrate the situation of my client, and the protection which, for your own sakes, you owe him. When, in 1687, King James removed several Protestant rectors in Ireland from their churches, against law and justice, and illegally and unconstitutionally placed Roman Catholic clergymen in their stead, would any of you be content that he should be simply called a partisan? No, gentlemen, my client and I, Catholic and Protestant though we be, agree perfectly in this, that partisan would have been too mild a name for him, and that he should have been branded as a violator of law, as an enemy to the constitution, and as a crafty tyrant who sought to gratify the prejudices of one part of his subjects that he might trample upon the liberties of all. And what, I would fain learn, could you think of the Attorney-General who prosecuted, or of the judge who condemned, or of the jury who convicted, a printer for publishing to the world this tyranny, this gross violation of law and justice? But how would your indignation be aroused if James had been only called a partisan, and for calling him a partisan a Popish jury had been packed, a Popish judge had been selected, and the printer, who, you will admit, deserved applause and reward, met condemnation and punishment!

Of *you*, of *you*, shall *this story be told*, if you convict Mr. Magee. The duke has interfered in elections; he has violated the liberties of the subject; he has profaned the very temple of the constitution; and he who has said that, in so doing, he was a partisan, from your hands expects punishment. But is not the controlling the election of members of Parliament a more dangerous violation of the constitution? Does it not corrupt the very sources of legislation, and convert the guardians of the State into its plunderers?

What gentler phrase, what lady-like expression, should my client use? The constitution is sought to be violated, and he calls the author of that violation a frightful partisan. Really, gentlemen, the fastidiousness which would reject this expression would be better employed in preventing or punishing crime than in dragging to a dungeon the man who has the manliness to adhere to truth and to use it.

Has the Attorney-General succeeded? Has he procured a jury so fitted to his object as to be ready to bury in oblivion every fault and every crime, every error and every imperfection of public men, past, present, and future, and who shall, in addition, silence any dissertation on the theory or principle of legislation? Do, gentlemen, go this length with the prosecutor, and then venture on your oaths—I charge you to venture to talk to your families of the venerable liberty of the press—the protection of the people against the vices of the Government.

And now O'Connell feels that it is time to close. He appeals in the name of Magee's patent disinterestedness. He harps on the calumny to both Protestant and Catholic in the practice of jury-packing. There is a final slash at Saurin, who had boasted of the Sheridan-Kirwan trials, "*Me adsum qui feci. . . .*" "But he forgot to add, gentlemen, the more appropriate remainder of the phrase, '*Mea fraus omnis.*' "

He would not have made this, I must say, disgraceful avowal, unless he were influenced by an adequate motive. I can easily tell you what that motive was. He knew your prejudices; he knew your antipathy—alas! your interested antipathy—to the Catholics, and therefore, in order to induce you to convict a Protestant of a libel for a publication innocent, if not useful, in itself, in order to procure that conviction from your party feelings and your prejudices which he despaired of obtaining from your judgments, he vaunts himself to you as the mighty destroyer of the hopes of Popish petitioners—as a man capable of every act within, as out of the profession, to prevent or impede any relief to the Papists.

For my part, I frankly avow that I shudder at these scenes; I cannot, without horror, view this interfering and intermeddling with judges and juries. It is in vain to look for safety to person or property whilst this system is allowed to pervade our courts: the very fountain of justice may be corrupted at its source, and those waters, which should confer health and vigour throughout the land, can then diffuse naught but mephitic and pestilential vapours to disgust and destroy. And yet it is believed, it is expected, that this system is fated to be eternal. Gentlemen, we shall all weep the insane delusion; and in the terrific moments of alternation, you know not, you cannot know, how soon or how bitterly the ingredients of your own poisoned chalice may be commended to your own lips.

No Irishman who reads this page of this history but must here pause and reconsider one current opinion—that which often blames the older Gaelic Ireland for its failure to produce a popular rebel, a Wat Tyler, or even a Langland. Here is a jury of Protestant settler blood, appealed to on every possible ground to defend their adopted country from sectarianism, to defend the Liberty of the Press, to denounce the machinations of an oligarchy—and they fail themselves. One blushes for those Dublin Protestants as one reads the last, desperate, generous appeal of O'Connell:

Let me transport you from the heat and fury of domestic politics; let me place you in a foreign land. You are Protestants; with your good leave, you shall for a moment be Portuguese; and Portuguese is now an honourable name, for right well have the people of Portugal fought for their country against the foreign invader. Let us suppose for an instant that the Protestant religion is that of the people of Portugal, the Catholic that of the Government; that the house of Braganza has not reigned, but that Portugal is still governed by the viceroy of a foreign nation. You Protestants shall form, not, as we do in Ireland, nine-tenths, but some lesser number—you shall be only four-fifths of the population; and all the persecution which you have yourselves practised here upon Papists. Your native land shall be to you the country of strangers; you shall be aliens in the soil that gave you birth, and whilst every foreigner may, in the land of your forefathers, attain rank, station, emolument, honours, you alone shall be excluded——

Only think, gentlemen, of the scandalous injustice of punishing you because you are Protestants. With what scorn, with what contempt, do you not listen to the stale pretences, to the miserable excuses, by which, under the name of State reasons and political arguments, your exclusion and degradation are sought to be justified! In this situation let me give you a viceroy; he shall be a man who may be styled, by some person disposed to exaggerate beyond bounds his merits, and to flatter him more than enough, "an honourable man and a respectable soldier," but, in point of fact, he shall be of that little-minded class of beings who are suited to be the playthings of knaves.

We shall begin with making his tour from Traz-os-Montes to the kingdom of Algarve—as one amongst us should say, from the Giant's Causeway to the kingdom of Kerry. Upon his tour he shall affect great candour and goodwill to the poor suffering Protestants. Enmity to them shall become less apparent, though only the more odious for the temporary disguise.

The delusion of the hour having served its purpose he shows himself in his native colours, selects for office and presents for his pension list men miserable in intellect if they be but virulent against the Protestants. He selects from his Popish bigots some being more canine than human, who with no quality under heaven but gross, vulgar, acrimonious, disgusting, and shameless abuse of Protestantism shall be promoted to some accountant-generalship. This viceroy selects for his favourite privy-councillor some learned doctor, half-lawyer, half-divine, and entire brute, distinguished by his unblushing repetition of calumnies against the Protestants.

These covert references to (probably) Protestant tools such as Gifford and Duigenan, one must feel both as a mistake and as a measure of the gap between real and half greatness in O'Connell as an orator; he should have kept his analogy clear from personalities. He goes on:

Next take his acts. The Protestants of Portugal shall be exposed to insult and slaughter. Behold him depriving of command and staying from promotion every man who dares to think Protestants men; promoting and rewarding those who insult and attempt to degrade the first of your Protestant nobility. Behold him in public, the man I have described.

In his personal revenue he receives enormous emoluments from the people he thus misgoverns. See the most wasteful expenditure of public money, every job patronized, every profligacy encouraged. See the resources of Portugal diminished. See her discords, her feuds increased, and lastly behold the course of justice perverted and corrupted.

Have you followed me, gentlemen? Do you enter into the feelings of Protestants thus insulted, thus oppressed, thus persecuted—their enemies and traducers promoted, and encouraged, and richly rewarded; their friends discountenanced and displaced; their persons unprotected, and their characters assailed by hired calumniators; their blood shed with impunity; their revenues, parsimoniously spared to accumulate for the individual, wastefully squandered for the State; the emblems of discord, the war-cry of disunion, sanctioned by the highest authority, and Justice herself converted from an impartial arbitrator into a frightful partisan?

At last he brings home his parallel; and we must remember that Magee was one of the ruling creed:

But if, at such a moment, some ardent and enthusiastic Papist, regardless of his interest, and roused by the crimes that were thus committed against you, should describe, in measured and cautious and cold language, scenes of oppression and iniquity; if he were to describe them, not as I have done, but in feeble and mild language, and simply state the facts for your benefit and the instruction of the public—if this liberal Papist, for this, were dragged to the Inquisition, as for a crime, and menaced with a dungeon for years, good and gracious God! how would you revolt at and abominate the men who could consign him to that dungeon! What pity would you not feel for the advocate who, heavily and without hope, laboured in his defence! and with what agonized and frenzied despair would you not look to the future destinies of a land in which perjury was organized, and from which humanity and justice had been for ever banished!

With this picture of yourselves in Portugal come home to us in Ireland, say is that a crime, when applied to Protestants, which is a virtue and a merit when applied to Papists? Behold how we suffer here; and then reflect that it is principally by reason of your prejudices against us that the Attorney-General hopes for your verdict.

When that last, hopeless, urgent appeal to manliness fell on deaf ears, well might Lecky (in tracing the rise of rational liberty in Europe) speak with contempt of the constant alliance between the Church of England and despotism. Puritans, Nonconformists, Catholics, Presbyterians—these might and often did stand for human liberty. The Protestant Established Church—never.

Is there amongst you any one friend to freedom? Is there amongst you one man who esteems equal and impartial justice, who values the people's rights as the foundation of private happiness, and who considers life as no boon without liberty? Is there amongst you one friend to the constitution? one man who hates oppression? If there be, Mr. Magee appeals to his kindred mind, and confidently expects an acquittal.

There are amongst you men of great religious zeal, of much public piety. Are you sincere? Do you believe what you profess? With all this zeal, with all this piety, *is* there any conscience amongst you? *Is* there any terror of violating your oaths? Be ye hypocrites? or does genuine religion inspire ye? If you be sincere, if you have conscience, if your oaths can control your interests, then Mr. Magee confidently expects an acquittal.

If amongst you there be cherished one ray of pure religion, if amongst you there glow a single spark of liberty, if I have alarmed religion or roused the spirit of freedom in one breast amongst you, Mr. Magee is safe, and his country is served; but if there be none, if you be slaves and hypocrites, he will await your verdict, and despise it!

And so he has finished. Outside the effect of that speech was immense. In the court it produced no effect. Magee was found guilty.

16

IT is understatement to say that Saurin was angry, and that Peel was angry. For Peel, also, had been abused, and in a manner which indicates that O'Connell's invective was fast perfecting itself in scurrility and venom. "A raw youth," he had been called, "squeezed out of the workings of I know not what factory in England, sent over here before he got over the foppery of perfumed handkerchiefs and thin shoes, a lad ready to vindicate anything—everything."

They held the unhappy Magee in mid-air until July gave way to November, when his appeal was heard and rejected. They dogged him. He had printed O'Connell's oration in full in the *Post*, and Saurin dragged him up again for aggravating his original libel by repeating it. The other newspapers had done the same thing but that did not trouble Saurin. O'Connell was rallying every bigot in Ireland against the Catholic cause.

The Lord Chief Justice was also angry. He had been told that the scenes of July had disgraced his court. Peel had further written to Lord Desart:

I hope the Chief Justice will not allow the court to be again insulted and made the vehicle for treason, but that he will interrupt O'Connell's harangue by committing him to Newgate for contempt.

All told, it was apparent that O'Connell had had his day and he would not at this new trial repeat his former defiance.

"What does all this mean?" cried Saurin, at the opening of the second trial, waving the record of O'Connell's speech. "How comes this blustering and bravadoing into a court of justice? If it is intended to intimidate me in the discharge of my duty the impotence and folly of the attempt is no justification of its illegality. For I do say such an outrage on public decency had not occurred in the memory of man."

O'Connell was seated opposite Saurin. He rose to his feet, while the court stared and waited. The young Kerryman addressed the bench and told it that it was as well that the Attorney-General had stored up his resentment for the four months' interval since July. "Because that interval also enables me to overcome the infirmity of my nature, and listen to an attack that, had it been made elsewhere, would have merited chastisement."

The bench swooped—Daly, Osborne, Downes. Daly could not believe his ears. Osborne warned the young man to have a care. O'Connell seemed oblivious of danger.

My lord, what I say is that I am delighted at the prudence of the Attorney-General in having made that foul assault on me here, and not elsewhere, because my profound respect for the bench overcomes now those feelings that, elsewhere, would lead me to do what I should regret—to break the peace by chastising him.

Daly rose in his wrath: "Chastising! The Attorney-General! If a criminal information were applied for on that word we should be bound to grant it."

O'Connell did not budge, though he did reshape his words. Osborne decided to take the opinion of the court whether he should not be committed. The Chief Justice told him that if that line of language were pursued they would call on another counsel to proceed. The amazing thing is that they did not do this at once. Old Judge Day, the fourth of the judges, intervened just in time with a mild and friendly remonstrance that Mr. Saurin could not mean what O'Connell was pretending he meant. "We did not understand that the Attorney-General meant you when he talked of a participator in the crime of his client." Saurin himself concurred, and so, while the court must have gasped at his escape, off with the young demagogue, safe for the time being, magnanimously declaring himself satisfied. Thence he launched an attack on the administration of justice not less heated than that of July.

Surely, however, no more barefaced, yet unassailable piece of evasion was ever used in any court as this abuse of the court and of Saurin before their very faces:

I conclude by conjuring the court not to make this a precedent that may serve to palliate the acts of future and perhaps bad times.

I admit, I freely admit the Utopian perfection of the present times. We have everything in the best possible state. I concede that we have the best of times and the best of all possible prosecutors. The things that be could not be better. But bad times have been heretofore and bad times may come again.

There have been partial, corrupt, intemperate, ignorant, and profligate judges. The bench has been disgraced by a Bilknap, a Tressiliam, a Jeffries, a Scroggs, and an Alleyblown. For the present there is no danger, but in the future such men may arise again.

At such a period it will not be difficult to find a suitable Attorney-General—some creature, narrow-minded, mean, calumnious, of inveterate bigotry and dastard disposition—who will prosecute with virulence and malignity and delight in punishment. Such a man will, with prudent care of himself, receive merited and contemptuous retort; he will safely treasure up his resentment for *four months;* his virulence will for a season be checked by his prudence, until at some safe opportunity it will explode by the force of the fermentation of its own putrefaction, and throw forth its filthy and disgusting stores to blacken those whom he would not venture directly to attack. Such a man will with shameless falsehood bring sweeping charges against the population of the land, and afterwards will meanly retract and deny them. Without a spark of manhood or manliness he will talk of bluster and bravado, and talk of these falsely where a reply would not be permitted.

If such times arrive, my lords, the advocate of the accused will be sure not to meet what I should meet from your lordships today, were I so attacked; he would not meet with sympathy and equal liberty of speech. No, my lords, the advocate of the accused will then be interrupted and threatened from the bench, lest he should wipe off the disgrace of his adversary, the foul, false calumnies poured over him.

Again we wonder at the patience of the bench. Possibly some will turn from it also in disgust, for there is truly in all this a certain amount of the "bandy-legged dancing-master," the cheap mountebank. How different it all is from, let us say, Robert Emmet with his plumed hat and his naked sword, or the eloquent brothers Sheares, or magnificent Smith O'Brien, and it even offended the gallant Mitchel, who wrote the most scathing of all attacks on the cheap and clever lawyer of the Four Courts. Everybody, indeed, who regards gracious living, nobility in thought and word and behaviour, must read this demagogue with a curl of distaste. Only the vulgar fellows down in Kerry laughed with delight, like the vulgar fellows they were, and whooping their hats in the air, and straightening their backs that had been bent with a century of cringing, cried out that he was their Man. And everybody who has since then been able to live in the grace and luxury bought by the sweat of these peasants has shuddered at them, and at him, and at the consequences. Heaven knows, they may well do so, for O'Connell did a great deal to kill gentle manners in Ireland, to vulgarize and cheapen us. One might even forgive them as one sympathizes with them if there had been any alternative. The trouble with gentle manners is that they become the "justification" of injustice.

But poor Magee had had enough. He had carried all he could for O'Connell and Ireland, and he bade his counsel Wallace pipe a softer tune, if necessary even to apologize for what had gone before. Wallace did so, and with a restraint that did not, however, save him from the rage of O'Connell and the animadversions of the O'Connellites—especially on the head of the unfortunate phrase—"Let not the guilt of the client be aggravated by the sins of his counsel." It was too late. It would have been futile at any time. Magee was sentenced to two years in jail, a fine of £500, and ordered to find securities of £2000 for seven years and lie in prison until it was paid.

17

IF O'Connell was in all this secretly trying to seize absolute power and push everybody else out of his way he had set about it effectively. His methods were met with abuse on all sides except the side of the common people. He was accused of foolish violence and intemperance.

Yet [he summed up later] amidst all this violence and intemperance, what was the consequence? Why, that in 1813 a bill was near to pass intending and purporting to give us all. Our enemies themselves consented to give us everything except seats in Parliament. They consented to give us situations and command in the army and navy, places in our bar and on the bench, corporate officers and dignities, places in the excise and customs—all, all except Parliament. They consented to give us all!

That was Grattan's Relief Bill in May. The Catholic aristocrats in England and Ireland were well pleased. O'Connell refused. There came the break with the peers, and there the people commanded rather than obeyed their own Church. His objections and the objections of the people were based on the "reservations" that accompanied Grattan's bill. These reservations included securities to the Protestants, possibly justifiable, but of a doubtful morality, and from the democratic, libertarian, point of view of tolerance and nationality, in every way objectionable.

By these "securities" Catholics were to take a new comprehensive oath abjuring the infallibility of the Pope—not then a defined doctrine—the alleged power of the Pope to depose monarchs, abjure obedience to his temporal power, and reject the doctrine that faith need not be kept with heretics; they were to swear to support the Protestant succession, and the existing social order as regards property; to reveal all treasons within their knowledge; never to attempt to injure the State or the Protestant succession; and never to nominate or elect a bishop of whose loyalty they were in doubt. Such an oath puts back English politics to the condition of sixteenth-century France; from an England full of Protestant refugees from the bigotry of Louis XIV it comes with a stale smell of the folly that learns and forgets nothing. On the other hand it is so redolent of the spirit of Gallicanism in its fear and dislike of the Vatican that one fails to appreciate the motives that induced some of the Irish bishops and English vicars to lend it, at least, a qualified support.

18

THE discussions that arose over this bill tore the Catholic Board to pieces all through that summer, and they were already in a vexatious condition over the Magee case which was going on meanwhile in the courts. From the comments, entirely derisive, of O'Connell's nineteenth-century biographers, it is clear that the aristocrats completely lost favour in these discussions. The two Bellews—especially the younger—came in for sharp raps even from O'Connell when the popular party found that one was in receipt of a secret government pension. Fingall fell from favour when he refused to divulge an emancipation pledge said to have been given him privately by the Prince Regent in Hugh Fitzpatrick's bookshop in Dublin. His refusal involved such others as Lord Clifden and Sir Francis Goold, whose fine sense of honour about semi-private conversations was above the heads of the democratic party.[1]

But it was the English Catholic gentry who drove in the wedge. The history of these Catholic laymen is peculiar. It is evident that they endured their servitude with impatience and, having none of the national spirit of the Irish to support them, were willing to go to grave lengths to obtain religious toleration. When the question of the Veto first arose in 1808 they were already, for several years before, inclined towards a reduction of episcopal and even papal power with a view to appeasing Protestant susceptibilities. They had begun to inquire into the conduct of their own vicars and to claim the right to

---

[1] O'Keeffe will do for Fagan, Luby, and others: "Such men as Lords Carysfort, Meath, and Powerscourt were, in the opinion of Lord Fingall, the Irish nation. They were the true constituents of the senators who, in the House of Commons, are supposed to represent the county Wicklow, but who really represented their lordships—they were the people—they were everything! For their sakes—to keep them in the possession of those vast estates and ill-gotten riches —Lord Fingall dodged, shuffled, equivocated, and played the informer; for their sakes Lord Trimleston fenced, schemed, hedged, and lied—for their sakes Sir Edward Bellew plunged his brother into the foulest perfidy—the most heinous corruption! They risked their eternal salvation to please such men as, for instance, the Marquess of Buckingham, who every year of his life swept out of the county Westmeath seven thousand pounds! These were the men they sought to serve—not the famishing Catholics whose interests O'Connell advocated. . . ." (*Life and Times of O'Connell.* Dublin, 1867; vol. ii, p. 180. No author's name is given, but it is attributed to Christopher Manus O'Keeffe by T. C. Luby in his *Life and Times of Daniel O'Connell.* Glasgow, n.d.; p. 259.)

conduct Catholic affairs independent of them. They objected in 1787 to government by the four vicars-apostolic who managed Catholic affairs in England, saying that it was contrary to *Præmunire*—an early assertion of kingly power as against papal; and they proposed that the vicars should be chosen by their own flock, contrary to that papal claim to nomination which is as old as the twelfth century. They even signed themselves Protesting Catholic Dissenters. In 1808 the vicars were on these laymen's Catholic Board, and had accepted the principle of government nomination and government maintenance with all its consequences to popular trust in the independence and honesty of the clergy. Now, with the promise of religious toleration— on whatever terms of an insulting and restrictive nature, should Grattan's Relief Bill go through—they agreed to the obnoxious reservations of the new oath. They had but one serious opponent, Dr. Milner, Vicar of the Midland District, the acknowledged mouthpiece of the Irish bishops. He was shamelessly expelled by the lay gentlemen of the Board, ignominiously hooted from the room, and one gallant actually offered to box the old man.

The other vicars then met, without Milner, in the October of 1813 and defended the pandering English aristocrats in a joint pastoral.

The praises contained in the pastoral [wrote Milner] will most unquestionably be considered, both by the public at large and the parties themselves, as applying to those leading and acting Catholics who first, under the name of Protesting Catholic Dissenters, endeavoured to force a heterodox oath on the Catholic body; who next, under the name of the Cis-Alpine Club, professed to restrain the usurpation of the Pope; and who lastly have laboured to give securities to the Protestant Church, and lately advertised against me in the most affronting terms for saving them from the actual guilt of schism.

In that atmosphere the Irish Catholics could not be blamed for regarding their own hierarchy with a considerable reservation of distrust. When O'Connell moved a test resolution that no measure should be presented to Parliament without receiving the assent of the Irish prelates, he had to withdraw it in the face of an onslaught from their theologian, Dr. Drumgoole, who said:

What is this, but to ascribe infallibility to the bishops—to bestow that attribute on them in civil affairs which is not allowed to belong to a general council? . . . The promulgation of such an opinion would give colour to the charge that is often falsely and maliciously brought against us that we follow them in the most slavish observance, and that our very religion is in consequence not the religion of revelation, but the religion of our priests.

A speech that should be remembered by those who speak of O'Connell's Ireland as priest-ridden.

All that year the Irish democrats lashed the English gentry without pity. "Catholic trimmers," they called them; "cringing, cowering, and complimenting"; "they do nothing, they say nothing, they get nothing"; "animals who clamour for securities." "How often," cried Phillips, the poet and orator, "have I seen them, their hands grasping the jug, and their minds grasping the constitution, hiccuping confusion to Christ for the sake of the Church, and drowning their memories out of compliment to King William's!"

These Irish democrats were, it is true, defending their own cause in defending tolerance; but they must be complimented on defending a reasonable and vital principle—the freedom of the State in relation to any Church, even their own. The dispute brings Ireland, democratic Ireland, into the European world for the first time since the fall of the Stuarts.

The year went in a welter of resolutions and meetings held all over the country. The most remarkable was a resolution proposing an appeal to the Spanish Cortes, passed and affirmed at more than one public gathering.

The usual price of democratic agitation had now to be paid in full. There was a truly miserable scene in Cork when a public meeting broke into pandemonium before the howls of the populace. The respectable, conservative men on the Board had to resign, and the meeting to adjourn into the open fields where the populace could hear and take part. For months after, the walls of Cork were blackened with placards and the newspapers with advertisements condemning one side or the other. Poor Magee printed an unusually inflammatory letter on the general topic of the bill and was again tried and sentenced for it. The Protestants became more and more disturbed. The sense of unrest became so great that an English provincial newspaper printed full details, down to the names of the regiments involved, of an imaginary rebellion. John Mitchel, in talking of the rage of the Dublin tories at the sight of O'Connell's "Papish horses prancing on a Protestant pavement," may have taken his cue from the Corporation member who declared:

Papists may get their emancipation! Papists may sit in Parliament! A Papist may preside on the bench! A Papist may become Lord Chancellor or Privy Councillor! But . . . never, *never, never,* shall one of them set foot in the ancient and loyal guild of Tailors.

When the Jesuits bought Castle Browne in Kildare for £16,000 the *Hibernian* (a bought paper, of course) raised a wail of rage and terror:

Ireland stands in imminent danger; if Popery succeeds our fairest plains will once more witness days worthy to rank with those of Bloody Mary, and the walls of Derry shall once more become the bulwarks against Popish treachery and massacre!

Against this general storm O'Connell held firm, backed by his democrats, Plunket, Scully, Nicholas Purcell O'Gorman,[1]

---

[1] Nicholas Purcell O'Gorman was for many years secretary to the Catholic Association. *The* O'Gorman Mahon is a totally different person; his life has been written by Denis Gwynn. Nicholas Mahon was a prominent member of the Catholic Board; "almost a millionaire," says the editor of the O'Connell *Correspondence.*

Nicholas Mahon, Finlay, half-winning, half-forcing the bishops to line up at his side. He denounced the Relief Bill, and he made no bones about his objections to the idea of suborning the hierarchy, or encouraging a priest-ridden Ireland. Would that his words were as heeded today when the charge might be as easily, if not more easily, made against the democracy he founded:

Does any man imagine that the Catholic religion will prosper in Ireland if our prelates, instead of being what they are at present, shall become the servile tools of the administration? They would then lose all respect for themselves, all respectability in the eyes of others. They would be degraded to the station of excisemen and gaugers, and the people, disgusted and dissatisfied, would be likely to join the first enthusiastic preacher of some new form of Methodism, that might conciliate her ancient prejudices and court her still living passions. The ministerial bishops of Ireland would become like the constitutional bishops of France, a means of uncatholicizing the land.

That he could so speak of an unreliable and pliant clergy and not be called anti-clerical, as he would today for far more sedate criticism, means only that the clergy were in no position to attack anybody. Had they dared they would have undoubtedly rebuked him. It is an old joke among Irish curates that "the Irish bishop stands on ceremony and sits on everybody." As it was, they had the spirit to back O'Connell and defy even the Papacy itself.

By that stand O'Connell laid down a law, ever since followed in Ireland, with one or two exceptions which damaged the influence of the Church in each case, that the Church in Ireland works through the people, not through secular institutions, and that if the Church differs from the popular leaders it does so at grave risk to its influence even in matters that concern faith and morals. It is one of his greatest heritages to modern Irish democracy.

The bill was withdrawn. Grattan gave up hope. The aristocrats drew apart one by one, Fingall and a few others hanging

on pluckily over 1814. But the real end came at the close of
1813 when O'Connell rudely burst in on and dispersed a caucus
meeting in the private house of Lord Trimleston where an address to the Prince Regent was being prepared over the heads
of the democrats. No account of the sequel can improve on the
contemporary account, with its final phrase that, even today,
bites like acid:

As a body they were as effectively dissolved as the Council of
Five Hundred was—with this difference, that moral influence compelled in the one case what military direction achieved by force
in the other. The next step the seceders took was to secede from a
secession; and as the Irish watchman once said to a nocturnal intruder:
"*Disperse yourself*," each retired within the glittering shell of his
title or his opulence, and like snails they left no memorial but the
slime of their proceedings to record them.

O'Connell might there have quoted what Napoleon said to
Barry O'Meara. "Your aristocracy always detested me because
I, placed at the head of affairs by the people, threw open the
career to talent."

19

THAT crucial year closed fittingly with a presentation to O'Connell of a service of plate worth a thousand guineas, as a small
tribute of gratitude for his intrepidity in asserting the rights and
vindicating the character of his fellow-countrymen. A peer and
a viscount collaborated with six esquires in the presentation.

The new year fittingly opened with another presentation from
the artisans of the Liberties of Dublin. This gift was a silver
cup "glittering and crowded with *bassi rilievi*"—very Hibernian,
since "grouped and contrasted picturesquely on the reverse were
a harp, a broken chain, a book, and a lamp, a scale of justice, a
Mercury's wand, a scroll and a pen," and lest any space should
be slighted by a vacuity, "a shield emblazoned with the arms of

the Clan Conaill." The cup was presented to him in his Merrion Square home, and he accepted it with his two little boys at his side.

"It is the widow's mite," said the chairman, "but it overflows with our affections."

These two gifts, both of an ugliness impossible to describe, are preserved in the shilling museum which Darrynane has since become. Looking at them now, in that dark house, with the garrulous guide admiring volubly, one feels that in presenting the one, the Irish aristocracy shook hands with its past, with all its lavish generosity, its easy open-handedness, its well-meaning ineffectuality; and that in presenting the other, Irish democracy shook hands with its future—with all its ingenuousness, all its goodness of heart, all its earnestness, and all its unlettered vulgarity that nothing but a touching simplicity and a native courtesy saves from being wholly objectionable. O'Connell gracefully dismissed the past. Warmly he received the future. Had one been there as the door closed, and the little boys began to paw the silver cup, and Dan to admire it, one might well have been inclined to murmur in his ear:

And now may God help us, Dan O'Connell! You have delivered Ireland to Demogorgon. Your real fight begins. . . .

IV: THE MAN OF THE PEOPLE

1814–1829

I

CHAPTER divisions lie—a sop to one's love of perspective. For O'Connell there were no breathing spaces. He had still the remnants of the aristocrats to fight, and the Veto question was one that dragged on for another fifteen years. The English gentry were now manœuvring in the Vatican, so eager to get emancipation on any terms that they would almost turn Protestants to be allowed to call themselves Catholics. The foreign situation was in their favour, too. Italy was under the heel of Napoleon, the Pope a prisoner, his cardinals conspiring in Rome. Consalvi, the Secretary for State, was, for political reasons, in favour of the compliant English; Litta, the prefect of the Propaganda, was on the side of the Irish, and it was freely rumoured, and later accepted, that Lord William Bentinck was feverishly pulling strings to get a favourable decision before Pius VII might be released by the French. O'Connell and his army of beggars had dragged "cowering" Ireland into the region of foreign politics.

In the end, before Pius was released in April 1814, the vice-prefect at Rome, Monsignor Quarantotti, signed a letter addressed to the vicar-apostolic at London, Dr. Poynter. It ordered the Catholics of Great Britain and Ireland to yield to royal approval (or rejection) of episcopal nominations, and the clergy to permit careful inspection and examination of all papers, other than those appertaining to matters of conscience, passing between Rome and Great Britain. O'Connell promptly called it the message of a slave to slaves, and without a thought Ireland revolted against Rome.

The laity were first appalled and then contemptuous. They called Quarantotti "Mr. Forty-Eight," and "An understrapper of the Propaganda." They said he got his name from a lottery ticket won by his father. A popular cartoon showed him carrying a basket of Irish mitres to the Pope, while George III grabbed at them as symbols of a new patronage. O'Connell snarled that Poynter ought to be called "Spaniel." "If the Pope himself," roared Nicholas Purcell O'Gorman, O'Connell's right-hand man, "if the Pope himself, with all his cardinals, uttered a bull to back the rescript, I should not obey!" and the whole meeting howled their approval. At the Catholic Board O'Connell uttered his famous pronunciamento:

I would as soon take my politics from Constantinople as from Rome. I put, in the present case, theology, of which I know nothing and desire to know nothing, out of my consideration entirely.

In other words, if religion was not going to be democratic in Ireland, then it was not democracy that would suffer. The contemporary story about the priest's housekeeper summed it up. "Oh, your reverence," she wailed, "is it true the Pope is after turning into an Orangeman?" The Catholic bishops here stood firmly by the people. They met in a two days' conference at Maynooth and rejected the command from the Vatican.

Emissaries were meanwhile passing to and fro from both parties, Macpherson from the English laity, Archbishop Murray from the Irish hierarchy; Cardinal Consalvi to London, Father Dick Hayes, the Franciscan, from Dublin to Rome, where he seems to have been so blunt and downright as to anger the Pope

himself, even to the point of having to be forcibly ejected from
the city. The Pontiff issued a fatherly rebuke to the Irish hierarchy. The Irish hierarchy read it and was unmoved. In 1818
yet another letter came from Rome, and though it did not end
the controversy, it sweetened it a little. Other events swallowed
it up, and it gradually became less exigent according as it became evident that the British Government had no wish to make
it a practical issue by introducing another bill along these lines.
The whole thing meant no profit to Ireland, in so far as she was
deprived of at least a qualified emancipation, but it preserved
her honour, and it consolidated the position of the O'Connellites.

2

BY 1819, however—to look ahead a few years—we find O'Connell writing in a tone that is far from the tone of a leader consolidated in power. He says (and had we turned over the pages
of his history in the hope of seeing him racing to his triumph,
the words must come as a shock):

The most perfect calm reigns around. "Nor leaf is stirred nor
wave is driven." Not one sound disturbs our death-like silence or
our drear repose. All is tranquillity, quietness, and peace. The enemies
of every liberty, civil and religious, say the English are seeking a
revolution. . . . The people of Ireland show not the least symptom
of a revolutionary tendency.

What has happened? The hero has almost overthrown all personal obstacles. His people begin to adore him. His personal reputation is high. He can exact obedience and loyalty. That he
should record "perfect calm" five years later seems to be the
wrong progression.

The history of an agitator is the history of his enemies, and
they are always varied and many. Just when O'Connell stood
without a rival, and having rejected all allies in order that the
democratic position should be clear, should have been feverishly

reorganizing, there came the European peace of 1814. It gave Peel a chance to strike at the Catholic Irish, their loyalty no longer important. He proscribed the Catholic Board.

Waterloo kicked O'Connell when he was down. It ended the war boom, threw thousands out of employment, made the war-time rents and prices intolerable to the cottiers, and revealed, suddenly, that the population of the country was out of all sensible proportion to its wealth. Competition for land had become cut-throat, and Peel's cheap Ejectment Laws made it all too easy for the landlords to fling the wretched tenants-at-will out on the road by the whole town-land.

On the top of this came the smell of the rotting potatoes in the fields when the blight struck the island like a sirocco in 1817; under the horrified eyes of the people, the potato leaves curled up, became black-spotted, shrivelled, and stank over the earth. They clawed away the earth and the death of the tubers, foul masses of putrefaction, imaged their fate, unless charity came to help them or they could fend off famine with such messes as the boiled nettles and the wild kale. With famine came desperation, wild outbreaks of violence, the recrudescence of secret societies, midnight raids, and the usual English balsam of Coercion.

There was something more insidious. Peel was not the mere boy O'Connell had rashly called him; he was a wily man who was to become one of England's great imperialists. He began in Ireland a policy that many of his successors copied and developed—the formation of a class that became known as "renegade Catholics," or, in mockery of their affected half-English accents, "Cawstle Cawtholics." These were the seduced Irish who turned their eyes—not unnaturally, Heaven knows, in so impoverished an island—on Dublin Castle and British rule as the only means and centre of preferment.

That class was, in every way, except in regard to their abilities, contemptible—the baboos of Ireland, neither flesh nor fowl, as aware of their inferiority, according to the social standards they

accepted, to the Anglo-Irish colonists as these were aware of
their inferiority to the aristocracy of the mother country. Nothing made it possible for them to rise but the harum-scarum, tat-
terdemalion condition of so many of the resident Protestant
colonists, from squireen up to broken-down peer—they who
were later to become the love and joke and delight of everybody, in novels from such competent people as Edgeworth,
Lever, Somerville and Ross. (The Catholic aristocracy, denied
emancipation, lived at least in dignity, even if it was the dignity
of a besieged city or a convent parlour. They might be pawky
agitators, but they were at least true to their own class.) Peel's
policy created for these squireens a new form of petty rural society, a new weight on top of the people—local Resident Magistrates and Petty Stipendiaries, with County Court Judges chosen
later (1821) from aspiring young barristers, the virtual guides
and rulers of a police force, also invented by Peel, composed of
the Catholic sons of poor farmers and cottiers, who became a
network of espionage among their own folk.

From these grew up in time a vast native sycophancy, always
taking their sanctions from English approval, often winning
honour at home and abroad. They rose to the highest rank; they
did splendid work within the system they had adopted—the system of British imperialism—until nothing so undid the work of
O'Connell as this willingness on the part of England to reward and admire the loyal Catholic Irishman. The end was that
poor, native democratic Ireland, with so few of her own to honour, could not but pride in these who outshone so many Englishmen at their own game. It was imperialism at its subtlest and
finest, an example of quiet absorption and denationalization for
which Peel deserves the highest praise from his countrymen. It
even began to sap O'Connell himself at the end, but, by then,
he had done his work—he had awakened a spirit of courage in
his people that was to survive everything, even his own decline.

Here then, O'Connell, at a crucial moment in his career, could watch his poor people become too hungry to heed him, and too cowed to follow him. He had beaten the gentry with their temporizing policy that seemed to achieve nothing. He had forced the Church to weld political and religious independence into one cause. He had rejected the support of English sympathizers. He had turned emancipation into a national demand. He had flung aside everything and everybody but the poor he knew. He had called up a democracy from the vasty deep of slavery. And now, just when he was about to mass his recruits into a mighty army of beggars—he found them prostrate. Well might the aristocrats, the English sympathizers, his own cautious friends like Keogh and Sheil, think he had done nothing else but create ruin and despair.

Yet this is the period of O'Connell's personal magnificence. Hammered without mercy he became like a man fighting single combat for his people. He was threatened with the gun and blackened with libel. If there is now no suggestion of a conspiracy—there was at the time—it is certain that a large number of people would have been pleased to see him ruined or "removed."

Early in 1815 he spoke of the "beggarly" Corporation of Dublin. The representative of the Guild of Merchants, one D'Esterre, a virtual bankrupt, took mortal offence. He was a brave, hotheaded man, who had been nearly hanged during the mutiny on the Nore; the mutinous sailors had strung a rope about his neck and asked him if he would, even then, join them. "Hang away and be damned to you," was his reply, and it possibly saved his life. He sent a letter to O'Connell; in his reply O'Connell refused to withdraw the word. A further letter from D'Esterre on a Saturday was returned by O'Connell's brother, who expressed his astonishment at not receiving a direct challenge. The thing was now public property and the gossip of the whole of Dublin. But Sunday passed without a challenge. On Monday it was rumoured that D'Esterre was trying to provoke O'Connell into being the challenger, that he intended to horsewhip him in the street, and that his friends had actually hired a window in Grafton Street to see the fun. On Tuesday it was reported that D'Esterre was parading the streets with his friends, and accordingly, about four in the afternoon, O'Connell emerged, with *his* friends. People were by this wondering why the law did not detain the opponents, a common practice; and many became still more suspicious when, later, the court definitely refused an appeal to restrain the aggressor, D'Esterre. That Tuesday nothing happened; the two paraders did not meet; but later on in the day O'Connell had to appear before the courts and guarantee, on pain of arrest, that he would not be the aggressor. That night a jostle in Grafton Street between O'Connell's brother and some buckish friends of D'Esterre passed over without a challenge.

At last, on Wednesday morning, the challenge was sent to O'Connell's second, Major Macnamara, a Clareman noted for trigger-work. He at once named the place and the hour, three o'clock that afternoon at Bishop's Court in Kildare. To repeated requests that the hour be put back to two the next day, or at least to the next morning, or at least to half-past four that afternoon, the terrible major turned a deaf ear. The most he would grant was a delay of one half-hour, but he was willing to limit the duellists to one shot each. By now angry with the major, Sir Edward Stanley, D'Esterre's friend, declared that five-and-twenty shots would not do unless O'Connell apologized. "Very well, by God!" cried Macnamara, "if it's blood you want, blood you'll get."

To the field there came a bevy of noted bucks, and famous killers, including Dick Bennett and George Lidwell; the pistols used were Dick Bennett's, notched on the hilt to commemorate their kills. A priest hid in a near-by cottage in case O'Connell fell. There were so many Catholics that O'Connell greeted his tailor, Jerry O'Connor, with, "Hallo there, Jerry! But sure I never yet missed you from an aggregate meeting." Macnamara was useful. He changed O'Connell's white tie for a black one; he removed some seals dangling on his stomach; he could not brush off the white stains from O'Connell's coat where he had fallen when crossing a ditch to the meeting-place. The press was in attendance, and special couriers were at hand to bring the news to Dublin, where the crowds were waiting in trepidation, and a squadron of dragoons stood under arms in case of riot should O'Connell be killed.

The affair had all the habiliments of drama. There was a light fall of snow in the evening, and the oil lamps threw their gleams on faces that looked unnaturally pale. The first news came that O'Connell had fallen, and the dragoons raced for the field to protect D'Esterre. They met on the way the jolting carriage of O'Connell and his brother returning to the city. They called on the postilions to stop, and James O'Connell put out his head to tell them they need not bother to go any farther. Then Dublin heard the fact. D'Esterre had taken the first shot in the groin.

That night Dublin blazed out with bonfires in the melting snow, while the bailiffs rushed for the house of the dying man, where his young and beautiful wife was in her first agony of grief. He died of loss of blood after two days, and the only thing that left the house was his coffin. He was buried at night by the light of lanterns, the bum-bailiffs at the window watching the hearse trundle from his ruined home.

It was the last duel O'Connell fought. He formed, soon after, so powerful a conscientious objection to the practice that no taunts ever got him to take the field again.

3

In August Peel challenged O'Connell to fight, stung to rage by his vulgar taunts. That affair had a comic core to its seriousness. The efforts of the antagonists to meet became so elaborate as to be farcical when they failed to be effective. Mrs. O'Connell, in

terror for her husband, informed on him to the sheriff and had
him arrested. Angry but powerless, O'Connell had to give re-
cognizances in the sum of £10,000, but he got Dick Bennett to
sign an agreement with Colonel Brown, Peel's friend, that they
would meet outside the kingdom of Ostend. The affair was further complicated by the eagerness of Lidwell, O'Connell's second friend, and Sir Charles Saxton, Peel's second friend, to meet
on their own account. These two, with a blatant Anglo-Irish
consciousness of the drama they were playing, wrote long letters
to the press about the conduct and details of the whole affair,
and Lidwell, in the best eighteenth-century tradition, addressed
a letter "To the People of Ireland," to the leitmotiv of:

I go to the continent in your quarrel, for I have none of my own;
I go for a people the more endeared to me by their misfortune, and
for a cause to which my last words shall bear evidence of my
fidelity. . . .

The papers of the day took sides, the Irish saying it was a national dispute, the English reservedly keeping it on a personal
plane. O'Connell, who was a good deal of a cynic, must have
felt much as he did in after years, when he would sit at Monster
Meetings with his hat over his eyes, and a sardonic smile on his
lips, listening to the windy orators who preceded and followed
him.

He had, however, to make every effort to "get at" Peel, and
dodge the police of the French, English, and Belgian coasts; he
may or may not have known that the Home Office had told all
the local mayors to apprehend the two fiery seconds, Lidwell
and Bennett. He did his best, but just as he was about to step into
the Dover coach from Holiland's in the Strand, the detectives
arrested him. (Old Norbury rubbed it in when, shortly after,
Dan had occasion to remark saucily: "I am afraid your lordship
doesn't understand me." "On the contrary," smiled Norbury,
"Mr. O'Connell is always very easily apprehended"—which was
one occasion when Dan had no retort.) In sum the arrest became

a fresh insult, for Peel was allowed to cross to Calais unmolested, and the thing looked very much like a general collusion. In dudgeon O'Connell returned to Ireland, "lying on the cabin floor, as sick as a dog, with three gentlemen's legs on my breast and stomach, and the sea water dripping on my knees and feet." Sorry and sore, he had to stand before Justice le Blanc, who told him that if he and Peel were to fight anywhere, at any time, the survivor would assuredly be hanged for murder.

The honour of duelling, and of Ireland, rested on Lidwell. He did meet Sir Charles Saxton at Calais, where, under the influence of his disposition, he received the shot, and then fired in the air. He then made a long speech, and the pair shook hands. Peel, still angry with Lidwell, challenged him, but they never met.

<h2 style="text-align:center">4</h2>

O'CONNELL's private morals were publicly examined. To this day the commonest gibe at him is that if you threw a stick over a workhouse wall you could not fail to hit one of his bastards. Another typical tale records how he was showing some English friends over Darrynane, and they were amused to see a small urchin following, peeking and hiding in the shrubs. "And who are you, my little fellow?" asked O'Connell. "I'm the son of the great Liberathor, Daniel O'Connell," said the child in his singsong Kerry accent. It is strange that Kerry folk-lore (says his Gaelic biographer, Dómhnall O'Súilleabháin) has nothing to record against him but one verse, that an old woman was heard to sing to a child:

> A watch of gold,
> A watch of gold,
> And a chain of gold to go with it;
> A watch of gold,
> A watch of gold,

For the little son
Of Daniel bright O'Connell-o.

But Kerry tradition, when one thinks of it, has nothing to offer
one way or the other, since they had made Daniel bright O'Connell-o into a legend. One local story about him says that he could
be killed only by wounding him in his heel. If they said he was
an adulterer it would be of a piece. And the same must apply to
all oral tradition, and to such stories as that given. Similar fables
were common with regard to Gladstone, and arise about the
name of every public man. The only thing that comes near to
being evidence relates to this time—the alleged seduction of
Eleanor Courtenay in 1817.

According to the pamphlet she published in 1832 while in the
Fleet Prison, she waited on O'Connell at his Merrion Square
home to ask his advice about a small leasehold estate in County
Cork left her under a mortgage by her father. She was then fifteen years old and felt an enthusiastic admiration for his talents
and patriotism. On a second visit, she alleges, he criminally as-
saulted her.

Vain were all my struggles, all my prayers, all my cries for sustenance; he sank the man in the brutality of the monster and desisted
not from his prey until he had accomplished the most remorseless
and flagrant aggression which ever disgraced humanity.

Her child, we note, was not born until November 4, 1818,
christened (she said) at O'Connell's instructions in the name of
Henry Simpson, in London. She appealed in vain to the father
for help, although immediately after the assault he had taken a
book with a cross on it and sworn to provide for her. His excuse
now was that he would have no money until Morgan died, when
she should have a yearly allowance. (As Morgan, his father, was
dead ten years at this time, she may have meant Maurice, his
uncle.) In 1825 she returned to Ireland, after having profited by
the charity of some ladies named Lynch, of Great Russell Street,
Bloomsbury Square, who opened a school where she could teach

needlework. She accosted O'Connell—her story goes on—on his way from the Four Courts and was referred to his agents.

He had at that time, ten or twelve wretched females whom he had seduced, hanging upon him for support, and who were compelled to visit him at his own house . . . or they would be deprived of the wretched pittance which he occasionally doled out to them as a compensation for their ruined prospects, their estranged friends, their fall in society, their blasted happiness, and their lost honour.

She next went to a priest in Clarendon Street chapel, Father l'Estrange, and got a bill for £20 payable in two months on condition that she would swear never again to apply for help to O'Connell; he also implored her to "destroy Mr. O'Connell's letters." She ended by becoming an actress, took several benefits, played with Booth at the Royalty, gave up her child to O'Connell's agent, apparently Major Macnamara, who put him into one of those "charitable institutions in Dublin that are favoured with many of Mr. O'Connell's illegitimate offspring," after which she went to France, and came back to London to be clapped into the Fleet Prison for debt. From that prison comes her pathetic narrative, written, it is likely, whether true or false, to earn a pound or two from some scandal-mongering job-printer in the Strand.

That pamphlet is evidence. It may be false and wicked, but it is still evidence. The woman existed; she prints a letter of recommendation, given her when fifteen, from the Bishop of Cork—presumably genuine or it would have been refuted. She had with her a boy, who appeared in court in 1836, in London, whom she publicly acknowledged as her illegitimate son and who claimed to be Henry O'Connell, the son of Daniel O'Connell. That was after the scene in Cavendish Street where John O'Connell struck the boy, and a warrant was issued, as a result of which John was fined twenty shillings and costs and the boy was warned to desist from following Daniel O'Connell. But even if we could check the various ancillary details of her statement, which it is impossible at this date to do—such as the true age of the boy, whether any boy of such name was admitted to any charitable institution in Dublin after 1825, whether any will referring to property of hers in County Cork was admitted to probate after 1817, and so forth, the truth or falsehood of the essential statement depends on her word. Eleanor Courtenay's *Narrative of Most Extraordinary Cruelty, Perfidy, and Depravity, Perpetrated against Her by Daniel O'Connell, Esq., M.P. for Kerry* is evidence, but it is worthless evidence. The woman was either unhinged, depraved, or telling the truth in the depths of her rage and misery, and that leaves us in the worst possible position, victims of the unfortunate suspicions that such charges always carry in their train. Even if O'Connell had fought the *Times*, which believed Miss Courtenay (and we have no means of knowing if *they* ever examined her evidence), and had defeated them in a libel action, some of the mud would still stick.

Irish opinion has paid O'Connell in his own coin. Following his own opinion that "sins against morals are less than sins against faith" it is light-hearted about the imputation of sexual promiscuity. Many believe that the whole thing was engineered by his enemies. That is based solely on Irish experience of the methods of imperialism, exemplified in such cases as Gladstone's hypocritical treatment of Parnell, of the deliberate campaign of libel carried on against Roger Casement by the Foreign Office during the European War.

I do not believe in the traditional light-hearted picture of a whore-mongering Dan O'Connell, and nobody would be more delighted than a novelist to come upon the bizarre, human puzzle of the contrast between the public pietist, now honoured by millions of pious Catholics, then writing the most loving letters to his wife, and the private man secretly living a wholly different life—*if it were true*. It is not his loving letters to his wife that make that contrast incredible; the human heart is capable of far greater self-deception than that, and the Irishman is an adept at fooling himself—and furthermore we are here in the presence of a man whose mind was a perfect onion of worlds within worlds. Such an Irishman could have lived six lives and reconciled them all. What rebuts it is the love with which his wife is writing to him in the summer of that year 1817 when he was supposed to be seducing Eleanor Courtenay and keeping "ten or twelve wretched females" at his command. A woman like Kerry Mary O'Connell would not have been fooled by false protestations. No woman would have been deceived. She writes, for example:

CLIFTON,
July 14th, 1817.

MY OWN DARLING DAN,

I assure you, my darling, you are our continual subject. When a kind husband or father is spoken of, Ellen or Kate will exclaim: "Mamma, sure he is not so good a husband, or father, as our father." You may guess, darling, what my reply is. You know what you deserve, and you are aware that in existence I don't think there is such a husband and father as you are and always have been. Indeed I think it quite impossible there could, and if the truest and tenderest affection can repay you, believe me that I feel and bear it for you. In truth, my own Dan, I am always at a loss for words to convey to you how I love and dote of you. Many and many a time I exclaim to myself: "What a happy creature am I. How grateful should I be to Providence for bestowing on me such a husband!" And indeed I am. We will, Love, shortly be fifteen years married, and I can answer that I have never had any cause to repent it. I have, darling, experienced all the happiness of the married state without feeling any of its cares, thanks to a fond and indulgent husband. . . .

To that may be added, finally, the words of his admiring and intensely patriotic biographer, Thomas Clarke Luby: "He is said to have not infrequently forgotten his marriage vows." Perhaps so. Although it is, surely, an impertinence to invade any man's soul to that extent. O'Connell never pretended he was a saint, and any such possible lapses or emotional disturbances concern nobody but himself and his Maker.

In this doldrum period from Waterloo to 1823 when, in his own words, "a moral lethargy hung over the country," and he was almost alone in the field for Ireland, we get a chance, like that of his London years, to observe O'Connell at our leisure. It was the period when dull days first began to be rounded off by lively nights at the banqueting-table, a habit consolidated later by the Irish Party. If the Catholics could not organize public meetings they could at least enjoy public dinners, and the toasts—their only political justification—became as endless as they were inventive. Yet there was more honest truth, sometimes, at these jovial affairs than at a formal meeting.

At Tralee a typical banquet was given to honour the pride of Kerry, and we hear him speaking out, once again, just as he thought and wrote in his Chiswick days. It is the submerged London radical coming to the surface, who had meanwhile gone so far to sublimate his eighteenth-century libertarianism in terms of Catholic Irish nationalism; he releases that submerged self to the surface in order to assure the Protestants at the banquet that he is no bigot.

My political creed is short and simple. It consists in believing that all men are entitled to civil and religious liberty . . . which, while it emancipated the Catholics of Ireland, would protect the Protestant in France and Italy, and destroy the Inquisition together with the Inquisitors in Spain. Religion is debased and degraded by human interference.

He then pleads for the Reform of Parliament, his new and long adhering interest, and after declaring that "the progress of rational liberty is manifest and cheering," with due mention of France, Germany, and South America, he gives the toast of "The Cause of Rational Liberty all over the Globe"—and sits down, well content at having justified his private conscience without jeopardizing his reputation for orthodoxy, a method dear to his heart. In that pleasant atmosphere of the Mail Coach Hotel of Tralee, of a fine June night, the wine flowing and all in a kindly humour, he could be assured that nobody would take more out of his speech than a lovable goodwill towards all men. Besides, there were, we are informed, thirty-nine other toasts, all equally vague.

Read verbatim it is a kind of speech that is not entirely pleasing today; it smacks of cant because it was not intended to be taken literally. It has the same quality as the toast which followed—" To Universal Benevolence." One can well understand, after reading the entirety of the proceedings, why John Mitchel, then a child, growing up equally ignorant of the terrible difficulties of the time and of what he was spared in his manhood by the manhood of O'Connell, should write in savagery of:

Poor old Dan!—wonderful, mighty, jovial, and mean old man! With silver tongue and smile of witchery and heart of melting ruth! —lying tongue! smile of treachery! heart of unfathomable fraud! What a royal yet vulgar soul! with the keen eye and potent swoop of a generous eagle of Cairn Tual—with the base servility of a hound, and the cold cruelty of a spider! Think of his speech for John Magee, the most powerful forensic achievement since Demosthenes—and then think of the "gorgeous and gossamer" theory of constitutional agitation, the most astounding *organon* of public swindling since first man bethought him of obtaining money under false pretences. . . .

But we may as well conclude that quotation from the *Jail Journal*:

And after one has thought of all this, and more, what then can a man *say*? What but pray that Irish earth may lie light on O'Connell's breast, and that the good God who knew how to create so wondrous a creature may have mercy upon his soul. . . .

It is easy enough for Mitchel to talk. This resilient and persistent man could not possibly have carried his work to its conclusion without serpentining to his end. He had to use every chance he got, of no matter what kind, to publicize his cause and organize the mind of Ireland. In that full period between the Famine of 1817 and the Famine of 1822 the unfortunate man tried, literally, everything that the human mind could devise to stir his people. Almost annually, he appealed for "yet one last effort." He offered a scheme for agitating for Reform, and said: "Let us wait another year and petition just once again." He would examine every half-hearted offer from the Government to see if they could honourably accept it, as he did, for instance, in March 1821, with two bills introduced by the Attorney-General Plunket (and thrown out as usual by the Lords), examined them at length, wrote to the papers to explain them to the people, and then we find him writing apologies to the papers for not having had time, while on circuit, to continue his instalments of explanation. We find him abused, next, by Sheil (and with the greatest scorn) for changing over from Petitioning to working for Reform, and he has to defend himself. This fraternal warfare and this paternal advice will next be interrupted to present an address to a Lord Lieutenant, or to propose a statue to Grattan, or to write long letters to Donoughmore to keep him in good humour. In January '22 he seems to see a ray of hope for another Petition, and out comes a "Letter to his Fellow-Countrymen" begging them to "make one more exertion." That is not the end of his invention; he is wrestling, next, with the old bugbear of the Veto, trying to devise some clever form of nomination of bishops that will be acceptable to both sides. He is now proposing to erect a bridge to commemorate George IV, now to form a Society for the Education of the Poor. And all that, and ten times more, goes on, we feel, on the initiative, and certainly on the propulsion of one man who has, nevertheless, to write in his public letters about the "miserable jealousies and dissensions" that torment him and threaten to destroy his followers. What these dissensions were it is not worth while defining now; perhaps one was Aeneas MacDonnell wining and dining and conspiring with Archbishop Troy, the "Castle bishop." "Here," said Norbury, "is the pious Aeneas coming from the *sack* of Troy." Perhaps another was Hay, "Honest Hay," the Catholics' secretary, holding back essential letters from the public, or, it was even rumoured, giving information to the Government. Another may have been Sheil himself conspiring still with the Vetoists—"Sheil has prepared an address full of the worst politics, rejoicing in the downfall of democracy." No wonder O'Connell groaned that "posterity never can believe the species of *animals* with which I had to carry on my warfare with the common enemy. . . ."

Then, in admiration, with that we must put his own private work, always referred to in a tone of harassed, but indomitable and indeed almost delighted energy. From Tralee he writes in the summer of '24:

I did not go to bed in Waterford till near two in the morning. I was up again at, or rather before, six, and travelled that day to Killarney, 104 miles, but I was not there till near three in the morning. I was obliged to be up again at six and came here [Tralee] before the court sat.

Or it suggests the same colossal energy, eating up the man, so that it is no wonder he died of softening of the brain, to read this kind of letter from his worried wife:

MY DEAREST LOVE,

I wish to God you could contrive to get out of court for a quarter of an hour during the middle of the day to get a bowl of soup or a snack of some kind. Surely, though you may not be able to spare time to go to a tavern, could not James get anything you wish from the Bar mess at your lodgings which is merely a step from the courthouse? Do, my heart, try to accomplish this, for, really, I am quite unhappy to have you fasting from an early hour in the morning until nine or ten o'clock at night. I wish I was with you to make you take care of yourself. I am quite certain there is not another barrister in your circuit who would go through half the fatigue you do without taking necessary nourishment. . . .

It was the divine energy of genius, so well expressed by his massive frame, that in turn suggests this energy of a bull—the pedestal of the neck, the brawny shoulders, the chest capacious and protruding, and the curls on the forehead butting like the curls on a giant Hermes.

Thinking of that ingenious search for labour one may forgive him for seeming to fawn on George IV when he landed at Dunleary and gave it its name of Kingstown; held to the time of the next George, when the descendants of the Young Irelanders restored the Gaelic name and lifted O'Connell from his bended knee. He has never been forgiven for that obeisance to the "gluttonous despot," as Byron called him in his bitter *Irish Avatar*, with:

> Wear Fingall thy trappings! O'Connell proclaim
>   His accomplishments—His!!!—and thy country convince
> Half an age's contempt was an error of fame,
>   And that Hal is the rascallest, sweetest *young* prince.
>
> Is it madness or meanness that clings to thee now?
>   Were he god, as he is but the commonest clay,
> With scarce fewer wrinkles than sins on his brow
>   Such servile devotion would shame him away.
>
> Till now I had envied thy sons and their shore.
>   Though their virtues were hunted, their liberties fled,
> There was something so warm and sublime in the core
>   Of an Irishman's heart, that—I envy *thy dead*. . . .

So, Byron. O'Connell thought otherwise. For the first time in two centuries, he boasted, the Catholics were received on terms of perfect equality with Protestants. The disingenuous term "perfect equality" is, alas, O'Connell's. And he went on:

The Catholic prelates were received by the King in their ecclesiastical costume, with their golden crosses and chains. It was the first official recognition of their dignity as prelates. To the Earl of Fingall, as head of the Catholic laity, was given the ribbon of the

Order of Saint Patrick at an installation at which the King himself presided.

*(Will thy yard of blue ribbon, poor Fingall, recall
The fetters from millions of Catholic limbs?)*

The rest of the Catholic laity was received and cherished precisely as the Protestants were. And to crown all, the celebrated Sidmouth letter was issued, full of present kindness and gratitude to the Catholics, and of future hope and expectation of conciliation—a conciliation which everybody knew could not be effected without legal and perfect equalization of political rights.

We may find it hard to forgive. There is a bit too much self-deception in the thing; the democrat using very odd means indeed to breed self-respect in his people; but whether we forgive or not, we must not forget that at this very time there was not enough money to pay for the rooms of the Catholic Board in Capel Street; that they had to move to a room or two in a back lane called Crow Street; that O'Connell had to put his hand in his pocket to pay for these; and, finally, that from those back rooms in a back lane the man who had with Napoleon and Cuvier such an immense life (according to Balzac) did—however ambiguous his methods—drag up his people, by his own efforts, to confidence and self-pride. If his methods were strange, even unpleasant perhaps, he knew their needs better than we do.

6

The fact that Byron should at least note O'Connell as a great man already, is significant, and eases the way towards a record of the same gradual acknowledgment abroad. For there—whatever the reason, a lasting European peace, the apparent quiescence of the Irish, the rise of Liberal opinion—O'Connell's persistence was beginning to influence intelligent minds, and these were now helping him by clarifying the issues for those who held or hoped for political power. Jeffrey, Sydney Smith, Cobbett, Moore, Sheil, were all writing in favour of Ireland, each in his own way; whether it was Cobbett's remarkable *Letters from Ireland*, a volume shamefully neglected in our time, presenting the most deeply cut pictures of Irish life in the most trenchant language; or Moore's *Captain Rock;* or Smith's humorous, almost Shavian, nudations of contemporary prejudices in *Letters of Peter Plymley;* or Byron's satires on titled sham.

What an excellent kind of propaganda Smith's book must have been! On that exasperating question of the Veto nothing comes so refreshingly as his sense of the comic; as when he describes the evil conspiracies that pass in secret missives every year from the Vatican to Armagh.

The portmanteau which sets out every quarter for Rome, and returns from it, is a heap of ecclesiastical matters that have no more to do with the safety of the empire than they have to do with the safety of the moon; and which, but for respect to individual feelings, might all be published at Charing Cross. Mrs. Flanagan, intimidated by stomach complaints, wants a dispensation for eating fish. Cornelius O'Boswell has inter-married, by accident, with his grandmother, and finding that she really is his grandmother, his conscience is uneasy. Three or four schools full of little boys have been cursed for going to hear a Methodist preacher. Bargains for shirts and toe-nails of deceased saints, surplices and trencher caps blessed by the Pope. These are the fruits of the double allegiance, the objects of our incredible fear, and the causes of our incredible folly.

Blessed English humour. Such a relief from Orange ponderousness and provincialism—from the Beefsteak Club of Lord Monck with his fantastic toasts like "The Pope in the pillory of Hell and the Devil pelting priests at him"—to which the inevitable wag offered the emendation, "or pelting *Moncks*."

Or, on another plane, Cobbett's artless realism cannot have failed to impress serious folk with its blunt, straightforward account of life in the fields (in his *Letters from Ireland*).

Such observers clarified the whole position. They were precisely to the point that O'Connell always stressed; for he also repeatedly minimized the religious aspect of Emancipation, saying that it was a question of simple justice—something that he would just as eagerly demand on behalf of the Protestants of Spain. It was for him, the private radical to whom all religions were equally good, a mere accident that he wanted justice for Catholics from Protestants.

The Orange order had no wish to see that point stressed. They were, in their own words, the enemies of the combination of "O'Connell, the Pope, and the Devil." To cloak the economic and social brutality of the system by which they profited, they linked up every mortal and immortal enemy they could safely involve, from Stuart Jamie to Maria Monk, from Chartism to Jesuitry, cloaking conquest in sectarianism, and defending the superiority, not of a religion, but of blue blood.

There was the usual disingenuousness on both sides. If what was really involved in Emancipation was place and power, the Orangemen did not wish to emphasize it: that would make a poor slogan. Neither did it suit O'Connell to as much as admit to himself that he was beginning what would, in the hands of others, become a fight for economic control. Both sides won something. Orangeism retired to the beleaguered citadel of the North, and the people won all they wanted, except the citadel.

Yet the hidden spring of the O'Connellite revolution *was* religion. It was, after all, much more than a smoke-screen for an economic rivalry. It was a symbol of contrasting concepts of life, values mutually contemptuous, and to underestimate this would be to accept a basely mechanistic view of human endeavour.

O'Connell had the awful task of formulating those values, since before O'Connell nothing was accepted in Ireland as normal or natural, except the normality of eighteenth-century English Toryism, i.e., the life-method of the planter. It was a fine life-method in a hundred ways, but instinctively the Irish rejected it, and not merely for material reasons. It suited the genius of the planter, but it outraged the racial genius, the native instinct for life. That native instinct was wild and uncultivated, haphazard, fumbling, largely negative, denying clearly, but not affirming clearly—as it is, to a less degree, even today. It could not affirm because it had no concrete way of affirming its genius, as free nations affirm their genius, in educational institutions, political institutions, great buildings, social behaviour, art and literature, and so forth. It had only one way of affirming what it instinctively regarded, and that was by political manœuvres, much as the Irish in America today, having no technical craft, can only try to express their racial genius in political craft—and the word is not, and should not be, used light-heartedly or cynically. Inevitably Emancipation had to mean more than permission to practise one's religion; that would reduce religion to formalism; it had to mean leave to project the whole native genius in every way. Otherwise the Irish Catholic would have continued to live more like an animal than a man, to live at the mercy of a landlord, stifle in a mud-cabin, eat potatoes, die of famine and typhus —*unless*, and that largely happened, he became impressed by the wealth and culture of the planter, became swamped in self-despair and self-contempt, and finally accepted these values, lived by them and rose by his loyalty to them, as in the army or the bench—all the while secretly miserable because all that he instinctively rejected and hated was warring in his broken heart.

O'Connell had to stress the formalistic side, having no concrete form of expression. So his famous doctrine that "sins against morals are not so bad as sins against faith," as if, which had truth in it, fine moral behaviour was the luxury of those who could afford it—usually at somebody else's expense, as in the case of imperial good deeds. He knew and explicitly stated the Catholic doctrine that to do evil to procure good is a false doctrine; yet he became an adept at so scholastically qualifying and defining in given cases, that the conscience almost became inoperative, and the end was to disintegrate all sense of reality. On the other hand, where he did get a concrete opportunity, he was magnificent in defining, for example, the relationship between the Church and the State, and, in a country where the Church could so easily become all-persuasive, established a most useful tradition. Again, where the letter of the law was so harshly weighted against the masses, that very elasticity of conscience which he encouraged became a kind of unguent against the literal-mindedness of the law; it introduced a warm, kind, human note into life, that to this day tempers justice with charity. In some things he was beyond his time, as when he declared that moderation is the true note of patriotism, which in a country that needed a revolution was not likely to be heeded, but deserves to be remembered—and with gratitude. His hatred of sectarianism was shared by men who preceded him, but by no Catholic before him was it expressed so rigidly and so often. In education he was long a Benthamite, but before the intransigence of Archbishop MacHale, who held the door of the West hard against him, he yielded on that question. In some things he was behind his time, as in his dislike of Trade Unions, and his detestable attitude to the Poor Laws—the bad fruit, both, of his latter-day subservience to English Whiggery. But, wrong or right, the fact remains that, by his actions, he did define in many ways what was "natural" to an Irishman as an Irishman. We may detest his ideas. But they were born of exigency, and they have become so founded in the soil of the Irish character that he has, in them, left his successors something solid to build on.

If he, therefore, kept the economic implications in the background, he was, on the lowest plane, doing no more than his enemies, and, on the highest, doing a great deal besides, by projecting in other ways his nation's instinctive life-method, hitherto undefined. That the whole process should also be a voyage through the jungles of his own heart was natural and inevitable. All we can ever hope to create is an image of ourselves.

Tourists and correspondents were already trickling along the edge of his battlefield. They came from France, Spain, Italy, various German states; there were even interested correspondents in British India, and the Irish had already sent a Foreign Legion, including his son Morgan, to fight for Bolivar in South America. Translations of speeches by O'Connell and by Sheil were being published on the continent, and a series of articles on Ireland appeared in *L'Étoile*. (France was naturally eager to see anybody jump on the lion's tail.) Belgium, in his words, "long the footstool of a gross Dutchman," and a Protestant at that, and further than that supported by Great Britain, as naturally wanted to lionize the defender of Catholicism and rational liberty in Ireland; he, too, was declaring for the freedom of the majority, and non-interference by the state in religious affairs. He was becoming a European figurehead.

Thus encouraged, he projected in 1823 a scheme that revealed his practical genius for agitation. Down to the last impoverished beggar in the streets the people were to enrol themselves in a vast army of the poor and downtrodden; and they were to gain pride from their power to pay—they, the starving!—the expenses of their army. The fee was one farthing per man per week. People mocked. The snobs roared their contempt. His own followers did not even discuss his scheme. In a few weeks this *Rent* for farthings, as it came to be called, as if in proud comparison with the rent paid to the landlord, amounted to several hundreds of pounds per week. Before the year was out he was drawing a thousand pounds a week, at which rate he could count, for the future, on over £50,000 a year. He carried his scheme to that point, however, only by constant fighting against the cynicism, the jealousy, the ungenerous carpings that are inevitable to every popular movement. At the earlier meetings, for instance, of the Association, Nicholas Purcell O'Gorman would insist, watch in hand, on disbanding within half an hour if there was not a quorum. Once O'Connell had to run out into the street, grab two clerical students caught looking into a bookshop window, and drag them after him upstairs to save the meeting—which they could do, being, as clerics, *ex officio* members. For he was now saying:

Without the priesthood we cannot succeed. They are not only the natural protectors of the people. They are the only persons who can make the people thoroughly sensible of their political degradation.

With his new war-chest his activities doubled. He fought test-cases in the courts, educated the poor, spread propaganda throughout England, and in a hundred minor ways agitated for the rights of the depressed classes. In 1824 he was arguing over such things as the abolition of church rates, monopolies, the power of levying money, party sheriffs, party juries, correct lists of magistrates, the limits of magistrates' powers, the reformation of various courts and other jurisdictions, the rights of ecclesiastics to make long leases, the powers of the Dublin Paving Board, the introduction of poor-rates, the right of Catholics to own graveyards, the right of clergy to officiate at funerals, the calumnies of the proselytizing Kildare Street Society, and a score (in one year) of other local and national grievances. Many of his letters can be read today, especially those to priests, only with feelings of dismay at the self-abasing humility with which he had to flatter and cajole these often timid men. There is a record among his published letters of an old parish priest who had lived all his life in utter seclusion, and who was persuaded to emerge from his dug-out and walk down the street of his parish. The poor man slunk along the walls, hardly daring to lift his eyes, wanted to lift his hat to everybody he met, and then, safely back in his presbytery, never could be induced to undergo the ordeal again.

Once, with all his tact, he overstepped the legal limit with a reference to Ireland's possible need for "a new Bolivar." The Castle pounced on him. To the eternal credit of the Dublin press, not a single reporter, even from the enemy papers who had often abused him, and were as often abused by him, would give evidence. Even the reporter who handed in the script to *Saunders' Newsletter* (from which the Castle took it) declared that he had fallen asleep just before the sedition was uttered—he well might, for O'Connell was long-winded—woke with the bang on the table that accompanied it, asked: "What's all this noise about?" and, as reporters will, took down from his neighbour the words of the alleged sedition. O'Connell was released and carried shoulder-high from the court to Merrion Square.

The King's speech of 1825 was the riposte, with its fears that such Associations would "retard the course of National improvement." At once a bill was passed for the Suppression of Unlawful Associations, and the axe fell on O'Connell's new army. With the usual folly of English statesmen this Coercion was accompanied by a half-hearted offer of a meagre form of relief, and even then the old exasperation of the Veto clauses was insisted upon to control ecclesiastical affairs. As if ironically, these clauses were called "The Wings." They would have not only controlled, but bribed. The Maynooth Grant, like the *regium donum* to the Presbyterians, had already seduced many priests. With the £1000 a year now offered to every bishop, £300 to every dean, £200 to every parish priest, and £60 to every curate—all contemptuously and gallantly rejected by the Irish Church—what a hold the British Government might have had over religion in Ireland!

7

BLANDISHMENTS followed Coercion. Before these the Irish whale seemed to behave like an Irish gudgeon. When Sheil, Sir Thomas Esmonde, and O'Connell visit London on a deputation, we are whirled forward, in Sheil's pleasant memoirs of their stay, to a period when other Irish delegates became for a time a curiosity in London society. We are also back two centuries to that time when the Great O'Neill and his gallowglasses held every Elizabethan eye, as we read of the fine figure O'Connell made with his large cloak folded about him like an ancient Irish mantle.

Sheil is as ingenuous as a boy about that visit. He tells proudly that he dined at Brougham's table with four dukes; that they were fêted at all the great Whig houses; that at the Duke of Norfolk's there were, "among the guests," the Dukes of Sussex, Devonshire, and Leinster; Lords Grey, Fitzwilliam, Shrewsbury, Donoughmore, Stourton, Clifford, and Arundel.

I was dazzled by the splendour of an entertainment to which I had seen nothing to be compared. I passed through a long series of magnificent compartments in crimson and gold. There was no glare of excessive light in this vast mansion. The massive lamps suspended from the embossed and gilded ceilings diffused a chequered illumination, and left the deep distance in dusk. The transition to the chamber where the company were assembled, and which was glaring with light, presented a brilliant contrast. The Duke of Norfolk came forward and received us in a most cordial manner.

The duke, we may recall, was one of those English gentlemen, earlier spoken of by the O'Connellites as "cringing, cowering, complimenting animals who do, say, and get nothing."

In this atmosphere O'Connell indulged, with a realistic sense of his own importance, but with a slackening in his self-humiliating tact, in the dangerous game of manœuvring in London without getting a mandate from Dublin; he agreed to the disfranchisement of the poor forty-shilling freeholders, who were the rank and file of his army. He went so far as to attend the Duke of York's levee, and it was felt that he had actually won over His Royal Highness. But old Lord Eldon played on the Duke; the Duke ran off to his brother the King, sought him out at the theatre, and in the royal box they snuffed out Dan's sanguine hopes between the acts. The bill was thrown on the same dusty shelf as all its predecessors, and O'Connell had to face back with empty hands, to an angry Ireland that had, meanwhile, been deprived by law of its only militant organization.

Never so much in his element than when in hot water, O'Connell was at his best and his worst back in Dublin. Mahon had organized a furious clique to down him. Jack Lawless had tabled resolutions condemning him. But he had the mob at his side and they took the horses from his carriage and drew him in triumph to his home. There at once he reconstitutes the banned Catholic Association under the thin disguise of the New Catholic Association, puts on the uniform thereof—yellow vest, white trousers, blue frock with black facings and gilt buttons—and sallies out to face the music.

Humorous, scurrilous, witty, handsome as the devil, cocking his eye here and there, he slowly wins the rebels to his side, never disdaining a dirty gibe at an opponent, or a trivial occasion to flatter or inflame his friends. He swept the meeting with him, as he swept almost every meeting. To his prætorian guard of Dublin coalies he roars, when lean-featured Stephen Coppinger heckles him:

Boys, will yez look at Stingy Stephen? Did yez ever see a more ugly or a more hungry-looking fellow? Oh, sure, wirrastrue, he denies us the light of his rueful countenance!

and so drowns the rage of the unfortunate man in the roars of his gangsters.

The Mahon clique meet in a caucus to condemn him, and he nicknames them the Bridge Street Gang. They were holding a meeting in a church and he climbed to the gallery and browbeat them from his perch. He abused them. He descended to charging Dick Gorman, a Mahon henchman, with being "detected in *a mistake* of twenty pounds" in the accounts. He flung William Bellew out of the Association, charging him with "receiving two, and I firmly believe [*sic*] three pensions from the government." He gave him the parting kick of "*Hic niger est, hunc tu Romane caveto!*" (Black-hearted, beware of him!) With merry jokes he glides on guffaws past the skirts of "The Wings," admits that he did agree to taking away their votes from the poor-freeholders, but only for the good of the cause, since he included only those paying a rack-rent or holding land in common, which would have made them the tools of the landowners at elections, voting only as they were bade.

Then he begs their pardon most humbly for any mistake of judgment he may have inadvertently made, assures them that it was all for the good of ould Ireland, and that he wishes to serve only her and them.

> "*Poor soul, his eyes are red as fire with weeping.*
> *There's not a nobler soul in Ireland than Antony,*"

cry the sweaty night-caps, and the meeting ends in a storm of cheers for their leader.

Surely the most successful mob-leader of all times, the father and mother of the Irish Parliamentary Party in its low-day, and of Tammany in its hey-day, the epitome of the peasant, the original, creative, disingenuous Irish politician. It is worth noting, however, that when a committee of twenty-one was elected to consider the general position, his name came sixth, and Sheil took first place. The Irish like their heroes to play the part.

8

HE had at least a million members enrolled in his army of beggars by the end of 1825. That is measurable from the weekly contributions, which amounted at times to £2000. Had that been evenly maintained, and no large contributions given, as they were, the total would have been £100,000 every year, or, counting each shilling as a member, two million members. It seems more than reasonable to halve that in order to arrive at his total of active followers among the poor.

Once more, as we realize how little we can know about those

millions, we suffer the old exasperation of ignorance. How they lived we know; it has all been gathered again and again from travellers' note-books, from the pages of Lecky—it has been excellently repieced in Daniel Corkery's *The Hidden Ireland*. But of what use are these externals of poverty, mud, lice, hunger, when what we want is to get inside the minds and hearts of these people? They are a blank page to us, for there was no novelist, no dramatist, who thought them worth his sympathetic attention; they lived, themselves, in a condition the nearest imaginable to illiteracy; and they seem—because of our ignorance—to be in such a morass of non-personality that they never emerge as critical, individual human beings. One pitiful ballad will do— written in this year, just after his arrest for his reference to "a new Bolivar," its references arcane, half of it insensible to annotation—to suggest the intellectual slough into which the people had fallen during the Penal Days. It is worth giving, however wretched, in full. It was printed in broadsheet at Newry, and is called:

O'CONNELL'S GARLAND

Ye true sons of Erin give ear to my fiction
Which I now dictate in the year '25,
The enemy's schemes, their plans and their fictions,
Thanks to kind heaven with them did not thrive.
To get under arms they raised the alarm
That on New Year's night we'd rise up in arms
With mischief well fraught they taught to harm
The true sons of Erin and Tarra's old halls.
See how they endeavour to snare O'Connell
By false accusations and flaming lies.
May heaven defend you, our friend, dearest Dan,
From machinations they daily devise.
On Catholic Rent they vent their whole malice
Saying they are rebels that respects the chalice.
But who stained Whitehall with the blood of Royal Charles?
Sure it was not done by the sons of the hall.
My boys, be advised, be obedient and study

> To your king most gracious, evading all plots.
> Let them be accursed that would touch the blood royal,
> We ne'er killed the lady Mary Queen of Scots.
> Though we lost our estates, court-gates, and towers
> When the renegade he defied royal power
> Defending our king in an ill-fated hour
> That surely undone the true sons of the hall.
> Is not all persuasions our neighbours and brothers,
> The man of Samaria the argument proves.
> I think it is right in the sight of our Maker,
> And is not practised by Swadler and Quaker
> Though we are condemned in each villanous paper
> Because we belong to the sons of the hall. . . .

To interrupt this wretched fair-day ballad-singer, it may be as well to say that by comparison with any score of political broadsheet ballads of the day it is not unduly illiterate; it is average. We note, however, that it repeats several of Dan's teachings: his hatred of sectarianism; his loyalty to the throne; his dating of Irish history from its true beginning—the defeat of the Stuarts at Limerick; and his horror of illegal societies. Even in this rude ballad-singer by the kerbs of Newry the essentials of his teaching are evident. Hear the bard to the end:

> O Tara my country I love thee 'tis certain
> Beyond any place on the face of the globe,
> And does not men love the place they gets birth in.
> Must we love the nation that did us disrobe?
> Five spacious roads to your door was completed,
> Your turrets were high and your stairs elevated,
> But now low in ruins, my jewel, you're prostrated
> Where the proud Dane he was slain in your hall.
> Without fee or reward the bard that composes
> For you dear O'Connell I'd ransack my brain
> To present you this as a garland of roses
> Mixed with the white lily and shamrock so green.
> If I would get leave to range I would rather
> To gather wild flowers in the bower of our faith

Around the bleak ruins of our courts and fine gardens
Before the sweet bloom was consumed in the halls.

It was such folk, so defenceless, so without tradition—the
crude repeated reference to the "sons of the hall" is the mark
of an already decayed race-memory—that O'Connell, in 1826,
asked to vote for his nominees in several parliamentary elections,
so daring a thing to ask that it was like flinging them to the
wolves. It meant that for the first time in history they must defy
their landlords who held power of life and death over them, who
had for generations bought and sold their votes as if they were
cattle. O'Connell showed that he knew what he asked of these
people when he organized a New Catholic Rent to defend vic-
timized voters.

The poor illiterate wretches rose to his fall. In Monaghan, in
Louth, and above all in Waterford they threw out the nominees
of their masters. Their defeat of Lord George Beresford in
Waterford was particularly gallant. Lord George had held the
seat for twenty years; he was one of a family of the greatest
power and influence not only in the South but in Government
circles in Ireland and Great Britain; he was one of a line that had
been a bulwark of Anglo-Irish domination all through the eighteenth century. The Beresfords could not believe it when they
heard that a rival had been nominated; he was, of course, a Liberal Protestant, a Mr. Villiers Stuart, for the people could not
by law elect one of their own. They stormed and raged, declared
it was "a palpable insurrection," abused Stuart in the most inso-
lent terms, said his action was "ungentlemanlike," and not only
felt but had the folly to declare that his nomination was an interference with the rights of property—the property being the
votes of the Beresford serfs and the emoluments and honours of
a rotten borough. Wyse, the historian of the Catholic Association, declares that O'Connell himself was incredulous as to the
chances of a victory, and threw himself into the election only

when he saw with his own eyes the fever of enthusiasm that had risen in the county. It may be so. Once in the fight his voice roused that enthusiasm to frenzy, and his work as agent for Villiers Stuart was as priceless as it was ruthless. The real credit, however, for the victory goes to the tenants who so bravely stood up to the Beresfords and defied their power, to the priests who organized and encouraged them, to Wyse and the other lieutenants of O'Connell who had for a long while previous been preparing the way—mainly middle-class people, for this class had begun to back O'Connell now, though chiefly in private. He may have resented so much autonomous activity—he was never a man to prefer colleagues to agents. He may well have felt that the power he had engendered was rising in a flood about him and was already passing out of his control, the common fate of the popular leader, whose only hope then is to keep ahead of his army or be lost in its dust. O'Connell may not have originated Waterford. He was soon so much the head and fount of the fight that he was, nominally, proposed as a suitable member himself, availed himself of the proposal to make a tremendous speech, and withdrew in favour of the candidate already decided on.

As agent for the candidate there was not a move by his opponents that he did not blast. When the Duke of Devonshire chartered a special steamboat to take his serfs from Lismore to the polls ("these degraded serfs," says Sheil, "are driven to the hustings as beasts that perish to the shambles"), O'Connell terrified the women by giving them the most outlandish accounts of the dangers attaching to sea-voyages in such boats as the *"Tay Kettle"*—his nickname for the ducal steamer.

A story of a different kind tells how the old Marquess of Waterford, then almost dying, was brought regular bulletins of the defections of his tenants, some sullenly and silently holding themselves against his agent, some boldly holding up in the courts their bribe-money. He bore it all until he was told that the bugle of his huntsman, Manton, was no longer being heard at Lord George's meetings. He sent for the old retainer.

"Are you, too, abandoning me?" he asked from his bed.

The old huntsman stuttered, and stumbled, his red cap twisting in his hands, almost crying to have to say it, yet resisting even this powerful appeal to his feudal loyalty:

"Long life to yer honour," he said, "I'd go to the world's end for yer honour. But sure, please your lordship, I can't go agin my country and my religion."

One would like to believe that the rest of the story lies when it records that Manton and his family were evicted after Lord George withdrew, in chagrin, leaving the field to his resurgent serfs. It is probably only too true, since after the election they were flung on the wayside by the hundreds. "Obey or starve!" had been the rule, and they had not obeyed.

9

THE tide was now storming in earnest. The democrats poured down to Clare when the sitting member Vesey Fitzgerald got a seat in the new Wellington Cabinet and had to recontest his constituency. They voted £5000 for the expenses of the election and cast about madly for a candidate. To their dismay they could get nobody. The local Catholic Dean was against them. So were some of the other lukewarm priests. In vain, emissaries posted to and from Dublin. The whole county was up for Fitzgerald, and the O'Connellites were told that no Clare gentleman would stoop so low as to accept their patronage against so fine a man. Angrily Tom Steele said they would fight Clare if they had to put up a Protestant grave-digger.

In the height of this disheartening impasse, and when it seemed as if they would not even get a Protestant grave-digger, the *Dublin Evening Post* suddenly appeared with an election address signed by Daniel O'Connell. This meant not merely that a Catholic commoner was daring to claim a seat in Parliament (a thing that could hardly have been more arrogant if a Russian serf had said he would dine with his Tsar), but meant that the Catholics were staking everything on one tremendous gamble. They were turning the Clare election into a symbol of such imaginative force that it must strike every observer in Europe as a decisive contest for the democratic ideal.

Perhaps the two strangest figures at the election, kindred and complementary types, were old Father Murphy from the mountainy parish of Corofin, and the young Trinity College Catholic bravo who called himself "*The* O'Gorman Mahon." The old priest struck those who saw him as another MacBriar, the covenanting preacher in *Old Mortality*. He was dark and lank-haired, pale and sunken of cheek, but "illuminated with eyes that blazed with all the fire of genius and the enthusiasm of religion." It was to his parish that Sheil drove straightaway on his arrival in Clare —a barren land of frozen lava and coarse grasses, with the rocky pools wrinkled and made dark by the Atlantic wind. There the wealthiest landlord in the county, Sir Edward O'Brien, the father of the rebel-to-be, William Smith O'Brien, controlled three hundred peasant votes. Hearing that Sheil was on the way O'Brien set out in his own barouche to forestall him, his horses galloping up the windy uplands to the stone-girt fields of his serfs. O'Connell had not yet arrived in Clare, but when he came he was to ask, flamboyantly, a question that these serfs were to answer even before it was put. That question was: "Are the forty-shilling freeholders the slaves of their landlords? Are they like Negroes to be lashed by their torturers to the slave mart, there to be sold to the highest bidder?" O'Brien met his "slaves" where they had begun to stream down in bands from the hills, carrying their green boughs to Dunsinane, preceded by fifers and a piper. As his carriage came near they fell sullen, divided, and watched it pass through them in silence. In silence O'Brien looked at them. He watched them stream down the road to where the dust of Sheil's car rose in the air and with it the wild cries of greeting from the cottiers. Dismayed, O'Brien did not proceed to the little Catholic chapel, the usual meeting-place for such occasions, but to the church door of the Establishment. There he drew up his horses where his carriage served merely to remind his people—*his* people—to what religion so ancient a Gaelic clan had shifted its loyalty to keep its wealth.

Across the cropped fields the old priest waited for his flock. With a voice like subterranean thunder (says Sheil) he silenced the moving balls of tatters that called themselves men and women, "the looped and windowed raggedness" of the emergent Ireland. Then he drew to the simple altar, as rough-hewn as the chapel itself, recited Mass, and spoke to them. He spoke in Irish, now gently as the wind, now wildly, now with a cold impassioned sarcasm for some renegade wretch who had abandoned faith and country, now raising shouts of laughter from his congregation, but all the time growing more and more inflamed until the sweat shone on his skull and his eye burned. At last, rising to his height, he laid one hand on the altar, lifted the other to the roof-tree, and in a voice of prophetic admonition bade them, by their land and their God, to vote for O'Connell. The shouts that answered told Sheil that three hundred freemen had been born.

Later in the week, on the night of the polling, the old priest was in and out among the winding streets of Ennis. The patriots were crushed into a humble tavern, drinking, devouring the piles of bread and beef on the trestled tables, with interlopers cadging a free drink, or young Whyte, the local barrister, mimicking, with legs astride a chair, the High Sheriff riding an elephant in Calcutta; other voices in a corner punning coarsely and crudely on the name of Father Coffey ("well ground"—"well roasted"), and others recounting the discomfiture of Sir Edward O'Brien, or the futile black looks of the gentleman's sword-bully, Hickman—all, it would seem, very like a later Sinn Fein election with a De Valera as candidate instead of an O'Connell. In on them bursts the voice of the old priest, deep as a voice from the tomb:

"The Wolf! The Wolf is on the walk! Shepherds of the flock, what are you doing here? Why should you sit in joyaunce while the freeholders are outside being tempted by Famine? Arise, I say! The Wolf is on the walk!"

Nothing could compare [says Sheil] with his aspect on such occasions but the phiz of Jack Lawless. The look of despair with which he surveyed this unrelenting foe to conviviality was almost as ghastly as that of his merciless disturber.

O'Gorman Mahon distinguished himself at the opening day of the poll, when nominations were being received in the court-house, by defying the High Sheriff, Maloney, a Mandarin who had spent most of his life in Canton with the East India Company. Looking up suddenly at the gallery of the court-house, he saw a beribboned figure underneath it, dangling on a ledge; he wore a blue shirt, open at the neck, no vest, a broad green sash with the medal of the Order of Liberators—one of O'Connell's propagandist inventions—hanging over his chest under his wild whiskers, and his hair brushed about his head in curls of the utmost profusion.

"Who, sir, are you?" demanded the Sheriff.

The fantastic-looking gentleman replied with bland arrogance that he was _The_ O'Gorman Mahon.

"I tell that gentleman to take off that badge," ordered Maloney.

Slowly and insolently "that gentleman" replied—and the reply seems to have caught the public imagination, for there is a portrait of him extant with the following reply inscribed below:

This gentleman tells that gentleman that if that gentleman presumes to touch this gentleman, then this gentleman will defend himself against that gentleman or any other gentleman, while he has got the arm of a gentleman to protect him.

Such were two of the many characters who prepared the way for O'Connell. They tore the sky when he entered Ennis after a triumphal march that had begun as far away as Tipperary; it was pouring rain, but the thousands had waited all day to see him, and, as if to reward them, he showed at once that he had come prepared to use every brutal and ruthless device he knew. That Fitzgerald had a good record, had been friendly to the Catholics all his life, did not now save him; and yet O'Connell hammered him only as the occasion demanded it, and not even slightly urged by ill-will. Here, as so often, one realizes that there is nothing whatsoever of the romantic hero about O'Connell—little to admire, or idealize. No wonder Balzac admired him, in zest—the absolute realist.

Because Fitzgerald had been seconded by one Gore, the reputed descendant of a Cromwellian nail-maker, O'Connell kept on making references such as "strike the nail on the head," or "put a nail in his coffin." To derision he added scorn, and roused hate; he spoke odiously of the dead minister Perceval, saying that the first political act of Fitzgerald had been to enlist himself under the "bloody Perceval." He thrust home that epithet like a spear, turned it like a gouge, left it sticking like an arrow.

This [with pointing finger] is the friend of Peel, too! The bloody Perceval and the candid and manly Peel! And he is our friend! He is everybody's friend! The friend of the Catholics *was* the friend of the bloody Perceval, and he *is* the friend of the candid Peel!"

In disgust Fitzgerald kept muttering: "It's not fair, it's not fair." It was *not* fair; it was hardly sense. But had not a barrister once blinded a jury by shouting at an opponent: "I will not be intimidated by the dark oblivion of a brow!" and said, when somebody protested that this was nonsense: "Yes, but it's good enough for the jury!" Above all, Dan galled the unhappy Vesey Fitzgerald by one brutal gibe. Fitzgerald had referred in his speech to his dying father, a man who had voted against the

Union near thirty years before, standing by the patriot party against the venal sabotagers of his country's Parliament. With brimming eyes Fitzgerald told the meeting that the news of this election in Clare was being kept from the old man, lest the ingratitude of it should mortally wound him. That reference had deeply affected the people. Another man would have respected such an emotion, but to destroy the effect O'Connell gibed at those tears.

"*I* never shed tears in public!"

(It recalls the more devastating retort of as able an advocate, but of a far colder heart and smaller mind, when an opponent closed his speech in tears for his client. "Me lard," said Tim Healy, "we have just witnessed the greatest miracle since Moses struck water fram the rock.")

The question now was, would the forty-shilling freeholders (with the spectacle of their evicted fellows down in Waterford to intimidate them) stand against their landlords? No picture gives a better idea of what was meant by voting then, or of the general conditions of life in the country, than the arrival in Ennis of the Vandeleur tenants from Kilrush. In came the hundred serfs trudging after their lord's carriage. Inside the bounds of the little market town Vandeleur halts the coachman, gets up, and addresses them for the last time. He stamps, shakes his clenched fist, waves his hat, and then motions his tenants forward to the booth. As the hundred men and women, in their shawls and heavy frieze, pass sullenly down the street the crowds watch them. Some shout: "Vote for the old religion, boys!" Some: "Vote for the old country!" And the hundred tenants must have dearly wished that it was going to be a secret vote, and that they need not speak out before their master their tremulous denials. They go to the booth—in their eyes not the sheriff, not the recorder, not the books and the pens, and the gentlemen sitting around looking at them, but their little cabins, their few chattels, their children at home—all in the balance of a Vandeleur's spleen. But they have to pass O'Connell's lodgings as they trundle into the booth, and a canvasser warns him. Out comes the great man, and on the little balcony erected before the house he looks down at them and raises his arm. On the spot the hundred sullen heads are lifted and they cry out their cheers. The cheers of a hundred more freemen; and perhaps a hundred more paupers before the night is down. . . .

On that little platform all O'Connell's lieutenants stood in turn. The people saw Father Sheehan of Waterford, who helped to beat the Beresfords, Father Maguire of Clare, Sheil, Lawless, Mahon—the Bombasto of the party—Kenney, the Waterford surgeon, men and names lost in the mass of names that come up to us from that time like the leaves of grass that make an old field. There Sheil saw a priest telling the crowd, in Irish, that the news had just come in that a Catholic had voted against his country, and heard the wild cry of rage and despair from the mob. The priest spoke again, and on the spot the multitude sank to the ground and prayed. The man had just died of a stroke of apoplexy, the sin of bribery and perjury on his soul. It is Sheil, also, who records the howls of detestation that greeted the name of Father Coffey. "It clearly proved," he wrote, "that a priest has no influence over the people when he attempts to run counter to their political passions."

The election, coming as a climax to a long and patient preparation of an untrained rabble, gives an idea of the thoroughness of that preparation such as we could get otherwise only by wading through the letters and speeches of O'Connell, filling in imaginatively the effect of the personal contacts made with the people in the intimacy of their homes by O'Connell's lieutenants, or in the intimacy of their hearts by the Man of the People himself. Of those lieutenants the clergy were foremost. They now kept a rigid discipline in the moment of conflict. Whisky was forbidden, and was not taken; meat and beer only were allowed.

The only man (an historical symbol, no doubt, and part of the fable) who got drunk was O'Connell's English coachman. The priests stood below the stairs at this and that house, giving out chits for food to the hungry people, many of whom had waited for hours to speak a friendly word and get a word of encouragement or praise. Never before, and since only in times of the greatest national excitement, was there such a warm and generous unity of hearts.

These were, in truth, the romantic heroes, fighting for a half-formed dream and supporting themselves in the name of an uncreated vision. O'Connell had all the joy of the creative artist in his life and work. He had moulded an Irish Atlas carrying a world on its back, but living muscles held the strain, and cracked beneath it.

10

HE was elected. He begged pardon of Fitzgerald for any harsh word he had said; and now, temperate again and far-seeing, he strove to cool the people he had inflamed. He might well strive. When Fitzgerald kept wandering around Ennis asking every friend: "Where will all this end?" he was asking a question of the future—and the future was in the hands of O'Connell and the people. Dublin Castle was asking exactly the same question. The British Cabinet asked the Castle. The King asked his ministers. "But what can I do?" was Lord Anglesey's reply to London. "I know the carrying of party flags and so forth is illegal. Put them down and what do you gain by it?—the meetings will continue." He felt with dismay the rise of public excitement; to Lord Leveson-Gower he wrote: "The final success of the Catholics is inevitable. No power under heaven can avert its progress." That was implicit in all his replies to Wellington. Why had he given interviews to O'Connell? Why had he seen Jack Lawless? Why had he not deprived O'Gorman Mahon of

his magistracy for publicly abusing the Clare Dragoons? Why
had he not indicted Lawless for adjuring the people to be tran-
quil "by their allegiance to the Catholic Association"? Why had
he stood by and done nothing when his own sons, and even
some of his staff, attended a meeting of the Association? It was
the last straw when the press, amazingly, published a letter he,
the Lord Lieutenant, had written to the Catholic primate, encouraging the Catholics to carry on their agitation—in the face
of another letter from Wellington asking them to slow down.
At that, Anglesey must have seemed the worst man for a tight
corner, and they recalled him in the January of 1829.

Parliament met in February. Wellington had the task of persuading His Majesty to allow him to introduce a Relief Bill, and
his last cast was a threat of resignation if the measure was not
supported. He had good arguments. Anglesey, as early as the
previous July, had asked for the withdrawal of the Irish troops,
on whom he could no longer rely, had said that the Irish leaders
could raise the people in rebellion at a moment's notice, that the
"probability of present peace rests on the forbearance of O'Connell." Meanwhile the Orangemen were playing into O'Connell's
hands. They were forming Brunswick Clubs against the Catholics, and the Catholics were forming Liberal Clubs against them.
Both were violent in tone. Jack Lawless was dispatched to the
North to spread the Catholic cause; he got peaceably as far as
Dundalk, but when he announced his intention of entering Monaghan with 140,000 men—figures meant nothing then (O'Connell would begin a speech as to 50,000 people and be referring
within ten minutes to an assembly of a quarter of a million)—
several thousand Orangemen massed to meet him. The magistrates flung General Thornton between them, whereupon Jack
turned back. It was wise and prudent of him; there might have
been another Sicilian Vespers in the South if blood had been
spilled that day at Ballybay. In Tipperary 50,000 men, wearing
green cockades and uniforms, entered Clonmel for a monster

meeting; one Cork firm sold £600 worth of green calico for those uniforms. To that meeting O'Connell cried:

Would to God that our excellent viceroy, Lord Anglesey, would only give me a commission. If these men of blood should attempt to attack the property and persons of His Majesty's loyal subjects, with a hundred thousand of my brave Tipperary boys I'd soon drive them into the sea before me.

The fierce yell that met those words showed how hungry his Tipperary boys were for the fight. It was known, too, that arms were hidden in the mountains and that the long knives were being sharpened on every cabin whetstone; while, as far back as 1813, O'Connell himself had been publicly attacking a host of Catholic secret societies—White Boys, Right Boys, Caravats, Shanavests, Thrashers, Carders, Ribbonmen, Defenders, United Irishmen, and what not. On top of that the Coercion Act of 1825 had not, on Anglesey's advice, been reintroduced. Wellington could not know—probably O'Connell himself did not know—that a great deal of this was sheer sword-rattling. It was no comfort that O'Connell recalled Lawless, and bade Tipperary be peaceful, or that he formed companies of one hundred and twenty men apiece, each under the rule of a Pacificator, who had to be a regular communicant. He was, at the same time, sanctioning a proposal for exclusive dealing with people friendly to Catholics, an early form of boycott, and a positive form of intimidation. He actually tolerated a proposal for a run on the banks. In Wexford, for instance, one of the directors of the Provincial Bank attended a meeting of the local Brunswick Club; two days later immense numbers of notes were simultaneously presented for payment, and in one week the bank had to lay in a million and a half of gold. So much uneasiness resulted that by the March following the banks had to hold five millions of specie to protect a note issue but two millions larger. Here, again, the middle-classes are seen lending a useful hand.

Briefly O'Connell had taught the Irish serf how to agitate.

He had invented a technique of peaceful revolt. To dissolve Parliament would mean a Clare election in every county in Ireland. To coerce was impossible, since neither peelers nor soldiers were to be trusted, and of England's 30,000 regulars as many as 25,000 were now crammed into Ireland.

All this Wellington put to his King in those fateful discussions of the February and March of '29. Lord Eldon's memoirs record the behaviour of George IV at these interviews with his ministers—his silence, his complaints, his distress, his wail that he was abandoned, his threat to leave England and abdicate the throne to his brother. He kept up his stubborn resistance to the night of March 4; in vain he tried to get rid of Wellington and form an alternative ministry. Not until then did he capitulate.

The bill was introduced on March 5 and given its first reading on the thirtieth. In introducing the second reading Wellington urged it in order "to avert Civil War." He felt that it would take 70,000 troops to control Ireland now; Peel said it was impossible to control Ireland; it was the popular feeling that even O'Connell had the greatest difficulty in holding the snaffle on the people—which, true or not, was precisely the popular feeling O'Connell wished to create. The Lords submitted to the bill, and on April 13 the King signed it. He broke and trod on the first pen handed to him, and for all history records, his tears may have been his last effort to dilute the emancipation of seven millions of his subjects. One may be pardoned such a fancy, for the thing was well diluted. To a large extent emancipation proved to be a sham.

In May, O'Connell crossed to London and claimed his seat in a packed Commons. To the end the Government was ungenerous, insisting that emancipation was not retrospective; accordingly O'Connell was given the old oath, which declared the King head of the Church, and declared the Mass impious and abominable. O'Connell said he was not bound to take the oath, withdrew, and three days later was given leave to argue his case; that done he again withdrew, and the Commons debated the position. A third time he came before the House, and was told he must take the oath. He took up the pasteboard on which the oath was printed, looked at it for a moment or two, and said:

In this oath I see one assertion as to a matter of fact, which I know to be false. I see a second assertion as to a matter of opinion which I do not believe to be true.

Tossing back the pasteboard, he bowed and retired. He was re-elected for Clare, unopposed, and took his seat.

I I

HERE, once more, every biographer will feel a natural temptation to close a chapter or a volume. There is no pause in the life of this man. There are only his scheduled holidays at Darrynane, where he became reinvigorated by the mountain air, chased the mountain hares, and drank in the spirit of his land from the wild loveliness of his home. Before that Parliament had dissolved in June 1830, on the death of George IV, ending the immensely long reign of the Tories, he had already made himself at home in the House, had moved for leave to introduce a Reform Bill (defeated by over 300 votes), made a new rapprochement with the Radicals—in five weeks he was more popular than the veterans Hunt and Brougham with the East End crowds, many of them exiled Irish—had planned a Repeal agitation, and was tempting the incoming Whigs. That summer, in addition, he fought an election, was returned for Waterford (beside a Beresford!), and went through many vexations over the behaviour of the wild O'Gorman Mahon in Clare. His son had to fight a duel with an old supporter. He himself had a fierce personal encounter with Mahon when that passionate creature met him on the road, two distinct triumphal processions in conflict, clambered into O'Connell's lofty car as if to oust him bodily, and found himself lifted into the air by his leader and hurled into the mob.

Darrynane came as a welcome rest in the autumn after all that hurly-burly. There he was, as somebody said, like a petty German king, with his hounds, his early-morning hunting, his red-coated men with their long staves hallooing from glen to glen. One would like to dally with him there, especially where we find him seated high up the mountainside greeting the postman from Cahirciveen who comes clambering up with his heavy post-bag. He would breakfast on the hills, going quickly but intently through his letters, strewing the grass with the *Times*, the *Universe*, letters from France or America, reports from Dublin, the *Oxford and Cambridge* magazine that contains some article of interest to him, begging letters, appeals from his poor folk in trouble . . . while, far beneath him, all Kerry sends its hills falling to the vast sea. The day's hunt over, he comes back at evening, down the slopes, followed by his shaggy dogs, his weary hunters, into the hospitable dining-room at Darrynane. There, as all agree, he was at his most lovable. Even that chilly creature, O'Neill Daunt, who had every reason to feel unenthusiastic about O'Connell, says so in his dryly impressive way:

O'Connell never appeared to greater advantage than when presiding at his own table. Of him it may be said, as Lockhart has observed of Scott, that his notions of hospitality included the necessity of making his intellectual stores available to the amusement of his guests. His conversation was replete with anecdote; and the narratives which possessed by far the greatest interest were those in which the narrator was personally concerned. His memory was prodigious; and not the smallest trait of character or manner in the numberless persons with whom, in the course of his bustling career, he had come in contact escaped the grasp of his retentive recollection.

Even there his people drag him from retreat, and one of the most famous incidents in his career began there one autumn morning at eight o'clock as he looked out to the sound of a horse's hoofs, and saw Burke of Ballyhea staggering to the door after an all-night ride of ninety miles. Burke begs him to come to Cork to defend some men on trial for their lives for what came to be known as the Doneraile Conspiracy. Four of them have already been sentenced to death, and the cry brought by Burke is that every man of them will die unless he comes to protect them. . . .

All that Sunday and all that Sunday night he drove alone, across the wild passes, through Glenshesk and Ballyvourney, their saviour, their rock about whom his people clambered as from a drowning sea. On he goes beside the sleeping hamlets, the rustle of the mountain streams, down the smoother valley of the Lee—nearer and nearer to the city, with Burke galloping ahead of him to bring the news. One might well imagine the murmurs in the street growing and growing to hear him come, a fable, not a man, until as Burke drew up his frothing horse outside the court the whole place had become one vast shouting of "Thank God! They're saved!" and it seems not a legend but an inevitable part of the drama of the thing that when his gig rolled in, and the Man of the People stepped from it, his horse should drop down dead.

In the court, which had refused to delay even an hour for him —there began a new enmity, with Dogherty, the Crown Prosecutor—they lifted their heads to hear the swelling roar. They paused as the passages outside seemed to become enlarged with it, burst their walls, echoed, drowned everything but the replications of that sound, and the fable again takes a hand to say that Dogherty grew deathly pale as the doors opened and O'Connell tramped in, followed by a crush of his admirers. He sits, dust to his eyes, and begs leave to drink a bowl of milk while a junior counsel pours into his ear the rough details of the case, and Dogherty rises to continue.

Almost at once O'Connell is on his feet, interrupting him, his mouth full of milk and meat, with "That is not law!" And wins his point. Or "That evidence is not admissible!" And wins again. Can not one see the mob? Hear the rumours pass in and out? "He's winning. Dan has them. Dan has them. DAN HAS THEM!"

"Alas," he had sighed, as the moon paled over the Lee and the roofs of Cork rose out in its little smoky valley, "in from all that heart-lifting beauty to the rascality of an Irish court of justice!" But once in, as always, there is no scruple. Again and again the image rises—it was like Mick Collins and his secret service built out of a million whispers. For O'Connell is working on a stolen copy of the original depositions and the Crown is suppressing half of them.

Using this knowledge of the difference between first evidence given in the privacy of a prosecutor's den and this oral evidence gently sieved by a Crown Prosecutor in court, Dan dogs his witnesses until, at last, one of them wails out: "Ah, Mister O'Connell, sure I never expected to have to face you here to-day!"

He mocks and upbraids Dogherty, imitating his polite drawl, teasing him when he lets slip something about "false facts."

"There's no such thing!" he scoffs.

"There are, and false men," throws back Dogherty.

"Yes, you and your case!"

He laboured over the evidence so successfully that the jury, though locked up for thirty-six hours, without food, could not agree—and that on the same evidence that had condemned the first batch of prisoners in the same case. (On identical evidence the third batch of prisoners were found Not Guilty, and in the end the first batch were reprieved.)

It was a gallant ending to a life spent in the "rascally" Irish law-courts, for from that on, with rare exceptions, he devoted all his energy to politics, his one aim the repeal of the Union, the restoration to his people of their full political liberty. Out of their pennies they recouped him for the loss of his legal income to the amount of a yearly average of about sixteen thousand pounds a year—known as the Tribute. Meanwhile they oiled their few muskets, and their secret societies grew.

V : THE SPHINX

1830–1840

"Use respectful language but threaten them as strongly as you can without direct menace."

O'CONNELL to the Trade Unions,
September 1831, on the Reform Bill.

I

IT is not now, in all probability, remembered by many that the Act of Parliament which emancipated the Irish Catholics purported to suppress all monasteries and institutions of Jesuits. It was, in O'Connell's words, an "inexecutable" clause, and nobody was troubled by it; but it gives an idea of the spirit in which the act was drawn up, and explains why it can be truly said that Emancipation earned no gratitude and deserved none.

It admitted Catholics to Parliament. That was the essential thing—an opening of the floodgates. It also admitted the people to every lay-office under the Crown except Regent, Chancellor, or Lord Lieutenant. But the stigma was not wholly removed, and even these last restrictions must in time have been felt as an insult. There were other petty restrictions, such as that no Catholic official could wear his insignia at Catholic ceremonies, and when O'Connell became Lord Mayor of Dublin he had to leave off his robes at the door of the pro-cathedral—easing the prick of that insult with a joke about robes that were Protestant but a wearer who was a Catholic. Catholic bishops were also forbidden to use titles of sees already in the possession of the Church of Ireland. When the new Catholic King's Counsels were chosen, the one man who most patently deserved silk was passed over deliberately. Six men were advanced to the inner bar. O'Connell was left in his stuff gown. The forty-shilling freeholders were disfranchised, the backbone of the popular movement. Worst of all, Catholics, nominally entitled to hold every office, were studiously kept out of as many as possible. There were, finally, many grievances still untouched, such as the payment of tithes by Catholics to Protestants. And the Government made up its mind that there should be no more O'Connellism. Inevitably the popular agitation went on just as before. Roused by a great victory, made aware of their power, the people were, in fact, champing at the bit.

2

THE disfranchisement of the poor was the great blot on the bill, and as O'Connell is to be blamed for not protesting more strongly against it, so he himself must have been aware that he had weakened on the question during that unfortunate visit to London several years before. In December 1828 he could not have been more violent in his words:

If any man dares to bring in a bill for the disfranchisement of the forty-shilling freeholders the people ought to rebel, if they cannot otherwise succeed. Sooner than give up the forty-shilling freeholders I would rather go back to the Penal Code. If an attempt were made to take from them the privileges vested in them by the Constitution I would conceive it just to resist that by force, and in such resistance I would be ready to perish in the field or on the scaffold.

(How fortunate, one thinks, for all politicians that the public has such a brief memory for public affairs! Also, may not Peel have had a longer memory, and begun here to form a suspicion,

that with the years became a conviction, that O'Connell's bark
had no bite?)

Now, all O'Connell could do was to write to his friends from
London:

The freeholders have no friends among the English members. We
must have many petitions from Ireland. We must put on record
our decided hostility in every shape and form só as to enable us
hereafter, and soon, to do battle in favour of a restoration of that
right.

He could not do less. In the Clare election one-fifth of the
electors had been the poorest people. In the Reform debate of
1831 he said that 190,000 people had been disfranchised by this
clause alone. This was, no doubt, a huge exaggeration, but the
importance of any large bloc may be measured by the fact that
out of seven millions, only some 300,000 were voters in 1829;
after it, only 26,000.

3

THE result was that O'Connell could not form a solid bloc of
Irish votes, an Irish Party, immediately after Emancipation, as
Parnell did later. The ground was cut from under his feet. Not
even in England was such a thing possible on a national or popular issue, until after the Reform Bill of 1832. That bill gave Ireland only five additional seats instead of the seventy-two O'Connell expected. So, the Catholic could enter Parliament—but only
if he was voted in, and the people who *would* vote him in were
gagged. The Irish members were of the most mixed type,
wrangled and broke into factions, and were never for long consolidated behind O'Connell. Even after 1832 the limitations on
popular suffrage did a good deal to nullify the effects of reform.
Municipal reform did not come to Ireland until 1838—and the
sign of its necessity was that O'Connell was at once elected Lord
Mayor of Dublin. The parliamentary vote was not extended to

lodgers and ratepayers in England until 1867, long after O'Connell's death; while the power of the landlord continued to be pervasive until the Land League and the Land Acts finally smashed it; even to this day, as anybody who has anything to do with elections soon discovers, it still continues in pockets of Irish life where the democratic tradition is weak. Not until 1872 did the Ballot Act establish secret voting. What between inadequate representation and a bad franchise, O'Connell was thus, in 1829, far from being in Parnell's position. The real issue was nevertheless in his own hands—the formation of a powerful national policy that would appeal to what electors he had, and impress what followers they gave him with the need for absolute loyalty. That national policy he did not formulate until, at the age of sixty-four, and within five years of the end of his active career, he established the Repeal movement.

In that Tory Parliament of 1830, under Wellington, who refused Reform, and the Whig Parliaments of 1830 and 1831, which fought for and gained it, he did collect a party of sorts —O'Connell's Tail as it was called. Of that tail six men were all he could count on when writing to Lord Duncannon in December 1831—at a pinch he felt he might rally twenty. It is odd to find him, so hampered, talking in a strain of virtual dictation—and the word is his. He says this clique must go, that man must be put down, the magistrates must be curtailed, the yeomanry must be checked, and so on. . . .

The Whigs have been in office for twelve months and what have they done for Ireland? There is but one way of governing Ireland, and that is by not preferring individuals to the people but the people to individuals. Ireland is sinking into decrepitude. In Cork, in three parishes alone, there are 27,000 paupers!!! And in such a state of things we have a ministry—bless them!—who prefer an individual and the gratification of his pride to the wishes and wants of a nation. Strike off the Tory Lord Lieutenants. Turn off Lord Lorton, Lord Wicklow, Lord Forbes, Vesey Fitzgerald. . . .

It is odd, but it is realistic too, because what he is banking on is the old thing—the moral power of his people's unrest. There can be peace in Ireland only if the people are at peace. "Reform our wrongs," he says in effect, "and you do govern Ireland. Otherwise . . ." The otherwise is the thing he gambled on for the rest of his life—Repeal of the Union, or, in one word, revolution.

4

THE times were against him. The European atmosphere of 1830–31, however favourable to English Reform, was far from favourable to O'Connellism, an entirely different thing. The King and his ministry had fled from France. A provisional government had declared the independence of Belgium. At Dresden the King of Saxony abdicated. At Lisbon and Madrid there were expectations of a revolution at any hour. William IV had arranged to dine at the Guildhall in the November of 1830, but cancelled the arrangement. "The interior of England," wrote O'Connell from London in that same month, "is in a frightful situation." In January 1831 twenty-three people were sentenced to death for rioting in Gloucester; at Norwich, forty-five; twenty-six at Petworth; hundreds in scattered places. "If firing had begun," wrote Wellington, "who could tell where it would end?" Had the aristocrats who had hitherto supported Reform not behaved like the Irish aristocrats who had supported Emancipation, that is, not fled in the hour of stress, the Reform Bill might have been carried that year. "O'Connell," wrote Cobbett, "is the only public man who retains the confidence of the English Radicals." It was in that year that O'Connell was nominated and voted for as first King of the Belgians.

The result was that O'Connell found his overtures repulsed, and had to take the offensive. His Anti-Union Association had been suppressed by Sir Henry Hardinge, provoking him to a scurrilous speech, in which he called Hardinge "a chance child of fortune and of war." The outrageous insult brought him a challenge which he refused, as he refused every challenge since he tried to fight Peel. He was stung by the contemptuous looks he met in every London club for months after.

When Anglesey was packing his bags in London at the end of 1830, on his way to replace Northumberland as Lord Lieutenant, he had to write: "O'Connell is my avant-courier; he starts today with more mischief in hand than I have ever seen him charged with." O'Connell might feel the same about his camp "follower." For, back in Dublin, he founded his Friends of Ireland Society, and saw it promptly suppressed. The next thing was a run on the banks for gold. The next was the Irish Volunteers for the Repeal of the Union. That, too, was suppressed. He established Repeal Breakfasts where the Irish democrats met and made speeches. They were suppressed. "Curse them," growled O'Connell, "we'll have Repeal Lunches. If they are suppressed we'll have Repeal Tea and Tracts. If they are suppressed we'll have Repeal Suppers." He established a General Association for Ireland to Prevent Illegal Meetings and to Protect the Sacred Right of Petition. It was suppressed. The Government, evidently, was also learning this technique of agitation. "Things have now come to that pass," wrote Anglesey from Dublin, "that the question is whether O'Connell or I shall govern Ireland." While O'Connell was thinking up a new Association, a Proclamation of January 13, 1831, forbade an Association under any name. "I'll make myself an Association!" roared O'Connell. And he did. He held a public breakfast, took ten minutes to disperse at a later meeting, and was arrested on January 19. Five others were arrested with him and two newspaper prosecutions followed.

"Please let us take a hackney," begged old Farrell, the peace-officer. "I have the gout."

"No," snapped O'Connell. "You and I shall walk. And the city will know that I am arrested like a housebreaker."

The cattle market butchers edged about them, their steel cleavers under their coats.

"Give us the word, Liberathor," they begged, "and let us get at them."

But if O'Connell was loud-mouthed, O'Connell was plainly in a stew. He had met his match in Mr. Secretary Stanley. He hated him for it ever after, baited him as Scorpion Stanley, and was often to feel his sting. Those three, Stanley, Peel, and Wellington, were the only men of his own size he met.

He began to write some of those private letters that are intended to be shown to everybody. To his old friend Bennett, afterwards Chief Justice, he wrote:

The country is ready to burst into action. The Government are not aware of the true state of the country. If my advice had not weight at least 300,000 men would by now have attacked Dublin.

The "at least" is ingenuous, but that Dublin was in a ferment there is no doubt. He wrote a much more important letter to his friend O'Mara, a "fighting lawyer," i.e., a duellist, and O'Mara passed it on to Lord Cloncurry with the remark that he had never witnessed so turbulent and angry a populace, not even in the height of '98. The letter he wrote O'Mara, on January 22, three days after his arrest, was obviously intended for the Government. It was ambiguous, evasive, diplomatic, a loophole letter, but it clearly implied his willingness to co-operate in a slowdown on Repeal. The Government read it with jubilation, and Stanley made its intent public—and was, of course, promptly given the lie by O'Connell. The essential parts of the letter speak for themselves as to the truth:

My dear O'Mara,
I do most anxiously wish to confer with Lords Meath and Cloncurry on the present awful position of public affairs, and the possi-

bility of calming the public mind. I would wish that this desire of
mine should be communicated to their lordships. . . .

I have had a communication from a person in the confidence of
the ministry, in England, but whose name I cannot disclose, who
states distinctly that all the ministry desires is to postpone the Union
question until those of Reform, abolition of corporate monopoly,
and reformation of Church abuses are disposed of, thus leaving the
"Union" for the last.

I think this may be done by Lord Cloncurry and Lord Meath in
such a manner as to carry with them the public mind, preserving
only just so much, or rather so little, of popular agitation as would
continue the confidence of the people in the prospect of legitimate
redress; such mode being in my mind the only mode of preventing
violence and outrage and preventing *probable* rebellion. . . .

There is more about this "probable" rebellion, but we have read
enough to measure the wiles and the lures. He proceeds:

I would respectfully wish to offer my assistance to Lord Cloncurry and Lord Meath. . . . I am most desirous of throwing into
their hands the full direction of all the influence which I may possess. . . .

This effort to inveigle the aristocracy into popular agitation
in order to throw a wall between himself and the Government,
at the price of a gearing-down in the Repeal movement, did not
succeed. The lords demurred when he asked them to join a Society for the Improvement of Ireland and to promote County
Reform Meetings. An effort to entangle Lord Duncannon also
failed. An effort to postpone the trial failed. "We have him so
far at our mercy," gloated Stanley.

But the Government did want his help, and the public was inclined to raise its eyebrows at the idea that he would ever be
tried, as it did at his vehement denials of the implications of that
letter. Naturally the Government declared that they would punish him without mercy, and naturally the whole thing vanished
in smoke when Parliament dissolved, the Coercion Act dissolved
with it, and they all slipped out of their several quandaries.

Then the old game began again, the irrepressible agitator establishing new associations, free of Coercion, and new alliances. He tried to make an alliance with the Trades' Political Union. He courted the Whigs. It was that wife-kissing, wife-beating policy inevitable to two islands joined by Force and sundered by Nature, which continues to our day, and which, no doubt, will end only either with a real marriage or a complete divorce.

5

THAT diplomatic letter to the Government via Lord Cloncurry, via Lord Meath, via Tom O'Mara, cannot be left there. It is too important. It marks the beginning of O'Connell's career as a Parliamentarian—at the ominous age of fifty-six—a career that lasted for seven years, deflected him from the source of his strength—his own people—and almost killed his own reputation and their spirit. One comes back to that letter, and back to it again, and ends by realizing that it reveals the fatal weakness in his character and his technique of living. A duality of nature, ambiguity, a serpentining evasiveness, may be all excellent as a way of living in hard times. But the serpent who climbs the pole has to have a pole to climb. For those seven years the people watched in wonderment the phenomenon of an O'Connell climbing a pole that was not there. They did not know what he wished them to do.

The partisans of O'Connell and of Parliamentarianism will greet this with scorn. They will say, and truly, that he was an opportunist, and that it was his business to get what he could get while never losing sight of his major intention; that he had desired for the last thirty years to live this life of the politician, and that he was now living it, doing good work as a pioneer for reform; or, it may be said, good work in familiarizing his people with parliamentary affairs. It is all quite true, and one could write an exhilarating account of his intrepid and persistent advocacy during those years. Indeed, as when one imagines, for instance, what the elegant inhabitants of Merrion Square must have felt to hear his voice echoing, from the windows of his house, over the mob surging against their railings; and as when one imagines what it meant to the pride of the people to see him living there, and talking to them there as an equal; one can also imagine what it meant to them to have a hero-personification of themselves baiting Parliament on their behalf. All that has to be remembered, and set against his substantial failure in the Commons. That it was a failure is the essential fact, and that the people became apathetic about it is a matter of history; at the end of it their subscriptions had fallen to nothing, and they no longer responded to his appeals. The rise of Young Ireland in 1842 is thus the natural corollary of his alliance with the Whigs in 1832. It was too soon for a Parliamentary Party, and the issues were not either realistic or defined.

Here, year by year, are extracts from his letters to show that he wavered on the subject of Repeal:

1832.—In this year a letter, of May 7, gives a perfectly honest definition of his position. "I do not urge on Repeal if it could interfere with Reform."

1833.—A letter of September 17. "May not Repeal be dispensed with if we get beneficial measures without it? I have made up my mind on that. There can be no safety for Ireland without a Repeal of the Union. That is my firm, my unalterable conviction."

1834.—Compare two months in the same year. May 7. "Beg Reynolds not to agitate for a Repeal meeting for the present. You may not suppose that there is the least relaxation in my opinions . . . but I will get what I can and use the Repeal *in terrorem* merely until it is wise and necessary to recommence the agitation." By June 17 he is in a rage over the Littleton exposure—to be mentioned later—and writes: "The Scoundrels!!!! Put this advertisement in *The Pilot.* 'Preparing for

Publication, The Speech of Daniel O'Connell on the Repeal, etc. I have begun and will proceed with Repeal. Can there be found a wretch so base as to consent to wait longer before he becomes a Repealer?' "

1835.—In a letter of February 27 he quotes his usual alternative terms, and adds: "*If that experiment fail*, I would come back with tenfold force for Repeal."

1836.—May. "Ireland in an equality with Britain, or no Union."

1837.—June. "My course is obvious—to insist on all, and get something substantial."

1838.—October 4. "The four principles of our new agitation are . . ." —and here follow the old reforms hoped for from the Whigs since 1831. On November 12 there enters a bolder note: "Our great resource, perhaps our only resource, is in ourselves."

1839.—August 21. He writes to Fitzpatrick that he wants the people to agitate for their rights, the improved franchise, an amelioration in the tithes question, and lastly, "quietly and cautiously for Repeal."

From that on he is finished with the Whigs and with his tentative and opportunist policy of conciliation. He founded the Repeal Association in 1840. Yet, even in 1843 there is a secretive letter to Lord Campbell that raises in us a frightened doubt. He says: "Why does Lord John Russell not prove himself capable of leading his friends into all the advantages to be derived from conciliating the Irish nation, and strengthening the British Empire?"

To return from that survey to his letter to—or rather through —Tom O'Mara, is to read it now without surprise. It is the letter of a man whose decisions are involved by the secret reservations of his mind. It must be said that he may, genuinely, have been appalled by the storm rising around him, the fate of every man who displays a force he has not planned to use. "We become that which we think," said the Indian sage. O'Connell had thought revolution. The people had become rebels. O'Connell had thought politics. The people were unable to follow him. In them the bigger idea drove out the lesser.

6

NOT that the alternative to Repeal was not an excellent programme, and that the British Government drove him from it, and did not fulfil it, marks their foolish stubbornness rather than his foolish optimism. Time and time again his alternative was to be tried. Time and time again obduracy, greed, and fear prevented it. "The Irish," said Grey at this very time, "must be taught to fear before they can be taught to love."

So the English would bribe, seduce, buy, but they would not listen. Run the eye along the footnotes to Fitzpatrick's edition of O'Connell's *Correspondence*, for example, and it is a litany of quietus. "Kyle, an undecided Tory, *afterwards* Bishop of Cork." "Sergeant O'Loghlen, *afterwards* Sir Michael O'Loghlen, Master of the Rolls." "Mr. Mullins, *latterly* known as de Moleyns, a branch of the family now ennobled by the peerage of Ventry." "Carew O'Dwyer, an able member of the Catholic Association, appointed to a High Post in the Exchequer, enjoyed to his death a pension of £3000 a year." They sank the wild and dangerous leader of the Irish Trade Unions, Mark Costello, in the orange groves of Gibraltar; they shackled even Sheil, as they had calmed Brougham with the Great Seal. They tempted O'Connell with a patent of precedence at the bar, and sounded him about the Attorney-Generalship, and in October 1831 he said to his friend Barrett, the newspaper proprietor: "I could be Master of the Rolls in an hour." But because they would give no promise of reform he refused to treat. All that they would try, and where the man was willing they would accomplish. They would not exert the same energy to remove the necessity for such bribes. The imperialist cherishes the luxury of cheap generosity.

So we watch the rise of the second of the three storms that swept Ireland in the lifetime of O'Connell. The first was before 1829 and Emancipation. This second storm is the tithe war of 1832–34. The third culminated at the Clontarf Meeting, when it was touch and go for O'Connell and Ireland.

Here, also, we watch a development in O'Connell's character that was not new, or invisible before this, but that he now begins to exploit ruthlessly. Or is it that it begins to exploit him? It is not pleasant. It is terrifying and exciting. It is the effect of his new labyrinthine mind on his fluent conscience. The man becomes a maze and it is impossible to track him. There comes into his face a mask-like quality, and the mobility of his mouth (in that pitiless lithograph made at the time) is matched by the cold Fouché-like secrecy of the right eye. For Minotaur and Sphinx lie in ambush in his countenance, where, as in that of most men, there is the differentiation of his double nature in the play of his looks; always that right eye had held its secret calculation; always the left had been a challenge and a doubt. One corner of the lip is likewise turned upward in a half-smile; the other is gripped downward with a horrible suggestion of latent ruthlessness and brutality. If one covers half the face, one side smiles but holds its secret, and the other challenges and offers no pity. There is almost a slaver about the heavy mouth. The hair is dry and matted. It is the face that Young Ireland was to fear and hate, the image that meant to their eager and open hearts everything hateful in the way of cabal and cunning plots, that made them shiver as before something that would destroy every dream by which they lived.

From this on he says little directly, and never holds tight to anything. He might be the embodiment of shiftlessness if he were not also the embodiment of perseverance. There is nothing noble, arrogant, or proud about him. He has made a dæmon of his country's genius, and it lives in his face; and mean and little men, men without his gigantic stature, will take from him more evil than good. He thus perpetuates that terrifying Irish type where truth is always in hiding and where the very soul ends by being in hiding from itself. Take from this half-brute, half-god, his animal power, his energy, his egotism, and the ennobling inspiration of a vast mass of people who cry out to him from the depths as to their saviour, and you are left with a man who might, without that inspiration, have been one of the villains of history.

No wonder Scorpion Stanley, a year or two later, frothed at him across the floor of the House that he was a man who led people into crime while teaching them to evade the law. Without considering the nature of "crime" (under the circumstances) it was otherwise true. For it was now the man's whole art to evade all obstacles. There is among his letters one shocking document which tells his friend Fitzpatrick how the people may take an oath without sinning. The purpose of the oath was to claim their votes as men who had paid all their taxes *up to* the previous half-year. He says:

Any man can take this oath who does not *owe* more than one half-year's cesses, and who has brought any *one* of the cesses to one half-year.

The words of the oath are clear. "I do not owe more than one half-year of my municipal cesses." That is clearly *all* of the cesses taken in the aggregate, not any one cess taken by itself.

The oath is not, "I do not owe the amount of more than one half-year of *any* municipal cess." The oath is: "I do not owe more than the amount of one half-year of my cesses."

Or, to elucidate—if a man stole forty pounds from a neighbour, managed to legalize his seizure of one of those pounds, he could swear without perjury: "I did not steal the money"—the word "money" being inclusive of that single note whose legal possession invalidated the accuracy of the word "money" by deflating the comprehensiveness of its plurality.

The plural [explains O'Connell eagerly] is strictly and critically true, if he has cleared off one cess. Remember the oath negatives the plural only, the plural conjointly. This will be clear if you suppose four cesses. You pay three. You can then most safely swear that you do not owe cesses.

It is horrible, but it is inevitable. It is the reply of wile to force; the reply of justice defended by a lie to injustice, defended by a phrase which conceals another lie. It is Irish approximation in answer to English compromise. Indeed, in the sense that all civilization implies the reservation of an appetite, and a subterfuge of recompense—aye, and all politics, all morality—what is this illustration of a capacity for mental reservation in O'Connell but a too brutal frankness in what all, especially his enemies, practise, but none confess? No nation which has won an international reputation for "perfidy," and no nation which, like ours, has in recent years played with oaths like shuttlecocks, can afford to throw a stone at O'Connell.

Yet, we note, this twisting advice of his was not to be given directly to the people, lest it discourage them from paying even the one necessary cess. Votes were too precious for carelessness, and he once lost an election in that way. "Keep it to yourself!" says O'Connell to Fitzpatrick: meaning that the mask must not be handed to the peasant until the last moment. The most ruthless touch of all comes when he considers how some of the Protestants may wish to impersonate against his voters. They will, he chuckles, without this magic elixir for deceiving themselves, the law officers, and God Almighty, "be hard set to take this oath *with truth* for an opponent"! In truth—in that "truth"— a Daniel come to judgment. Surely a man to make one shiver, thinking what sense of strength he must have felt, what a dark serpentining power, what capacity for good and evil, and what a world of folly and of deception he must have seen when he closed his eyes and surveyed from within the ragged Ireland he controlled, and had, without exaggeration, taught how to exist; surveyed, too, the erect images of empire that were but the gilded masks of exploitation, to his eyes glittering abattoirs.

One telling anecdote sums up that side of the man. He went on a deputation to the Chancellor of the Exchequer—another Irishman—and was received so cordially that his friends were charmed and became optimistic. Outside the door O'Connell said to his friend: "Did you observe, Pierce, how he took me by the hand?" "Indeed I did," said Pierce, "and I thought it augured well." "Did you observe how he took me by both hands?" "Indeed I did. It was a good sign." "That," said O'Connell, "means that he is going to deceive us. . . ."

In that spirit he handles the war against the Church tithes. He does not provoke it. He does not condemn it. He does not admit to himself what he himself desires. Recall that marvellous soothering letter he wrote to his uncle as a boy in St. Omer, and compare it with this diplomatic murmur in the echoing ear of his devoted Fitz. The date is 1834.

MY DEAR FITZPATRICK,

There is something in the *contentiousness* of the last year [The italics are his, as if in admiration of the word.] . . . more stimulating than in the acquiescence of the present. And perhaps general approbation may be followed by neglect. We shall see. And yet it would be a pity Ireland did not afford me one more opportunity of being of service.

There is no doubt that if the people generally, and in particular the Presbyterians of the North, resist the payment of tithes this year generally, they will be abolished or much reduced next session. The bill rejected by the Lords will certainly be passed unless there be an acquiescence in the payment. I am deeply anxious to know how the people will act. You know, however, that it is criminal to *advise* people not to pay tithes, or to *combine* for non-payment; but each man separately and by himself may refuse to pay, and not be liable criminally for prosecution. . . .

Thus with one last bit to explain what special "secure spots" are safe from distraint under—or beside?—or around the corner of?—the law the man has fanned on the war and yet left not a loophole for a charge of incitement. "Blessed be God," he concludes, "I am buoyant with the expectation of crushing faction and producing solid advantages for the people of Ireland."

The hint was enough. The people issued from their houses in every corner of Ireland. Ever since pre-Emancipation days they had got the taste for organization—as they still have it, learned from him—and in open, secret, and informal societies of a dozen kinds they gathered their wretched forces together. They had the impulse of a real necessity. There had been a bad petit-famine in 1830. Cholera had come in for the first time, ravishing the ill-nourished. They saw that Emancipation was a barren fruit. They saw, when they refused to pay tithes, that their hovels were knocked, their cattle distrained, and their pots and pans flung on the grass until the whole process of tithe-collecting became a series of scenes where there was always wailing, always bitter hatred, and often the spilling of blood.

The tithe war was mostly a night-war. The sons of the labourers dressed strangely, with a straw rope about their waists, or their coats turned inside out, or a white band of rag about their hats—their only attempt at uniform. They had odd nicknames for their bands—the Terry Alts, the Blackfeet, the Right Boys, the White Boys, the White Feet—and they gathered under the apocryphal leadership of a Captain Rock as they were afterwards to band under Captain Moonlight—and that was their attempt at ritual. Their weapons were crude and cruel, a shortened pitchfork, a scythe-blade, or a slasher, and one man in ten might have an old muzzle-loader. They were pitiless, and they had the cruel inventiveness of driven men. In Kerry, for instance, they carded their victims. They took the wire brushes between which the wool is pulled and teased soft in order to make ready for spinning, and they applied the system to the human skin. They stripped a man naked and they pulled and teased him until he was raw. It was not uncommon to burn a house and its occupants. To maim cattle was almost humane. Carleton has left us many pictures of their doings that still scrawl the nerves. Frequently they came into daylight or early morning conflict with the armed police and military, warned by bonfires that sent from hill to hill the news that a raid was approaching. As a result the bailiffs began to come earlier and earlier until every conflict stole out into the dark before daybreak. Carrickshock was typical. There one night two fellows in shabby greatcoats and greasy comforters landed from the mail-coach and drew out twenty-six armed police. They stole into the fields only to find themselves landed in a countryside that was already wild with excitement. In a narrow lane the raiders found themselves, near dawn, facing a mob armed with every kind of weapon, and the end was that the police were cut to bits, and O'Connell found himself defending twenty-five peasants charged with murder.

In his usual way he led a witness, a policeman, to swear that he had never even known a sheep-stealer, and then suddenly confronted the man, from secret information, with the fact that his own father had been a convicted sheep-stealer. From that breach in his victim's integrity he went on and on until he so weakened the evidence that the trial was abandoned.

On these lines the irregular warfare went on until in one year there were 9000 political crimes and 200 homicides, and while O'Connell kept on publicly beseeching the people to be calm and peaceful, the Viceroy became so exasperated that he actually threatened a blockade of the ports and a suspension of all intercourse between Great Britain and Ireland. (It was to this threat that Bully Boynton, the leader of the Protestants, replied in Swiftian terms, renewed in our day, that Ireland would thereupon eat her cows and England could eat her carpets.)

In England the struggle was fought on other lines. After the election to the Reformed Parliament O'Connell led a bloc of forty-five pledged Repealers, out of a total of one hundred and five Irish members. But the Whigs had an enormous majority of their own and they chose to give Ireland not Reform, but Coercion. O'Connell led the attack at once, so often speaking of the King's Speech as "bloody and brutal" that the Speaker had to remonstrate. He declared that after four years of Emancipation not one single Catholic judge had been put on the bench. Out of thirty-four paid magistrates, thirty-two sub-inspectors of police, and five inspectors-general not one single man was a Catholic. Church taxes were crushing a supposedly emancipated people, so that there were as many as 151 Protestant incumbents without a single parishioner, and cases were known where cess had been levied on poor peasant communities to build Protestant churches for which there were no congregations. The poor who paid these taxes from their light purses actually saw fine private houses being built in view of their hovel doors for Protestant individuals. On top of this injustice, he went on, the law was now to be given an almost unlimited power of raid and search; the police would be able, under martial law, to close every cabin door in proclaimed areas from sunset to sunrise, invade these homes at any hour of the night, and transport as felons any member of the family found out of doors.

Night after night he battled against Grey, Brougham, Stanley, Peel, Macaulay. Once he spoke for over four hours. He ended one speech by telling the Whigs they had "brains of lead, hearts of stone, and fangs of iron." If Peel had dreadful stories to tell of the brutalities of the peasants, he had examples to quote of the sufferings of those same peasants under martial law. He told them how, on one occasion:

A witness, named O'Grady, looked at a prisoner at a court-martial and said: "That is not the man." What was the result? O'Grady was ordered out, stripped, and given a hundred lashes. Then they brought him back and said: "Now can you identify him?" Still O'Grady refused. They ordered him out again, and gave him a hundred more lashes. In all they gave him three hundred lashes, and the trial only ended because he fell in a faint from which it seemed that he would not recover.

"Yes," Peel could retort, calling up the evils that follow on agitation, "but what of the informer who returns home after giving evidence?" He recalled one such case.

Nine or ten men broke open the door of this man's house in the night, called him out, and killed him by stabbing him with pitchforks. Inside was his wife and his only child, aged nine. The mother placed the child in a recess by the hearth and said to it, with an extraordinary fortitude—for her husband's screams were heard outside—"My child, you hear the cries of your dying father. I will be the next to go, for when they have finished him they will kill me too. I will struggle with them as long as I can to give you a chance to do what I am putting you here to do. See! I am putting a lighted turf on the hearth. By the glare of it you mark these men. Mark them well. Watch them closely. So that you may be able to tell who they are and revenge your dead mother and father."

"So it fell out," went on Peel, creating in the horrified House a sensation impossible to counteract:

They dragged out the mother. She struggled as long as she could in the kitchen. Then they murdered her on top of the dead body of her husband. By the child's evidence five of these wretches were arrested and convicted within the month. The child was under my care for some years after.

Stanley's speech, based on official records, was equally devastating, for there is nothing so potent on the mind as the account of one or two dreadful deeds of blasting impact, combined with figures that suddenly multiply their effect. He read out the crimes of two typical counties for the year just ended—1835.

	KILKENNY	QUEEN'S COUNTY
Murders or attempts at murder	32	60
Injuries to property	34	115
Burglaries	519	626
Serious Assaults	178	209

The total suggests the aggregate of about 35,000 crimes in the whole country in one year.

To meet that sort of thing, went on Stanley, in one of his most forcible and pungent speeches, the Government had offered £120,000 in rewards for information; only two awards had been paid. It was then that he so bitterly voiced the real reason for English detestation of O'Connell. "Can," he cried, "the honourable member put his hand on his breast and say that he had not given his ignorant countrymen advice which led them to transgress the law whilst he cautiously told them to avoid going beyond it?" He was equally to the point when he declared that the poor were now being savaged by the still poorer. That had been admitted by O'Connell himself as early as May 1831, when he wrote to Lord Duncannon that in Clare "the poorest class have got the masterhood, and even the small farmers are now enduring an atrocious tyranny." He had even said that he would go down there and pacify the people or "satisfy myself on the necessity for harsher measures." Stanley was right, too, in objecting that O'Connell had taught the people to hate the Government for its supposed favouritism against Catholics while teaching the people to hate every Catholic who took office. It was all so reasonable on the English side. Always it is all so reasonable! If one agrees on the premises! Stanley went on, furthermore, to quote figures showing that out of eighteen recent legal appointments nine were Catholics, to which O'Connell retorted that he spoke of those who enforced the law, and that out of the twenty-six stipendiary magistrates appointed within the year not one was a Catholic.

In that debate O'Connell got no real support. He was fighting an almost solitary combat, though Sheil came to his aid, later, to show how the law was being over-enforced. He pointed out that at one Civil Bill court in Cashel ten thousand cases were tried, and in some of these cases against the peasantry the claims did not exceed 2½d. and 3d. The Marquis of Sligo thought to help the Government by proving that the West was peaceful enough. (O'Connell never succeeded in penetrating far beyond the Shannon.) He offered the averages of policemen per head of population in Roscommon, Sligo, and Mayo, where the ratios were one policeman to every 390 people, one to every 460, and one to every 1900. Today, Mayo apart, these figures would be considered appalling. Even in the present Northern Ireland area, which is more disturbed than the South, the figures in 1926 were one to every 550 people; and, in the same year, in Scotland, one to every 750.

Besides Sheil, the only other outstanding supporter of O'Connell was the Chartist leader Feargus O'Connor, a wild man who knew no mortal form of restraint. He was really a thorn in O'Connell's "tail," the only man, except O'Gorman Mahon, who ever defied him. He had already gathered, and was to go on gathering vast concourses in England, and he was to ruin Reform by his extravagance. He passed his life under a series of triumphal arches, saw his name flaming on every banner, even floating in the sky on balloons, high and wide as his own soaring imagination. He turned the heads of millions and ended by going mad in his own. Yet O'Connell admired him for his brute force. "He was a man!" Outwardly he was another O'Connell, an annotation of O'Connell's greatness. With his red curly hair brushing his coat-collar, his fluent tongue, his brawny bulk, his tireless energy, his cajoling grin, his rage, and his futility, he was a grand example of an explosive without a container, wasted energy, a meteor that falls as a burnt-up cinder into a small hole. He had no real brainpower. The result was that his speeches poured from him with more sound than sense to such easy rhythms as "the people are wrecked by disunion, torn by discord, revolutionized by faction." He was the sort of wild man who could reply in a fury to some Whig opponent of Repeal:

The honourable member has declared that rather than consent to Repeal of the Union he would face the bayonet. I reply that rather than submit to the oppression of Ireland I would encounter swords, blunderbusses, pistols, guns, muskets, nay, firearms, of every known sort. . . .

From him little useful aid was to be expected in the House. His work was done outside it among the poor.

Inevitably the Coercion Bill was passed, and O'Connell was left without any machinery for agitation. "The die is cast," he wrote back to Ireland. "We are slaves."

7

IT was the clause against every form of public organization that really angered O'Connell, and in a savage mood he prepared for revenge against Grey. During the debate he had said that "as long as I see the utility of a British connexion, and an immense utility may exist, I should prefer to see this House doing justice to my countrymen rather than that it should be done by a local legislature." The speech had been bitterly resented by his extremists, and he now willingly ate his words. Or, rather, in his typical way, he denied the obvious meaning. Emphasizing the restrictive word "connexion," he elaborated a scheme for Federal Government, with two Parliaments, one in England to deal with national affairs, such as defence, peace, and war, and one in Dublin to deal with trade and commerce. On this basis he started a campaign which, unfortunately, he had to lay aside almost at once under pressure from behind. There O'Connor threatened to lead a revolt against him if he would not introduce a motion for a whole-hearted Repeal.

Cursing his followers' impatience he did so. The half-heartedness of his management of that debate, the genuine sensation of timidity he expressed to his friends, the feelings akin to fear with which he faced his enemies, are interesting. Though full of inventiveness, and most resilient in a crisis, the man never could fight in any large political situation he had not himself carefully engineered. His motion was debated drearily and defeated by almost five hundred votes. More than half the Irish members voted against him. It numbed Repeal for many years to come, and it encouraged him in his temporizing policy.

Leaving O'Connor and the rest to their own devices, he now seized his real chance, which was just over the page. Urging on the tithe war at home, he waited for the Cabinet to break on a choice of policy, as they did. He knew that Grey and Stanley trusted in Coercion, while Brougham and some others wavered towards Reform; he was not surprised when Stanley resigned and the Government was left dependent on the Irish vote. Here Littleton, Chief Secretary for Ireland, unwisely began a private *pourparler* with him, actually promising that the objectionable clause against public organizations would be dropped from the Coercion Bill on its expiry in August (1834). In delight O'Connell swore fealty to the Government, and then sat tight. In due course, however, Grey discovered these secret negotiations, and insisted on re-enacting the old bill in all its fullness, and at once O'Connell struck.

Shamelessly he exposed Littleton. He revealed to an infuriated House every word that had passed between them. The exposure produced a disagreeable scene, Littleton charging O'Connell with blank perfidy, O'Connell charging Littleton with breaking his word. O'Connell's friends upbraided him for his breach of confidence, but he waved them aside. He knew he held the Cabinet in his fist, and he had no intention of letting the bird go. "I knew," he exulted, "that from the minute Littleton told me that Lord Wellesley and himself were adverse to Coercion the game was in my hands if I did not throw it away." The Prime Minister could not ask now for a Coercion Act which neither his own Viceroy in Ireland nor his Chief Secretary desired, and the Cabinet resigned.

Without a qualm he now allied himself with Melbourne, Grey's successor, and fought for a Tithe Bill that would have abolished arrears, diminished the amount payable, and commuted the tithe itself for a land tax. He won his point, only to have the bill thrown out by the Lords. Still, full of hope, he laboured on, and his letters home are a succession of encouragements. "Wait a while." "One more year will put an end to our anxieties." "I do think we are approaching a great National triumph." "I am convinced all will be for the better." It is a litany familiar to every student of the history of the Irish Parliamentary Party during the last hundred years.

Less familiar is the arrogance of his comment on the departure of Lord Grey.

The dexterity of the ministry in trying to deceive me has been their ruin. It was I who turned them out of office. And if the next Government do not improve I will turn them out too.

Melbourne he did not turn out. Instead Melbourne resigned and the Tories came back. Here O'Connell held the balance of power and forthwith he used it against Peel. "O'Connell," wrote Disraeli, "is so powerful that he says he will be in the next Cabinet. It is the Irish Catholic Party that has done all the mischief." Gloatingly O'Connell wrote back to Fitzpatrick that for his three R's—Reform in the Church, Reform in the Franchise, Reform in the Corporations—he was prepared to hang Repeal behind the door.

Upon getting these terms I am prepared to give a full and fair trial to their efficiency. If the experiment failed, I would come back with full force for Repeal. . . .

To the people he issued a manifesto which read:

People of Ireland, let us show ourselves worthy of the present all-important crisis. Let us forget all bygone dissensions and injuries. Let us rally around a ministry which promises a new era, an era of justice and conciliation to the Irish people. . . . We are, after all, a generous and confiding nation. May our generosity be met with a congenial and reciprocal spirit. . . .

The people did not disobey. But he was to learn that without the people he was a man of straw. Four years later when he founded the Precursors Society, the antecedent to his real Repeal Movement, his objects were still the same, and it is possible that he made the fatal error of continuing his parliamentary policy just that four years too long. Then he was to get his last chance, and learn his first real lesson. There was nobody to warn him, however, that the greatest enemy of all politicians was ranging his forces quietly against him. Not even Hercules can murder Time, and not even an O'Connell can evade or circumvent it: he was now sixty.

8

THESE years are the peak of his parliamentary success. He had a genuine influence over the Government, and it gave every promise of being beneficent. He saw a Catholic become Attorney-General for the first time in under two-hundred years. Lord Mulgrave, the new Lord Lieutenant, was a man of Liberal ideas. Morpeth and Drummond gave every satisfaction as Chief Secretary and Under Secretary. The law officers, too, were admirable. In fact, he could truly say to Fitzpatrick that what patronage the Government had would be "disposed of only to sincere friends of the country." *Delenda est Carthago* became his motto for the Orangemen. "I will never support the ministry if they leave one of them in place or power." Alas, he never solved the problem of these Irish Tories, or Orangemen, they who became in later days known as Unionists. He had tried successively to conciliate them, reform them, and crush them. Each way was fatal to Repeal. To conciliate them, obviously so; to reform them, since that meant conciliating a Government little interested in Repeal; to crush them, even more so, since that meant not merely conciliating the Government but combining with it. All failed, as they failed until Repeal came to metamorphose them. Not until he found every other method impossible did he, in his day, turn to Repeal, and then he wrote sadly: "They have perfected my political education."

Otherwise his influence continued to be immense. The *Times* proclaimed that henceforth he would be the real Prime Minister, and he wrote himself at the end of 1835: "I am beginning to think I shall be a Cabinet Minister next session." Such dallyings with office need hardly concern us. Offers of place naturally excited and flattered him. The fact remains that he never accepted them, although at times he cannot but have grown sick to death of the strain of agitation, and he worried constantly over his financial position. His expenses were always enormous. "Frightful" was his own word, in 1835, when, for one election petition, he had become personally responsible for something like £20,000. Yet, even had he taken office, we may be certain, he could not have held it long, so much did his whole nature depend on the people for a life-interest. Whenever such offers were rumoured or made he always said he rejected them because Ireland needed him. That was half the truth, the other half being that he needed Ireland even more.

His wife knew that. She wrote him, four years before, when he refused the Attorney-Generalship:

Had you been betrayed into an acceptance of the terms offered by the Government, you would die of a broken heart before six months had expired; you may now stand firmly in the affections and in the love of your countrymen, and depend on it, they will strain every nerve to reward you.

But that influence, his hope of various reforms, and his idea of putting Orangeism in its place, were the end of whatever good arguments there were for his alliance with an English ministry, and presently even these ceased to be good arguments. His parliamentary career, if judged solely by the major advantages he gained for Ireland, was barren. Year after year a Tithe Bill came before the Commons and was rejected by the Lords. Reform became a will-o'-the-wisp. Corporation Reform was always eluding him. He found himself supporting bad bills for the sake of a well-meaning Government, and losing all influence at home as a result.

One of his immovable critics was Archbishop John MacHale, the great power of the West of Ireland, and another was Sharman Crawford, member for Drogheda. We find O'Connell constantly wooing the one and never budging him, and abusing the other, both for the same reason, i.e., that neither of them would tolerate his policy on tithes. That policy was, frankly, a weak one. O'Connell fumbled the tithe war.

Tithes were a fundamental injustice. Originally no more than a manorial endowment given voluntarily to the local regular clergy, they had been early resisted by the monasteries, who were made subject to them. Up to the dissolution of the monasteries their objections were being regularly argued at Rome; after their dissolution tithes became a secular grievance for the rent-paying tenants, among whom this tax was divided in proportionate sums. That they should be even more bitterly resented in Ireland was only natural, since the Reformed Church was not recognized there. A large pamphlet-literature against tithes remains to us from the time of Swift, and the varied provenance of these pamphlets makes it clear that tithes were resisted by every nonconforming Church in and out of Ireland. A curious but important element in the fight against them was that the tax became divided with the subdivision of the farmlets, and this, though the amount might not be more than a few pence in each case, made tithes an assault on the whole nation, down to the poorest. O'Connell had small hope of abolishing this unjust imposition of a tax on members of one Church for the benefit of another; he aimed, rather, at a reduction in the amount, abolition of arrears, and an appropriation of the surplus for popular education. He did, after long manœuvring, get the reduction. The appropriation idea was opposed by Archbishop MacHale, who would not touch popular education, on the ground that it was sectarian if not pagan.

Finally the principle was not only left entrenched, but was doubly entrenched, because the tithe payment was now changed into a rent payment, and the landlord and the Church were flung into one another's arms. O'Connell left the tithe as firmly rooted in the soil as private property.

Against this Crawford and MacHale and others fought without rest. MacHale was downright in his condemnation of the Appropriation Clause. He said it was a curse rather than a blessing. He denounced several members of the Education Board as "rank infidels," and said their school-texts were "forms of proselytism," as, indeed, many of them were. In all his time there was never a National School in Connemara, and he did not die until 1879.

He was a great old fighter, and as a Nationalist he was always to the front, but he was also one of the first Irish priests who made it easy for more progressive minds to dub the Catholic Church in Ireland as obscurantist. Looking at his portrait today, one is oppressed by that stubborn, tight mouth, and the small, hard eyes. There is no gaiety in his face, no suggestion of an expansive character—a man hard to persuade; and to unpersuade once his mind was made up. When he so rigidly opposed the Queen's Colleges scheme later, against the more diplomatic efforts of his colleagues to find some *modus operandi*, his attitude shows what difficulties O'Connell had to face in his task of trying to make a nation out of a rabble. He actually forced O'Connell to present a petition against the Tithe Bill he was privately and publicly supporting, and it measures O'Connell's private rage to see him working off on Crawford the abuse he dared not vent on the bishop. For O'Connell, as we have seen, was at bottom a Benthamite, a progressive, a "radical," a reformer, an educationist, and his attitude to religion was that of a politician as much as of a zealous believer. He would have agreed thoroughly with Burke—"The only man I know is the civil social being, here in such a place, now at such and such a time; such a one has the right to enjoy the result of his labour, he has a right to be protected by the law for whose social protection he has given up some of his individual liberty"—and agreeing, declared himself, in Ireland, in his time, a Catholic. To have to yield so much, therefore, to the fears and prejudices of his more doctrinaire Catholic colleagues was galling.

As a result, that year, 1837, was a particularly bitter year for them all. They were beginning the task that still goes on in Ireland of finding a *modus vivendi* between opposing interpretations of Irishism and Catholicism. The controversies were endless, and the effect on O'Connell's popularity was in the main seriously detrimental. The comments of his almost contemporary biographer Fagan make that clear, and even his own paper, *The Pilot*, was hardly vocal in his defence. "Expediency," says Fagan, "came and whispered in his ear. . . . Crawford, influenced by no such motive, was, therefore, on the abstract principle, right. . . . O'Connell was guided by prudence, considering it the part of a good tactician to yield at the proper moment. When he could not get all he wished he took what he could get and then looked for more. *In the management of details he was guided by expediency. In the assertion of principle he was unflinching.*"

So far had this policy of expediency taken him that we actually find him supporting a renewal of the Coercion Bill, the fight over which had so nearly sent him to jail in 1831. Again Crawford is against him, and this time *The Pilot* does not make any comment and suppresses the debate. One might almost say it hung its head for shame. All that O'Connell could do was to abuse Crawford with further clumsy mockery about his white waistcoat, or to rally him with buffoon jollity like, "What brings you here, Sharman, me jewel?" while the people looked on in a dull bewilderment.

It is in equal puzzlement that we watch O'Connell, the one-time Radical, oppose the Poor Laws. He had opposed them, however, quite early on in his career, and we may give him the benefit of the doubt as to his sincerity. In this year he absolutely denounced them, saying that no person had a right to be supported by the industry of another, that Poor Laws lessen capital and lower wages, and that Poor Rates must end in confiscation. He shouted down his opponents, particularly the priest, Father O'Malley, and became abusive and insulting when called to order by the chair. On other matters he was clashing with Smith O'Brien, to whom he refers, in all his letters of the period, with unbounded contempt; but that was an old quarrel, dating from the Clare election, and it continued, though somewhat assuaged by the necessities of the times, into the years of his fight with the Young Irelanders. "Trifles," sighs Fagan, "but most injurious to the cause of free discussion." Injurious to more than that, since he appeared to most people to speak against the Poor Laws rather as a landlord and a banker (as he had now become) than as a Man of the People. But it must be said that he held his opinions on this question most stubbornly, boasting to the very end (see his letter of February 13, 1847) that he had warned the landlords of the dangers inherent in that kind of legislation, and he did not yield a jot even when Dr. Murray, Archbishop of Dublin, declared that the Irish hierarchy were *una voce* in favour of legislation for the poor.

Likewise he spoke and fought against the workers, and these, unlike O'Malley, were not shouted down. That controversy deserves careful study, since O'Connell has been generally represented as condemning Trade Unions or Combinations. He undoubtedly disliked their methods, but that he condemned them absolutely is not a fact. In 1837, when he condemned a strike by shipyard workers in Dublin, he was heard patiently by the workmen, whom he faced in public to state his case, and they even allowed him to move a resolution condemning "a system of illegal combinations pervading several of the trades and many of the working classes." Not until he became more particular was he howled at, attacked in his person, and after trying in vain for a whole hour to shout down the men, he had to leave under police protection.

One can well understand the rage of the men. In '38, when five cotton-spinners were punished with the customary savagery of the times for violently defending their claims to the right to combine, and a Commission of Inquiry into the conditions prevailing in that kind of work was proposed, O'Connell opposed the motion, saying:

There is no tyranny equal to that exercised by the Trades Unionists of Dublin over their fellow-labourers. One rule of the workmen prescribed a minimum rate of wages, so that the best workman received no more than the worst. Another part of the system was directed towards depriving the masters of all right in their power of selecting workmen. The names of the workmen were inscribed in a book and the employer is compelled to take the first on the list.

It was precisely for condemning these features of combinations that the Dublin workers attacked him. On the minimum wage nobody would deny, today, that they rightly attacked him, and they might have attacked him with even greater reason for his professed belief that Irish trade was being adversely affected by Trade Unions in general.

His name will not, for that attitude to the city workers, ever be greatly honoured by an urbanized Ireland, and he has been roundly condemned in James Connolly's *Labour in Irish History* —the Bible of modern Irish Socialism—as a renegade who set Class before Liberty. John Mitchel, later on, used the same arguments against him in the pages of *United Ireland*, though O'Connell was by then no more. As against that condemnation of O'Connell may be set the fact that the Irish Catholic Church was invariably opposed to Trade Unions—on which Connolly savagely, but justly, observes that the Church had been almost universally silent when illegal combinations were being used in the tithe war against the levies of "a rival priesthood." But O'Connell's position might be best understood by reference to another matter affecting the workers.

That was an Act moved by Lord Ashley to prevent infringement of the existing Factory Laws, which since 1833 had prevented the employment of children under nine except in silk mills, and those under thirteen from working more than nine hours a day. By barely two votes the Government threw out his measure, O'Connell voting with them against the more humane. He was promptly called a Malthusian Whig, which was unjust. His defence was that of the Benthamite opportunist.

I acted for the advantage of the children, and would to God that children under thirteen years old in Ireland could earn the money the English factory children might have earned.

In other words he was not a humanitarian; he was a brutal realist occupied with the present conditions of his own country. His vision of an Irish democracy was limited by those conditions, and we have little reason to ask him to vision that democracy as a kind of Workers' Republic, seeing that no Irish politician of our own day so visions it. He saw his people as a free people in the sense that they would have their own Parliament, a popular franchise, popular education, security of tenure on the land, freedom of speech, and freedom of worship, and it was his aim that they should be able, with these institutions, to choose their own modes of life. This he did to a large extent, and his work was continued by his successors along those lines. What happened when his seven million Irish got a majority in their own Parliament was outside his sight as it was outside his time; evolutionary politics would, no doubt, create their own problems, and create new vested interests. That was none of his immediate concern; it was the concern of future Irishmen in a free Ireland. In brief, he was a political revolutionary first and foremost. He was a social revolutionary only in that he would first provide something to revolutionize. Long after he wrote *Labour in Irish History* Connolly followed exactly the same path—political change first, social change after.

In his own time and in his own place, however, there is no doubt that being, as we have seen, an inclusivist who accepted all grades and faiths as the material for a free Ireland, O'Connell accepted a hierarchical society as the proper order for Ireland. It would seem that his successors to the latest date agree with his ideas about democracy.

That is important, and a welcome qualification of his ideas of a democratic Ireland. One could easily over-emphasize it—tracing it to his instinctive regard, as a Catholic, for certain values inherent in the Catholic insistence on the importance of the individual, the inequality of human nature, the importance of authority. It may have come from an entirely different source— from the feudal tradition of Darrynane; or from his sheer common-sense view of the crudity of Irish life in his time—something that absolutely necessitated leadership, and an intellectual if not social gradation. Wherever it originated it is there.

It is quite different, we must note, from the English gradation, which, so human and so pliable in the time of Shakespeare, even in the time of Pepys, had become dehumanized by the end of the eighteenth century—Johnson the mid-type from whom might emerge either (as did emerge) the harsh Tory snob who does not talk to his servants, or a tolerable patriarchal form of authority like, let us say, that of an Austrian landowner, or a Renaissance archbishop. O'Connell represents the still warm and human idea of a hierarchical society. It is being lost in Ireland where the modern *bourgeois* is an imitation of his English prototype, and where the Church is, in its Jansenistic aridity, without the Jansenistic elevation of soul, or intellectual strength, severing itself from the people, by severing itself from their natural gaiety, and so losing the authority that should be based on love.

So much for his then unpopular opinions.

Tergiversations, or logicalities, it was not these, nor his little success as a parliamentarian, that caused his decline in power. He was fading out of the Irish picture because his people had real needs, and he was not exploiting them. He was merely playing with their lesser grievances. "Brutal and wretched," a parliamentary commission had described the condition of the peasant in 1833, "their children during the day struggling with the pigs for food, and huddled at night on damp straw under a roof of rotten thatch." Such men and women could hardly be interested in a tithe war that called for no warfare, or be expected to rejoice in a Tithe Bill that asked them to do sums in percentages. What they wanted was a hero who would incarnate them as a nation, and in whom the nation could triumph by proxy. The last thing they wanted was a politician *simpliciter*. To this day the poorer regions of Ireland cannot afford a penny daily paper; in those days Ireland was one vast poorer region of the United Kingdom, and his House of Commons speeches and controversies hardly reached the people at all. That they nevertheless continued in these years to subscribe for him twelve, thirteen, or fourteen thousand pounds every year is an immense tribute to them, to him, and to the men who served him as his lieutenants.

9

SLOWLY O'Connell came back to the main question, though hardly because he had the wit or objectivity to see all this. Does a great popular leader ever realize the extent to which he is nothing in himself, everything as a symbol? He came back to them in the end simply because the Tories were coming in and the Whigs were going out.

What a ten years he had to look back on! What toil, what little fruit! He had laboured for all those years with an energy remarkable in any man, amazing in a man who was fifty-six at Emancipation, when he began his life of complete devotion to his people, and sixty-five when he abandoned Parliamentary Reform to commence a new war at the head of his race. He had had an endless round of meetings and speech-making in and out of the House of Commons, a correspondence of the heaviest, two hundred letters a day he computed in 1837, monstrous private and public quarrels with his friends and his enemies, business affairs to manage—his own bank (now the National Bank), his son's brewery (now manufacturing O'Connell's Dublin Ale), his ancestral farm in Kerry, scandals to crush, newspapers to feed, journalists to keep informed and active, people to interview—the Dublin publicans today, the Dublin clergy tomorrow, the Dublin grocers the day after, jobs to cadge for friends or relatives, with "Tell J. D. Mullen he may depend on me," or "The office of Clerk of the Hanaper has been offered my son-in-law," or "I did what I could for Mr. Birch," or "I used every exertion for Charles Brennan, but without success," until, once, he cried out in comical despair that there was not an office from Lord High Admiral down to scavenger that he had not been asked for, and that the one word he loathed to hear was the request for that "one word" that would unlock some post or other to an optimistic place-hunter. Add to this an endless routine of petty affairs impossible to record, of little interest now, if of great moment then. "I was never in bed before two" sums it all up.

As to his private quarrels, some have been mentioned. One more will do; that with Lord Alvanley, whom he publicly called a bloated buffoon, a miscreant, a liar, a disgrace to his species, and heir-at-law to the thief on the cross, all because he was a Tory member of the exasperating House of Lords. The usual challenge followed, and the now usual refusal to fight—a thing that then needed great moral courage. The London clubs tried, as usual, to expel him, and the usual secondary challenge followed, this time from Disraeli to his son. As to his public quar-

rels, the greatest nuisance he suffered was petitions to unseat him
at elections. One whole year was wasted in this way when the
Dublin Tories tried to eject him in Dublin, an annoyance that
cost them, among them, almost £70,000. At another time he and
his sons had to face simultaneously as many as five such petitions.
Finally, in 1838, driven to distraction by these tactics, he openly
charged the parliamentary committees who tried these petitions
with being "corrupt perjurers." So they were, in that they acted,
despite their oaths, solely as loyal party men. But the House of
Commons could not brook the insult, which was in any case entirely disingenuous, and he was publicly reprimanded. Disraeli
records that while being reprimanded he cut a sorry figure, but
whether he did or no—and it is most unlikely—he got up immediately after and repeated the charge. It must be added that he
himself refused to pay tithes, and was at one time almost out-
lawed by the Court of Exchequer.

In the end he lost heart completely, for he realized suddenly
that during those ten years of tireless labour he had lost ground.
He blamed it on his lack of lieutenants, saying in bitterness that
"the apathy of our public men, of our men of sense and discretion, is most disheartening—how is it possible to serve such a
country?" He looked back, and he must have seen that what the
Melbourne ministry had accomplished was not accomplished for
Ireland. They—and he had fought for many of these things—had
mitigated the law on death punishments, passed laws reforming
the legal conditions of wives, improved the jail system, spread
vaccination, to some degree regulated child labour, reduced the
duties on newspapers and on pulp, established commissions of
inquiry into the conditions of the destitute and the workers,
founded New Zealand, and opened the trade route to India and
China. They left in Ireland exactly the same vested interests and
exactly the same rooted evils they had found. All they had done
was to reduce tithes and then root them, institute some form of

popular education, and give the Catholic masses an entry into official responsibility. And these were mainly by virtue of his influence.

If he needed final proof that he had lost ground, he got it in '38, when, with his undaunted optimism, he founded yet one more organization, the Society of Precursors. These were to agitate for the old reforms, failing which, as their name indicated, they were to be the final preliminary to a nation-wide drive for the Repeal. The people hardly noticed the effort. Connaught did not respond at all. There, Archbishop MacHale stood stubbornly in the way, and the whole province was dead and apathetic. It seemed to O'Connell then as if he were finished at last, and his letters of the time are pathetic in their despair. To Fitzpatrick he writes, in August 1839:

> I am very unhappy. I look upon myself as in danger of ruin. The country is plainly tired out of my claims. I am, indeed, unhappy. I will write to you again on the painful, painful subject tomorrow. I do not believe I will survive long the blow I apprehend from the desertion of me by the country at large. It weighs upon my heart and interferes with my health. At my time of life mental agony is poisonous.

10

HERE in the declension of his egotism he reveals his softer and more amiable side. We may have felt, for instance, in spite of his many pious phrases, that his religion was always vitiated by the natural crookedness of his conscience, the native obliqueness of his mind, or been unable to believe that he could easily shake off the theistic rationalism of his early manhood. We may have applied his own scepticism to himself and found in his love for evasion a treason-felony to the truth. Of such dishonesty, watertight examples are, in the nature of the man, almost impossible to find, but it so happens that we find him—in 1837—challenging

Sharman Crawford to prove or retract the charge that he had ever procured a job for any man!

I call on him to retract the charge he has thus brought forward, or to sustain it by a single fact. I challenge him to name one appointment given in consequence of my interference; or, in fact, that I took any part at all in the transaction.

The most hurried glance at his published correspondence proves him a brazen liar.

But now, however much anyone may have hesitated to take his religiosity at its face value, there seems to be no room for doubt that after his wife's death in 1837 he surrendered to his God. In the wild winter of '38 he went on a pilgrimage to the Trappist monastery of Mount Melleray, and there the thought of retiring for ever from the world seems to have invaded his mind. Later he wrote: "God help me, what shall I do? I think of going to Clongowes to spend the rest of my life there. I want a period of retreat to think of nothing but Eternity." From that time also comes a document, preserved by his daughter, in which he lists twelve spiritual reforms he must make, and not even the thought of the tricky lawyer can induce one to use it against him, its sincerity is so patent. There are, besides, two letters of the most moving from the summer of 1839 written to his daughter, and they silence all one's lingering doubts.

This girl, apparently, had been battling with some undefined temptation, and written in despair to her father. To read his replies is almost to eavesdrop.

My dearest, darling Child,
I have complied with your wish. I have procured Masses to be said for your intention, and after my communion tomorrow I will offer up my wretched prayers for the daughter on whom my fond heart dotes with a tenderness that is not to be described or known to any but the heart of a parent.
Represent to yourself your darling boy in mental agony, and then

you will read my feelings of utter misery at your state of mind. This, I own, is the severest blow that ever I experienced, to have you, my angel daughter, consuming your heart and intellect in vain, idle, and unprofitable scruples. . . . Despair is your danger, your only danger. O Generous God, protect my child from Despair. . . .

Is your scruple such that you can communicate to your father? If it be, tell it to me, and you yourself, when you write it, will probably see how idle it is. Can my child think that the God who, in the lingering torment of the cross, shed the last drop of His blood for her, is a tyrant, or that He does not love her? Your greatest love for your babe is nothing to the love God bears for you. . . .

You would pity your poor father if you knew how miserable you make me. I fear for you with the most agonizing fear in your trial. . . . Write to me, darling, darling child. I enclose ten pounds to pay your expenses to France. If you do not go there use them as you please. Ever my own, own dearest child.

> Your fond, though distracted father,
> DANIEL O'CONNELL.

The girl wrote back, confessing the nature of her sin—an O'Connell sin, if not an O'Connell confession—pride of heart that murdered her power to admit any contrition. What incident gave rise to this arid condition we do not know. Mingling tenderness with legalistic theology, rather comically when we know the old rascal who writes, her father replies:

MY OWN DARLING, DARLING ——,

I write to you by your pet-name to recall to your own tenderness your fond father's affection.

I see your case clearly and it breaks my heart to think of it.

There is one remedy, and *only one*; that is, absolute unqualified submission to your director—unreasoning submission. Do not argue with anybody. Do exactly what your director requires. In your case your director may—and I think should—compel you to go to communion without going to confession at all. Many persons in your condition have been perfectly cured by perfect submission.

Believe me, my own idolized child, you have ease and happiness here and hereafter in your own hands. Submit, my own ——. Do not think on anything but implicitly obeying your director.

The moment you receive this letter tell your director you submit to do everything he desires—to pray or not to pray, to fast or not to fast, to confess or not to confess, and above all, to go to communion whenever he advises or commands you.

By that simple process your mind would be restored to tranquillity and the love of God—submission, the first of virtues, the corrective of pride, of subtle pride, that wants us to think *we* are perfect.

I believe it will kill me if I do not hear that you take my advice. I would call it, darling child, my command; but no, I give you your father's blessing if you submit to be ruled by your director without reasoning or arguing. Cast your heart and mind in humble thought into the loving hands of God, who in the excess of His love, died on the cross for *you*. Do not argue. Tell the priest not to argue with you, but to command you, and obey to the tittle, and you will be at once and for always relieved.

The moment I can leave this I will go to you, my own darling child. I will go to you to hear you say you have obeyed me. I am sure, if you do obey, I will find you happy in your sweet family, and in the spiritual delight of the love of God. *Obey*. You know you are safe in obeying your father and director.

May I not tell you, darling, that you seem not to know what the theological virtue of contrition is?

Contrition, darling, is a belief and conviction that it is a great evil to have committed sin. It is the knowledge that in committing sin we did that which was a great evil, and the consequent regret.

Contrition is not such a grief or sorrow as you would feel if your child was sick, or as I do at your mental affliction. It is a conviction of the evil of sin in offending God, and subjecting us to deserve punishment hereafter. Ask your director how accurate this is, but obey him, and you are safe and well. May God bless you, ever my own darling child.

> Your afflicted and most fond father,
> DANIEL O'CONNELL.

11

WITH the end of Whig power rapidly approaching, the position of O'Connell was sardonically reversed. Time was when he used to threaten the Whigs to resign if they did not grant his demands. Now it was the Whigs who threatened to resign if he did not satisfy them by his conduct. Accepting the inevitable, he abandoned them. In April 1840, at the age of sixty-five, the old giant turned his back on Parliament and came home to his army of poor Irish. Choosing the Royal Exchange for his meeting-place, he announced that he was about to found a Repeal Association, and call the people to a new and, this time, relentless war.

When he arrived at the Exchange he found the hall almost empty. He sat for half an hour glowering at the half-empty benches, and then he got up, addressed them magnificently, and went home to plan his campaign.

He thus ended ten years of what one must call (in terms of material results) barren labour. But while he sits in his wifeless home in Merrion Square, let Sheil say what had been achieved in those years, as he said it across the floor of the Commons in 1836.

If we were seven millions of mere, dull, uneducated, degraded serfs, a mere mass of helotism, to our seven millions little regard should be paid. Once, indeed, we were sunk by the Penal Code. But a marvellous change has taken place. Men often talk of the great improvement which has taken place in Ireland, and in doing so they refer merely to its external aspect. Its moral one has undergone a still greater alteration. Not only has the plough climbed to the top of the mountain and cultivation pierced the morass, but the mind of Ireland has been reclaimed.

You educate our people, and with the education of our people, the continuance of unnatural and unjust institutions is incompatible. But if education has done much, agitation has done more. Public opinion, which before did not exist, has been created in Ireland. The minds of men of all classes have been inlaid with the great principles on which the rights of the majority depended. This salutary influence has ascended to the higher classes, spread among the middle, and descended among the lower. The humblest peasant has been nobly affected by it.

Even in the most abject destitution he has begun to acquire a sentiment of self-respect. "He venerates himself a man." I remember the time when, if you struck an Irish peasant, he cowered beneath the blow. Strike him now, and the spirit of offended manhood starts up in a breast covered with rags. . . .

No, sir, we are not what we were. We have caught the intonations of your rhymes. Englishmen, we are too like you to give you leave to keep us down. Nay, in some points we have surpassed you.

"We are," he said in proud conclusion, "an undecaying and imperishable people."

VI : THE "COME-BACK"

1840-1847

I

THE Whigs did not give up the ghost until the summer of 1841, and then the elections spread O'Connell's cry in every county in Ireland. He was thrown out in Dublin, and had to take refuge in Cork, and he found his "tail" reduced to twelve, of whom four were members of his own family. Thus truncated, he found himself facing his oldest and most bitter enemies, now in power—Wellington, from whom he had wrested Emancipation, Scorpion Stanley, Graham, whom he had thrown out over the Littleton affair, Hardinge, and the young man whom he had, at the time of the Magee trial in 1813 (over a quarter of a century before), mocked at as "Orange Peel," now Prime Minister. In that long ago Peel had been at a disadvantage. He was thirteen years younger than O'Connell when he first came to Ireland as a young and inexperienced stranger. Those thirteen years were now a handicap on the old fighter staging a "come-back," and time and experience had made Peel into a hard, cold, calculating statesman. He had watched the career of O'Connell almost from the beginning. He had had many opportunities to measure him. He must have asked himself many times during the next few years whether he was still dealing with the same man who, in 1813, had defied the Irish Government, deliberately challenged

its power, almost banked on its cowardice. In so far as he ought
to have asked himself that question, and his behaviour during the
following three years is the behaviour of a man who is carefully
weighing the chances, it was because he could see rising up again
behind O'Connell's bulky frame the shadow of that old army
of the Seven Millions. Soon the choice would not be (as it was
in 1813) between tolerating O'Connell and sending him to Newgate, but (as it was for Wellington in 1828) between O'Connell
and civil war.

2

On O'Connell's side there were questionings of another kind.
He had three enemies—lack of time, lack of money, lack of men.
As for the first, he hoped to get the Tories out of office by the
time his new movement had come to ripeness—but he was growing old and the race was telling on him. For money, he founded
a Repeal Rent, although he well knew that it must diminish his
own income, since the poor could hardly create both a fighting
fund and pay him his usual twelve or fourteen thousand a year.
That Rent, as late as 1842, came to little more than £50 a week,
and his letters to his faithful treasurer, Fitzpatrick, are despairing
on his own account. "Want is literally killing me," he wrote
from London in July 1841. As for the last thing, men, Cobbett
had well named him the Member for all Ireland, meaning that his
work was essentially a personal work and a personal triumph.
He had with time, it is true, gathered about him hundreds of
lieutenants, some in Dublin, most scattered throughout the country, and attending to their own affairs for the greater part of
their time, none of any stature.

He had O'Neill Daunt, a literary man more fitted to be a recluse than an agitator, a gentle and sensitive soul who never
really trusted his master—he was O'Connell's private secretary.
There was a young man named Ray, who acted as General Sec-

retary for the organization. There were several unscrupulous tongue-bullies like Somers, or Dillon Browne. There was that lovable and grotesque character, Tom Steele, who, without using any cliché, almost adored O'Connell, whose language became Biblical when referring to the Liberator (he never referred to him in any more personal terms), whose brains were more like mice running around than steady grey matter, and whom O'Connell had, in Tom's words, "in the stupendous workings of his awful spirit," crowned as Chief Pacificator of Ireland. Steele can hardly be called a lieutenant, although his goodness was such that the people often obeyed him out of loving kindness, and there is not on record a harsh word spoken against him, or, at most, nothing more than a bemused sigh. So, on one occasion at a Tralee meeting, O'Connell's daughter saw a poor harper, dressed as an ancient bard, strumming by the kerb with coldblue fingers. She begged Steele to do something for the poor man, and was told: "Set your mind at rest, daughter of Ireland's Liberator, I have taken care of the bard." "What have you given him?" she asked cautiously. "I have made him immortal," cried Tom Steele. "By virtue of my office as Chief Pacificator of Ireland, I have constituted him O'Connell's chief musician." "Yerrah, for God's sake, Tom," laughed O'Connell, putting his hand in his pocket, "run after him and give him this half-crown." To this list of useful but scarcely inspiring lieutenants we may add Richard Barrett, the journalist, who had served a period in jail to shield O'Connell from a libel action at an awkward moment; and, most useful and loyal of them all, Fitzpatrick, who worked tirelessly to keep him supplied with funds. After that there were a few small men who, without his force, brutality, and magnificent genius, imitated his bombast. These were the orators who, at public meetings, made Dan pull his hat over his eyes to hide his amusement, and sink back in his chair during their speeches, his chin buried in his cravat and a sardonic smile playing about his heavy lips.

But presently there were to be others, far more valuable, essential indeed to O'Connell's last fight. These were the young men who not only did not hide their contempt for O'Connell's lieutenants, but included in it O'Connell himself. They were avowed Repealers, ready for any extremity, who had only a very inadequate idea of the immensity of their debt to the man they always feared and sometimes despised. These Young Irelanders had never known what it was to be an Irishman cowering under the rags of slavery, never known the slime out of which O'Connell had lifted the entire people. To these, in their high idealism, his appeals on the score of Ireland's material poverty were almost base; they thought of glory, not of finance, and they ransacked the past that O'Connell had kicked aside. They tried to learn from little books the language O'Connell spoke as a child, and thereafter only when addressing the peasants of the western seaboards. They would meet on the roads old men who were to O'Connell so many votes and little else, and because of the memories these old men preserved they saw, behind the apparent illiteracy, the superficial roughness or even boorishness, something like the last rays of their sun-god. How angry they would have been to hear O'Connell called King of the Beggars—not because they could deny his kingship, but because they felt themselves as the descendants of kings. These—James Clarence Mangan, Thomas Osborne Davis, Charles Gavan Duffy, Thomas Francis Meagher, John Mitchel, Michael Doheny, and others—created in verse and prose, for they were all able men of letters, image after image of the legendary greatness of their people, and they appealed to the country in the name of its former glory.

That winter of 1841, while O'Connell was enjoying one of his spectacular triumphs, his election as Lord Mayor of Dublin, standing on the balcony of the Assembly Rooms in William Street in his red robe, gold chain, and cocked hat, guffawing as the mob roared beneath him—these young dreamers would surely have been gathered together, at a distance, in one of those little back-rooms from which emerge the rebellious movements of every country in the world. Down the street they would hear how Dan bellows to the mob: "Boys, do yez know me now?" and the roar coming back: "Ah, sure, aren't ye our own darling Liberathor?" "Does the hat suit me, boys?" with a comical cock of the old head, and the street roaring with laughter and cheers. The roaring would have penetrated to the attic under the roof of the presbytery of St. Michael and John's on the quays (where Father C. P. Meehan so often gave shelter to those young men) as their eyes roam through the low window over the smoke-laden roofs of the old Dublin all about them—the Dublin of Lord Edward, Robert Emmet, Wolfe Tone, the conspirators and spies of '98, or across the Liffey to the tower of St. Michan's, in whose graveyard lay, and lie, the bones of the brothers Sheares. They would have heard the mob cheer their "darling Liberathor," and groaned that a mob should be so deluded as to believe utterly in him.

So the contrast forms in the imagination, and the imagination is merely an emphasis of the fact—the tar-barrels escorting the Catholic Lord Mayor back to Merrion Square in all his borrowed regalia, and the firelight flickering in the face of young James Clarence Mangan as he creates—some may say *invents*—for his people a past they had never experienced, unless in the dying and ravelled memories handed down from their fathers' fathers, old memories, hardly only half-alive, of a time before the Gaelic world was broken for ever on the wheel at Limerick.

He would whisper:

> O my land, O my love,
>   What a woe, and how deep
> Is thy death in my long mourning soul!
>   God alone, God above
>   Can awake thee from sleep,
> Can release thee from bondage and dole.
>   Alas, alas, and alas,
> For the once-proud people of Banba. . . .

> The high house of O'Neill
>   Is gone down in the dust,
> The O'Briens are clanless and banned,
>   And the steel, the red steel
>   May no more be the trust
> Of the faithful and brave in the land. . . .

Cannot one hear the throat-gulp that answered such poems, see the clenched fists, the hot tears of rage; or a like answer to that other magnificent song, "Dark Rosaleen"? Yet it rests with the calmer eye of history to note that that poem, so lovingly translated from the Irish, was written originally by the Egan O'Rahilly who called the common Irish "boors"—those poor relics of Limerick and 1691 who had been left behind to live on in slavery for the awakening touch of Dan O'Connell!

There is the clash of ideas and ideals come again—the clash of old Keogh and young Wolfe Tone, of young O'Connell and old Keogh, young Davis and old O'Connell. It is all part of a long groping towards what Ireland could be and should be, one image after another of Life Eternal, all half-legible, all half-false, all half-true, that are always being added to one another by the young and the old of every land. It was the pity of it that their striving to bring Past and Present into a unity should breed more rancour than affection.

Charles Gavan Duffy had his song of the past, too, and it has the same flash of the drawn sword.

> O never fear for Ireland, boys, for she has soldiers still.
> For Rory's boys are in the wood, and Remy's on the hill,
> And never had poor Ireland more loyal hearts than these.
> May God be good and kind to them,
>   the faithful Raparees,
>   the fearless Raparees,
> My jewel were you, Rory, with your Irish Raparees.

To his song he appended the note:

When Limerick was surrendered, a multitude of the old soldiers and some gentlemen remaining in the country were long a terror to the new and old settlers and a secret pride and comfort to the trampled peasantry, who loved them even for their excesses. It was all they had left to take pride in.

There, once more, is the historical imagination of these young men typified in Duffy's ignorance. Because he did not know Irish he did not know that the older past, the Gaelic lords, had, in the person of David O'Bruadair, spat on the selfsame Raparees. It marks the difference between the Young Irelanders and O'Connell that he had the greater strength, because he had the greater realism: he had the power, lacking in them, and the pride and self-belief, to admit poverty and nothingness as the true fact from which to start to build. But it is easy to appreciate their difficulties if we remember that they came mostly from an urban life, or a landowning class; the best of them, Doheny and Mitchel, had the strength of a more intimate background; so that when the break with O'Connell came finally, and the Young Irelanders established an Irish Confederation, it is no surprise to find Duffy writing to Smith O'Brien:

> The sole security we have *for keeping the Confederation from becoming purely democratic* is the gentry's junction; every additional landlord that joins it will be an additional check on movements such as you fear.

That has to be borne in mind by anybody who may have formed an unfriendly opinion of O'Connell on the basis of the frequent animadversions of Arthur Griffith. Griffith also was urbanized and undemocratic, and very naturally has no words flattering enough for the Irish Confederation, or hard enough for O'Connell.

In this way the Young Irelanders created a blazing picture, false or true, weak only in its inability to face the essential fact; strong because generative, electric, fecund, able to give the people that superflux of racial pride without which few people can fight, suffer, or die. That O'Connell managed to do without it is amazing: not as for himself, for he was a giant, but as for his army of beggars. But that his army of beggars would have loved him all the more had he given them this, in addition, is evident from the reception given to the Young Irelanders' weekly paper, the *Nation*, founded in October 1842. It was sold out in a day.

In this paper they printed their heartening songs and poems and essays, and expounded their policy of self-dependent Nationalism. It is not correct to think of them as Republican separatists like the United Irishmen. Their canon was much looser, and they were willing to work with O'Connell for the restoration of the old Irish Parliament which acknowledged the Crown. Since their paper, in addition, is a landmark in the development of modern Irish literature—from it dates the rise of Irish letters in the English tongue—they have in that way contributed also, indirectly, to the development of the modern democracy set on its road by O'Connell. Many have found in that cultural work their best contribution to Irish nationalism.

Looking about them they found in the metropolis of Ireland not one single statue to an Irishman; in the shops of the statue-makers they could find only a bust of Wellington. Not one street or square was called after an Irishman; they commemorated instead a Harcourt, a Sackville, an Essex, a Dorset, the instruments of official English rule. Whatever literature existed revelled in gibes against the native Irish; the stage-Irishman was already flourishing in the novel and the drama. To the journalists in the popular press "Irish ideas were like Irish diamonds, the worst of their class." Gaelic songs still circulated in many of the cabins, but, as we have seen, they were unrelated to modern conditions and they were never heard in the workshops and in few taverns. No school-book on Irish history was in use in any Irish school. Of Irish heroes the people knew only three or four —Sarsfield, Grattan, Lord Edward, Emmet. In all that spiritual desert there were, then, only the rudest ballads, and the speeches of O'Connell, or better still, since he was flowery and poetical, Richard Lalor Sheil.

Of the popular ballads, in English, we have seen a typical example, "O'Connell's Garland." One glance at the others shrivels the heart at the sight of the void the Young Irelanders had to fill. From a people living on such an exiguous spiritual fare, wrote Duffy, "there might be drawn an army; for a civil contest they were unprepared." The civil contest for Emancipation gives the "No" to that, but it was certain that the Young Irelanders did excellent work as a kind of spiritual commissariat to the nation. Selflessly they devoted to the business of propaganda and popular education talents that in a more fortunate land might have been carefully garnered and patiently trained for the creation of pure literature. They were alone in their splendid work, or almost alone, since apart from them, and possibly the earlier Cork poet Callanan, we can record only one other man who fed the starving hearts of the people in their way—Tom Moore.

Looking back at it all, forty years after, in a temperate mood, Gavan Duffy makes it clear that the Young Irelanders felt they were bringing to Irish life something essential to its well-being that was not there before:

Marvellous as were O'Connell's energy and resources, they were not sufficient to move the mass of prejudice and dumb indifference which confronted him. The bulk of the people were gifted with a generosity which shrank from no sacrifice, but they were ill-equipped. . . . The majority could not read or write. They had got a political training which in some degree compensated for their want of culture or self-knowledge—they had learned concert, self-reliance, the necessity of making mutual concessions, and the invaluable secret to a suffering people, the secret of their own power, but they had been taught for the most part as men are taught before the invention of writing. Their courage was not fortified by knowledge, or that pride of place which feeds the self-respect of nations.

It was, as far as it went, quite true; and it was to become more and more urgent as time went on and the complexities of Irish problems became intensified by her incursions into the modern arena. If one adds to that feeling of Duffy's the Young Irelanders' dislike of O'Connell's crude methods, his flattery so gross that it savoured of contempt, his preference for agents rather than confederates, his preference for obedience rather than a concert of minds, his bullying ways, his coarseness, his—to them —degrading and sycophantic expressions of loyalty to England, his conservatism and his parliamentarianism, is it any wonder that the young men who did so much to change, or start a change in, all that felt themselves as real originators, more original than the man who gave them their audience, with whom they worked as against the grain, whose tremendous power they feared, whose fall they would have regarded as the removal of an obstacle—if only all did not fall with him; but by whose death they were to find Ireland sinking into a tomb, there to lie until the child who was born in the year before he died, Charles Stewart Parnell, came to his manhood to replace both them and him? Parnell was to carry on neither tradition alone; he was to carry on the double tradition of brain and fist, the bloody night-fields and the screaming hustings, that tradition which O'Connell at least postulated (if he did not thoroughly exploit it), for the ever-growing Gargantua of which (including even Young Ireland?) he was the father.

3

ORIGINATORS or not, the young men were the generators of O'Connell's last campaign. They supplied so much emotional electricity, so galvanized the people, that, were he a dozen years younger, he and they might have made something like the combination that Davitt made afterwards with Parnell. Their greatest success was with a planned series of Monster Meetings. These were a Young Ireland idea, their purpose being to discipline the people. Doheny says in The Felon's Track that he, with Davis and John Blake Dillon, had long before designed them "to train

the country people to military movements and a martial tread
. . . an object unsafe to announce, but to be effected through
other agencies than drill."

So playing into one another's hands, he, with these vast meetings, his loud voice, his brutal tongue; they, with the papers,
clubs, songs, flashing idealism, hurled the eight million souls into
action. In one average week O'Connell spoke in Charleville, on
May 18, to, it was computed, 300,000 people; sitting down that
night to a banquet of 400; on the twenty-first in Cork to a gathering, it was said, of 500,000 people; on the twenty-third at Cashel
to 200,000; on the twenty-fifth at Nenagh to 400,000; on the
twenty-eighth in Longford to 250,000—and after that, within
another week or two, he was at Drogheda, Kilkenny, Mallow,
and Clare, always addressing vast gatherings. The figures are
doubtless unreliable. He would begin a speech by referring to
"this vast gathering of 50,000 Irish men and women," go on to
". . . and when I look about me at this meeting of 100,000 people," and perhaps end up with a figure three times that with
which he began. But the increasing rate of subscriptions to the
Repeal Rent gave proof enough of the return of belief in his
cause. In January 1843 the average weekly Rent was about
£150. In February they collected £342 for the last week of the
month. March brought in £366 in its second week; the first
week in April brought in £473; the last, £683; the last week of
May, £2205; and the third week in June, £3103. For the year
the total was over £48,000. In Conciliation Hall, the new home
of the Repeal Movement in Dublin, there had been nine clerks
in 1841. There were forty-eight at the end of 1843. Even more
agreeable to him, and disagreeable to the Government, was the
debate on the Repeal question in the Dublin Corporation, in
February 1843, when O'Connell as Lord Mayor of that one-
time impregnable stronghold of Orangeism carried a motion
against the Union by forty-one votes to fifteen. Disturbing, in
another way, was the peaceful nature of these vast, semi-seditious

meetings, as well as the rise of Repeal Police and Repeal Arbitration Boards that, between them, kept a check on the inevitable secret societies that follow on every political movement in Ireland. These "courts" bade fair to usurp, in the unassailable name of peace, the functions of British law.

Add, finally, to this evidence of the success of the return from Elba the fact that in the same year of 1843 his own personal tribute came to over £20,000. When Thackeray was in Dublin he saw it being collected at the church doors.

Every door was barred, of course, with plate holders, and heaps of pence at the humbler entrances, and banknotes at the front gates told the willingness of the people to reward their champion. The carboy who drove me had paid his little tribute of fourpence at the morning Mass. The waiter who brought me my breakfast had added his humble shilling. And the Catholic gentleman with whom I dined and between whom and O'Connell there was no great love lost, pays his annual donation out of gratitude for old services and to the man who won Catholic Emancipation for Ireland.

On the educational side James Duffy, the publisher, was meanwhile issuing thousands of little books at a few pence apiece on Irish history, literature, art, music, while Repeal Reading Rooms sprang up in hundreds of parishes all over the country. From that time dates the general acceptance of certain symbols first distributed, if not created, by Tom Moore, and not yet killed in popular Irish thought or commercial design—the round tower, the harper and harp, the wolf-dog, Eire with her broken chain, the leaning Celtic cross, the wreathed shamrock. Time has decried them, and proved them synthetic, but where they freely decorated the Repeal Card they were then tucked away reverently in many a tattered vest.

4

FOR long Dublin Castle had been listening to and measuring this rumble of popular agitation, though all it did so far was to see that no meeting took place without a small army of police and dragoons on its outskirts. The *Times's* brief comment on a meeting at Enniscorthy gives us an idea of British impatience with this tactic.

There are stated to have been 200,000 people at Enniscorthy last Thursday. There was first of all the usual irruption of soldiers hurled across the country to put down an outbreak which everyone must have known would not occur. They were then cooped up in a temporary barracks from which they could witness the procession and join in the shouts of the mob.

A German traveller describes the effect these Monster Meetings began to make on other observers. Speaking of a meeting at Dundalk in June he says:

Never did I see anything like it. I have seen princes make their solemn entry into Cologne. All was child's play to this. There was no walking in the streets; all were either borne or pushed. I looked down and I saw nothing but heads—not even shoulders were visible. Never did I hear anything like that prolonged, that never-ending *Hurrah* for O'Connell. He descended from his carriage and instantly a large broad path opened for him, and as instantly closed when he had passed. It was the passage of Moses through the Red Sea to the very life.

Lytton wrote a fine description of that O'Connell as heard speaking "to mobs and on his mother earth."

> Once to my sight the giant thus was given,
> Walled by wide air roofed by boundless heaven;
> Beneath his feet the human ocean lay,
> And wave on wave flowed into space away.
> Methought no clarion could have sent its sound
> Even to the centre of the hosts around;
> And as I thought rose the sonorous swell
> As from some church-tower swings the silvery bell
> Aloft and clear, from aery tide to tide
> It glided, easy as a bird may glide,
> To the last verge of that vast audience sent

It played with each wild passion as it went;
Now stirred the uproar, now the murmur stilled
And sobs or laughter answered as it willed.

Then did I know what spells of infinite choice
To rouse or lull, has the sweet human voice;
Then did I seem to seize the sudden clue
To the grand troublous Life Antique, to view
Under the great rock-stand of Demosthenes
Mutable Athens heave her noisy seas. . . .

And yet, in all those meetings, thanks to the priests, to O'Connell's hold on the people, to the work, too, of Father Theobald Mathew, the "Apostle of Temperance," never once was there a serious brawl through drunkenness, even though in the hot weather, and in these dusty, compressed gatherings the temptation to drink copiously must have been strong. Gavan Duffy records that he heard three men loitering in a village, twenty miles from Tara, being asked why they had not come to the meeting; to which they replied that they had been prevented by the teetotallers of the village because they had broken their pledge of abstinence. It may have been a joke, but Duffy believed it as something not unnatural, though striking. The sellers of liquor must in those days have felt like the old woman who, after the suppression of the Faction fights, used to lean over her half-door and sigh: "Ten o'clock in the morning and not a blow sthruck yet!"

O'Connell's handling of this campaign followed his usual method. To the warning that the Government would interfere, sooner or later, he laughed that they would not dare raise a finger. In any case, it was not the Government he feared; it was the inevitable push from behind. As a result his language became a mixture of cautious appeasement and veiled threat, with the caution and the veil alike becoming more and more faint, as the meetings grew in size and the barometer of public excitement rose. In May (1843), at Mullingar, he heard the Bishop of Ardagh say to the people, and he interrupted him repeatedly to echo and emphasize his words:

I defy any minister in England to put down agitation in the diocese of Ardagh. If they attempt to rob us of the daylight we will retire to the chapels. . . . If they beset our temples we will prepare our people for those circumstances. . . . And if for that they bring us to the scaffold, in dying for the cause of our country, we will bequeath our wrongs to our successors.

John O'Connell even wrote in the British press: "We will not attack. I do not say we will not defend." Clearly it was a time when the Parnell of the day needed his Davitt as no man ever needed one, a Land League, a fighting force, a—Young Ireland?

All through the spring of 1843 the Government watched in silence. Then in reply to a question by the Grand Master of the Orange Lodges, Peel threw down his glove.

There is no influence [he said], no power, no authority which the prerogatives of the Crown and the existing law give to the Government that shall not be exercised for the purpose of maintaining the Union, the dissolution of which would involve not merely the repeal of an Act of Parliament, but the dissolution of this great empire. . . . I am prepared to make this declaration, that, deprecating as I do all war, and especially civil war, there is no alternative which I do not think preferable to the dismemberment of the empire.

To the delight of the Young Irelanders O'Connell at once dared the Government to begin the war. He repeated it a week or two later with: "Where is the coward who would not die for such a land? I do not like fighting, but let our enemies attack us if they dare." To that the mob rose in one great roar; it was the kind of talk they had been waiting to hear these twelve years.

As promptly Peel retorted. Twenty-three Irish gentlemen were deprived of their offices as magistrates for having attended Repeal meetings. The effect was an angry debate in London, while at home the insult stiffened the lukewarm. In the House, Peel followed it up by an Act which proposed to limit the holding of weapons only on licence and if they were branded, the police being given authority to search for hidden arms. To the surprised dismay of Peel, and the delight of O'Connell, it was fought, clause by clause, step by step, by a strong combination of Irish Liberals and English Radicals, and held up for three months in committee—an example of that kind of obstruction which Biggar and Parnell so effectively used in later years. When the Act did become law, it was used shamelessly to prevent the Catholic nationalist from holding arms, and to allow the Tory and landlord to arm himself to the teeth.

That month, at Kilkenny, O'Connell surpassed himself in the skill with which he uttered veiled threats of resistance by force. This was the method he followed:

I stand today at the head of a group of·men, sufficient, if they underwent military discipline, to conquer Europe. [*Cheers.*] Wellington never had such an army. [*Cheers.*] There was not at Waterloo on both sides as many brave and determined men as I see before me today. Tell them what to do and you will have them disciplined in an hour. [*Cheers.*] They are as well able to walk in order after a band as if they wore red coats.

But at Mallow, three days later, he went farthest of all. Michael MacDonagh, in his *Life of O'Connell*, quotes from the reminiscences of a reporter present at the meeting the statement that O'Connell was surly arid preoccupied before the meeting, and that Steele explained his moodiness by saying that the previous day's *Times* announced an approaching meeting of the Cabinet to consider the state of Ireland. "Our next move," said the Chief Pacificator, "may be to take the field." Later O'Connell approached this reporter, Maurice Lenihan, and bade him ask his colleagues to be particularly careful to note his words that day. "I do not know whether I may speak the particular things I consider most important at the dinner," he warned, "or at the meeting." But he asked the reporters to be particular in taking a verbatim report of what he said at both. His speech at the meeting was statesmanlike and temperate; he lauded the discipline and orderliness of the people, and said that it was impossible to credit that any government would try to crush such a constitutional and so loyal a movement.

Whether this was what he considered of particular importance or not we cannot tell, or whether the scene at the dinner was a piece of careful stage-management. But at that dinner, the galleries thronged, every seat shoulder to shoulder, a singer had just come to the end of Moore's verses, which begin:

> Oh, where's the slave so lowly,
> Condemned to chains unholy,
>   Who, could he burst
>   His bonds accurst,
> Would pine beneath them slowly . . .

when O'Connell jumped to his feet, his arms in the air, his eyes ablaze, and shouted out:

"I am not that slave!"

Whereupon the whole company rose and echoed him again and again with:

"We are not slaves! We are not slaves!"

The speech that followed was the speech of a soldier, not a politician, and it became known as "The Mallow Defiance." In the course of it he said:

Gentlemen, you may soon have the alternative to live as slaves or die as freemen. [*Prolonged cheers.*] In the midst of peace and tranquillity our Saxon traducers are covering the land with troops. [*Groans and hisses.*] On Thursday the Cabinet was considering what they should do, not for Ireland, but against her. [*A voice:* "We are ready to meet them."] Of course you are. Do you think I suppose you to be cowards or fools? Are we to be called slaves? ["No, no!"] Have we not the ordinary courage of Englishmen? ["Let them try."] Are we to be trampled under foot? [*Loud cries of* "No, no!"] Oh, they shall never trample on me at least! [*Tremendous cheering that lasted for several minutes.*] I was wrong, they may trample me under foot. [*Cries of* "No!" *and* "They never shall!"] I say they may trample on me, but it will be my dead body they will trample on and not the living man! ["Hear, hear," *and most tremendous cheering.*] Cromwell, the only Englishman who ever possessed Ireland, sent 80,000 Irishmen to work as slaves, every one of whom perished beneath the ungenial sun of the Indies. Peel and Wellington may be second Cromwells. They may get his blunted truncheon and enact —Oh, sacred Heaven!—on the fair occupants of that gallery, Cromwell's massacre of the women of Wexford. But I am wrong. By God, they never shall. [*Tremendous cheering, and waving of handkerchiefs by the ladies.*] Remember that deed! Three hundred women, the beauty and the loveliness of Wexford, the young and old, the maid and matron. When Cromwell entered the town, these three hundred inoffensive women, of all ages and classes, were collected around the cross of Christ, erected in the part of the town called the Bull Ring. They prayed to Heaven for mercy, and I hope they found it. They prayed to the English for humanity and Cromwell slaughtered them. [*Cries of* "Oh! Oh!" *and a great sensation.*] I repeat it. Three hundred of the grace, the beauty, the virtue of Wexford were slaughtered by those English ruffians. [*Cries of* "Oh! Oh! Oh!"] Sacred Heaven. [*Cries of* "Oh! Oh!" *and great sensation, many of the ladies screaming with terror.*] But, I assert, there is no danger to the women of Ireland, for the men of Ireland would die to the last in their defence. [*Wild cheering, the entire company on its feet.*] We were a paltry remnant in Cromwell's time. We are nine millions now!

MacDonagh, quoting Lenihan, says: "The excitement in the room was intense; every sentence was greeted with frantic shouts; all were convinced that civil war was at hand, and the thought evoked tempestuous outbreaks of mingled terror and rage from the audience." What O'Connell thought about that speech when he read it in the morning with a cooler head, one would dearly like to know. One may, at any rate, think that this man must have lived on a knife-edge of apprehension all during that year, he who had said that a country's freedom was not worth a drop of human blood, and was, while he thought so, playing with slaughter.

The whole situation was, in any case, passing from even his

iron control. One Repealer, O'Connor, was already proposing a scheme that was to fling Parnell into Kilmainham Jail forty years after—that the people should pay no rent whatsoever until they got perpetuity of tenure. That would have revived the Tithe War on an even more immense scale, and O'Connell had to crush the idea instantly. Even the mild O'Neill Daunt, infected by extremism, was proposing that people should receive, on their freedom, a military education like the Prussians.

Abroad it was worse. In America the Irish held vast meetings like those at home, and they collected money to pour into the Repeal treasury in Ireland. One contribution of two thousand dollars was accompanied by the significant message: "Whilst we say little, we are prepared to do much. We are ready to render to Ireland any assistance, consistent with our duties as American citizens, that *any* exigency in Ireland may at any time require." President Tyler wrote:

I am the decided friend of the Repeal of the Legislative Union between Great Britain and Ireland. I ardently and anxiously hope that it may take place, and I have the utmost confidence that Ireland will have her own Parliament in her capital in a very short time. On this great question I am no half-way man.

In Canada and Newfoundland the growing influence of the Repealers made the British governor write home that any aggression in Ireland would be "fatal to the tranquillity if not the security of the North American provinces." In France, at a dinner attended by such men as Carnot *fils*, the son of the Organizer of Victory who aided Wolfe Tone, Arago, Garnier-Pagès, Marrast, and Ledru-Rollin, Left deputies, Radical journalists, and officers of the National Guard, some of whom were to become members of the French Government four years later, Rollin declared that "France is ready to lend to an oppressed people, in their decisive struggle, experienced heads, resolute hearts, and sturdy arms." (*Le National*, commenting on a report in the *Times* that French officers were training the Irish peasantry, said: "The statement is premature rather than false.") France was always toying with the Irish pawn; writing in his reminiscences of an incident that had occurred as early as 1840, Colonel Miles Byrne says:

I remember one day, after a conference General Corbet [a fellow-exile] had with the Minister of War, on the situation in Ireland, he told me that the minister wanted to have a conversation with me respecting the reliance which could be placed on the leader of the Irish when a French army should land in Ireland.

When, likewise, the Prince de Joinville published a pamphlet, in 1844, foreshadowing an invasion of Ireland by the new French navy, it was treated by the European press as a prime event. An invasion of Ireland and Irish wrongs were always a common enough theme in the French press.

This kind of verbal aid both pleased and embarrassed O'Connell. He exulted in Rollin's speech, and bade the British Government note it; but when Rollin came to Ireland to offer armed aid, he hedged uncomfortably, and came up, for the first time, against the Young Irelanders; it was the only occasion on which his authority was questioned, or (says Doheny) "his advice audibly condemned" before the debacle at Clontarf. Even on that matter of Rollin's offer he was driven to say in public that "if the British Government used force, trampled their rights, and set the law at defiance, they would be glad to get allies and supporters everywhere": a statement received with so much applause that he hastened to mitigate the enthusiasm of the people as best he could.

He was, after all, a constitutionalist, and though he might have, in certain circumstances, taken the last course open to a leader of an oppressed people, it is most doubtful if he would ever have acknowledged that those circumstances had (under any circumstances) really arrived. He was too much of a realist, too, to trust these offers of armed aid. On that even Tone's experience chastens wild ideas, and Tone had hit the most favourable period for an invasion in the history of modern Europe. How far the people themselves were in the least way prepared for an armed revolt is impossible to say, probably not more or less than before the '98 Rebellion and more eager; which reduces, as it reduced for O'Connell, all such questions to the one: "What useful repercussion would have been produced by a slaughter?"

Had O'Connell therefore, for any reason, led or blessed a revolt, he would, in satisfying a natural human desire for the magnificent ending, be remembered for an even greater man than we now confess him; he would have died in prison or died on the scaffold. He would have shown a larger variety of character, added the fire of the gambler to the caution of the politician, and rounded his immense life by a great gesture. Instead, less romantically, more human, the old man was to fall in love with a young girl in her twenties, die in exile in the arms of his priest, muttering his terror of eternity, while the young men groaned with misery at home, and his people died by the roadside of the pangs of famine. As a result our sympathy wavers from him to his more ardent followers.

Let us not, however, forget how much of a gambler he was. By July 1843 what was his whole campaign but one vast gamble for everybody concerned? As the weeks went by, it ceased to matter to anybody whether the man was bluffing or not, as it ceased to be a fact, even in his own ambiguous mind, that he was, to his own knowledge, working a gigantic political swindle. All that was certain, by the autumn of 1843, was that he had lit a trail that somebody must either stamp out or take the unpredictable consequences. One could have drawn a fine cartoon to illustrate that position—O'Connell juggling with percussion bombs while Peel watched and wondered what action of his was the less likely to produce an explosion. In that cartoon Peel might say to O'Connell:

"Are they *real* bombs, Dan?"

To which O'Connell should reply:

"I wish to God I only knew!" and glare at the Young Irelanders standing in the background with eager eyes and clenched hands.

5

THESE Monster Meetings were all symbol. What was said hardly mattered, since no orator, even the bull-throated O'Connell, could possibly be heard by a hundredth part of the people who swarmed to them. The largest of them was held at Tara, the centre of the ancient Irish monarchy—that was a Young Ireland touch—the very ground sacred, the choice a covert threat. There, in August 1843, in the estimate of the *Times*, a million men and women came to see, hardly to hear, the Liberator. All night long the crowds poured across the plains, camped on the hillsides, slept under the hedges; and when dawn lit the countryside there was not a road for miles around but was blackened by trudging men. In the morning, forty-two bands were playing to the people in the fields about. Not a vehicle of any sort was left in the city of Dublin.

When O'Connell appeared at the foot of the rising ground, men computed with pleasure that his carriage took nearly two hours to cover a mile of ground, and when he approached the hill-top he saw there a priest saying Mass to a gathering that one may hope to see—since figures become powerless at this stage—only as a host of ants. That he should speak was necessary, but it was not essential; it merely completed the symbol that had already been fashioned by the devotion of the people who had come from such long distances and waited so patiently for his voice to toll its bell across their heads. Many of them did not even pretend to listen. As all the contemporary drawings show, they would sit or lie on the trampled grass, far beyond the radius of his voice, playing with their children as if this were some popular festival, or some sportive occasion like a race meeting organized by experts, glorified by the multitude. It was left to him merely to define, and then to personify. He could in one sentence do the one with:

The overwhelming majesty of your multitude will be taken to England and will have its effect there.

He did the other with:

I mean no disrespect to the Queen's soldiers, but I feel it to be a fact that Ireland, roused as she is at the moment, would if they made war against us furnish women enough to beat the entire Queen's forces . . .

by invoking there the memory of that old Limerick fight of a hundred and fifty years before that began the life of the Ireland to which he spoke.

Symbol followed on symbol, and the thing that had begun with the appearance of danger seemed to be ending as a reality. Peel watched O'Connell being crowned at Mullaghamast in Kildare. He saw several more vast meetings follow in order. Still he did nothing, although the autumn was coming on when these meetings must end, and the people, their harvest safe, be left with the winter months and that early darkness that is the friend of all violent men. At last he heard that this procession of symbol and sedition was to end on the ominous site of the battle of Clontarf, on the outskirts of Dublin. There, in October, O'Connell would address a hosting before which Tara was to look like a caucus. There, where the Irish under Brian Boru had driven the Danish invaders into the sea, the Repealers declared they would astound Europe by a demonstration of the unanimity of the new Ireland's demand for liberty. Peel proscribed the meeting.

That Saturday eve of the meeting there were warships in the bay, troops with artillery at Clontarf, and anything up to a million souls on their way to the meeting-place. The proclamation was pasted on the walls of the city at three o'clock. At five the sun would set and it would not be read by any wayfarer until dawn. In those few hours O'Connell had to decide between obedience and resistance. In Conciliation Hall he met his followers and made his decision. He called off the meeting. On Sunday morning Clontarf was deserted except for the guns pointing on Conquer Hill, the soldiery cooking their breakfast, or down in Dublin Bay the ships champing at anchor. The imperial symbol had been replaced.

So one sees it now. But such was the influence of the man and such was the spirit and trust of the people that nobody saw it so then. Long accustomed to such interruptions, they regarded this as nothing but a momentary setback. The Counsellor would beat the Castle lawyers; the campaign would hurl itself forward on the wind of his victory. Yet, here at least, one sees the rightness and foresight of the Young Irelanders. Those vast meetings could never be more than a preliminary to an extended resistance, and that slow, long resistance of the will must be tactful, various, co-operative, a resistance of mind against mind, an endurance supported by every form of spiritual defence.

The Government struck again. With six others O'Connell was charged with conspiracy and incitement to sedition, and called for trial. The indictment, a hundred yards of parchment, contained eleven separate counts and referred to forty-three overt acts. It was so intricate and so inclusive that it was of a confusion impossible to elucidate, and no precision emerged from its phrases on which anybody could ever hope to agree, or ever did agree, or from which any victim could conceivably escape. "Criminal justice," exulted the *Quarterly*, "once fished with a hook; she now fishes with a net." To ensure a verdict the jury, as everybody expected, was packed. There, by every known and hitherto unknown device, the Crown lawyers justified the disrepute with which English law has always been smirched in popular Irish opinion. Prevented with difficulty from using an antiquated and corrupt register which listed twenty-three Catholic citizens instead of three hundred, they yet managed to extract from an amended, though still mutilated list, forty names of whom only eleven were of the people. The jury, taken from this list, consisted ultimately of eleven Irish Protestants and one English Protestant. Of the four judges all were Protestants, two were acknowledged Tories, and one was an Englishman. When one considers such methods one humorously wonders whether O'Connell did not learn most of his wiles from the same source, and whether the true parentage of Tammany Hall might not be traced to British law in Ireland.

With such methods the result was never in doubt. A special steamer took the verdict of guilty from Kingstown to London where it was blazed on the pages of the English press even while it was being formally delivered in Dublin to O'Connell in the dock. That was February 1844, O'Connell in his seventieth year. The sentence was not delivered until May. He was to be imprisoned for one year and had to pay a fine of £2000. Meanwhile, unknown to anyone, his brain was being gnawed at by a secret disease.

6

AND now for the pitiable debacle, the decline into horror. To some, at least, of the young men O'Connell's speech in his own defence had been ominously weak. "Lamentable," one called it. "Weak as sillabub," said another. In cold fact it was quite an effective speech, but nothing like the speech he would have made twenty years before, nothing like the speech demanded by the occasion. But all were dismayed at the last meeting of the Repeal Association held between the verdict and the sentence. At that meeting O'Connell, as if in despair, proposed to disband the Association, and abolish the Arbitration Courts—and that even before sentence had been pronounced. After a bitter debate with his Left Wing he yielded so far as to be content with the resignation only of all newspaper editors on the Association, and the severance of all official connexion between the parent body and the Arbitration Courts. Then he left for England, much, it must be admitted, to the relief of everybody. Davis declared that the trial had terrified the old man, and Doheny condemned his proposals as "false, craven, and fatal." "Imagine," said Davis, "the sad effect of ten such speeches from O'Connell in his present state of mind."

In England he courted public opinion, addressed many meetings, and made an excellent impression. But he found himself abandoned by both Whigs and Radicals, and when he returned to Ireland to receive his sentence he can have had but little hope that he had mitigated it by his campaign. Neither had he glorified his position in the least: it had been no time for manœuvring when a great symbol was at stake. To everybody it must have become apparent that the lion was in his cage, his claws cut.

The behaviour of the young men in that extremity makes one of the really inspiring chapters in Irish history. They sustained, with a real magnificence, the continuity of the Irish struggle. A long way back Davis had, in one of his essays, pleaded for a series of plays or historical novels showing Ireland resting between tide and tide, often driven down, never conquered. The O'Connell cubs lived that theme now. Under the leadership of Smith O'Brien they kept the flag of Irish resistance flying at least as gallantly, and with far more dignity and arrogance than O'Connell had any right to hope for. With great pluck they cushioned the people from the worst effects of O'Connell's weakness, and however stunned in their hearts, they held the position like men born to fight. The *Nation* not only refused to tone down its defiant style but exaggerated it. It kept on urging resistance even where there was no longer anything tangible to resist until Sheil, manful to the rescue, taunted the Tories with:

You have imprisoned three newspaper proprietors but the Irish Press is as bold and as exciting as it was before. Eleven thousand copies of the *Nation* circulate every week throughout the country, and administers the strongest provocation to the most enthusiastic spirit of Irish nationality which the highest eloquence can supply.

The day O'Connell was accompanied to jail by a procession of his followers some of the daily nationalist journals came out in deep bands of mourning. The *Nation* came out in blatant green. It had no compunctions about printing a song like:

> Conspire! Conspire!
> Singly ye shall be weak as water,
> Singly like sheep to slaughter.
> By tyrants evermore be led. . . .
> Sorrow and shame and death,
> These are the portions sent
> To nations by divisions rent.
> Therefore Conspire!

The Young Irelanders set out to increase their Repeal Reading Rooms from 300 to 1000. They faced, and urged the people to face, a long and arduous struggle, and tried to adapt new agencies to old ends. Nowhere was the true value of their work better defined than in the contemporary summary of the *Tablet*:

Never were the leaders and the led more deeply assiduous in their labours. The contest has become less noisy and deceives the vulgar, but it has, in exactly the same proportions, become more real, more true, shall we say it—more honest, more respectable. It has now become a recognized fact that the struggle for Repeal may be a long one, and all parties are girding themselves for that march through the wilderness which is to prepare them for the possession of the promised land. . . .

In the meantime the years of pilgrimage will not be wasted. They will be spent in earnest, anxious, painful efforts to acquire knowledge and discipline, and every moral, spiritual, and intellectual quality which can adorn freedom. Instead of the pike and the drum with which we were distracted last summer, this shows us the reading-room, maps, books, papers, the furniture of the mind, not the barracks. Instead of battlefields and assembled myriads we are to have a more peaceful discipline, combinations against the excise, against all manufactures that are not of Irish Production. When to this we add a very possible revival of the arbitration boards, we have described a system of agitation which, if properly and heroically worked into practice, will succeed.

The details of that adaptation of the fight begun by O'Connell belong to another history, that of the armed rising of '48, the rise of a native Irish literature (with such names as that of Ferguson to link us to the times of Yeats), the welding of men of various religious and antagonistic politics into a broad national movement: but that it *was* an adaptation, a refraction and not a rejection, must never be forgotten.

He would not have been O'Connell if he had not resented the refraction. Yet the ensuing quarrel, as the word implies, was largely a personal one, and it was the old intriguers on the skirt of the movement, rather than O'Connell himself, who made the pace. So while he was in jail, his bully Dillon Browne, a typical Tammany thug, was trying to knife Davis in the back by proposing, at the Repeal Association, motions that would (if passed) have abolished the Reading Rooms. He induced the boy Daniel O'Connell to second him, and got Barrett of the *Pilot* to applaud him. Against that kind of intrigue, poor, straight-forward, Anglo-Irish, inexperienced Davis was no match. He complained bitterly to Smith O'Brien that he could not use these weapons. "There are higher things than politics," he wrote, "and I will never sacrifice my self-respect to them." Before he finished his brief life he was to feel those weapons on his spine many a day.

That was the tragedy of the Young Ireland movement. It had no man, not even Mitchel, to stand up against the O'Connell machine. Doheny, the sturdiest of them, had no mental equipment fit for the task, though he, perhaps alone among his colleagues, knew his Ireland, and his courage was unbounded. Smith O'Brien was of a totally different kidney from the O'Connellites; a cold, vain man, with a rationalized character, a fine moral sense, but no sense at all of the reality of the human forces with which O'Connell dealt. He was almost a provincial recluse, and his enormous post-bag—his correspondence has recently been presented to the National Library—shows how little he was in the thick of things in Dublin between 1843 and 1848. On the other hand, Doheny's *Felon's Track* gives many examples of the astuteness and perseverance of the O'Connellites, and it makes bitter reading, alike for the foolish cleverness of the older men, the ineffectual nobility of the younger, and the frittering irrelevance of the general warfare between the two that followed on that arrest in May 1844.

In so far as O'Connell had fostered that type of political warfare the ultimate blame does, of course, lie on him. It was doubly unfortunate that the responsibility for the application of that form of intrigue was out of his hands at a time when new men were rising to purify his methods.

He was now out of the game, not only because he was a prisoner, and not only because he was the victim of an unsuspected brain-disease, but for the most pathetic reason that, at the age of seventy, he had fallen madly in love with a young Protestant girl who might have been his daughter. He kept his correspondence with this girl, Rose MacDowell, locked in his desk to the end, and it is a pity that the editor of his letters, Fitzpatrick, suppressed it. The girl could hardly have been expected to feel the slightest sentimental affection for the hard-faced, hard-mouthed, blubber-jowled widower, but though she was naturally flattered by his admiration and visited him in prison, and wrote to him, she must have tormented his mind and heart during his last years. She certainly embarrassed his sons and his colleagues. In Richmond he shared the most comfortable quarters with these, ate with them, walked with them in the gardens, and had absolute freedom within the jail as the guest rather than the prisoner of the warden. Her visits, under these conditions, were equivalent to the public wooing, and the public folly, of a national leader— a joke, possibly, to some smirker like Somers, or a shame to his son, who would hide away in his room until she left, but they were a calamity on the highest ground to men like Charles Gavan Duffy and Doheny.

They knew that outside the jail the Repealers were spending anything up to £50,000 to fight an appeal in the Lords; here inside the jail the O'Connell who boasted in his hey-day that he could drive a coach-and-four through an Act of Parliament seemed atrophied. He refused to interest himself in the appeal. He believed Peel would never release him until his time was up. He could not credit that the Lords would reverse a decision so necessary to Government prestige. When Sir Thomas Wyse proposed a sub-committee to inquire into the case, he pooh-poohed it contemptuously to Sheil—though it must be said he did it well, despising all the workings of the English Parliament and chiding Sheil for not coming back to fight in Ireland. (He was disingenuous there, conveniently forgetting his own ten fatal years of servitude to the Whigs.) The result was that nobody was so astounded as O'Connell when the Lords quashed his sentence, and did it in vigorous anger, the Lord Chief Justice using a famous phrase to express his contempt of the Dublin courts. If such practices continued, he said, trial by jury would become "a delusion, a mockery, and a snare."

It was Ford, the Irish attorney, who dashed to Dublin with the news. At each big station it is said that he shouted to the people—the story has an apocryphal air—"O'Connell is getting out!" which made them all look hopefully up and down the line of carriages. He had a special engine chartered at Kingstown to bring the news to Dublin, and this engine carried a flag which bore the legend of victory. The prisoners were at dinner when the Repeal messenger burst in on them with the cry: "You're free, Liberator; you're free!" and it indicates the general unpreparedness for such news that everybody at once either burst into tears, staggered, grew pale, or, as happened to the governor of the prison, fainted. All O'Connell could say when Ford embraced him was that the hand of Providence had been lifted in answer to the prayers of the people. Then, clouded and gloomy, he walked home from the penitentiary; he would not wait while the young men tried to salvage the position with an enormous reception at the jail gates. "His spirit was broken," wrote Doheny.

But the young men clenched their teeth. There was going to be a reception and a procession whether O'Connell liked it or not. They made him come back to the jail and be imprisoned again the following morning—which the governor kindly permitted. With God knows what feelings of mingled hope or sardonic rage they spent the night rushing around Dublin to prepare the Triumph. The old triumphal car was dragged from its stable, and rubbed up and rubbed down; an itinerant harper was sought out in the Dublin slums; they got little green tunics for all O'Connell's grandchildren, and they put white feathers in their caps. Then, when the prisoners had breakfasted with their jailer, the gates were flung open—oh! for a film of that scene! —and out stalked O'Connell in his great cape, and the green, wreathed cap with which Hogan the sculptor had crowned him on Mullaghamast. While he mounted to the topmost tier of the trireme chariot, his eldest son John—the Young Liberator—beside him, his grandchildren were ranged below, and the harper, seated in the prow, struck up a martial air from Tom Moore. Then Tom Steele, the Chief Pacificator, stood out with his green bough, the crowd roared, and the wagon lumbered away.

The procession was immense, but historical pageants broke its monotony. They went down the quays, left the Four Courts behind, crossed the Liffey, jeered in passing at Dublin Castle, and then the great moment came when they halted the chariot for a moment in College Green, and with one silent gesture O'Connell tore the sky by lifting his cap and pointing to the old Houses of Parliament. The young men were delighted. It was a scene of "public rejoicing," wrote Doheny, "never surpassed on any occasion in his life," for not until long after did he begin to realize

what he then called the "demoralizing effect inherent in a lie."
As they watched and cheered the splendid gesture in College
Green they did *not* realize that under that green cap and those
matted grey locks the old brain was giving up the struggle; that
the machinery of that once perfect engine was now milling about
and about mere fragments of dreams; that he was living in a
world that was fast slipping into a gigantic miasma where all
things wavered in the fumes of an approximate madness; that they
and Ireland were backing a man whose powers were already in
decay.

7

THE next few meetings of the Repealers told the tale: they had
managed to give Peel a serious blow, and it became apparent
that there was nobody to follow it up. For two hours O'Connell
rambled and wandered to a packed audience, who wanted to
be told but one thing—what next to do. He vituperated, he denounced, he abused, but still he did not come to the point. He
prophesied and recapitulated, but still he would not define. The
audience cheered him loyally, but it was with difficulty that his
lieutenants held control of their nerves. At last, when he did
come to it, they found that there were three mad thoughts in
his head: they could hold that interrupted meeting at Clontarf;
they could summon a Council of Three Hundred as a kind of
preservative society, initiating nothing (these were his own
words: "it should initiate nothing, but correct and control everything"); and lastly—and he made it clear that he preferred
this scheme—they could try to impeach the Attorney-General,
the Queen's Bench, and the entire Cabinet for having wrong-
fully imprisoned him! For this last dear scheme he declared that
he would travel England from end to end, town to town, county
to county, and if the English people did not impeach the foul-
mouthed letter-openers, and the monster liars, and hurl Peel into

oblivion with the finger of scorn pointing to him as he went adrift, etc., etc., he would have no faith in England "any more." Having said which, he retired to Darrynane to hunt real hares, and the young men retired to their office of the *Nation* to weep tears of blood.

They knew, and all Ireland must have feared, that to invite another Clontarf was to invite another surrender; that to call a Council of Three Hundred in the now cooling atmosphere of definitely constitutional politics was impossible; but to think to impeach the British Government was surely the fancy of a lunatic, as well as being suspiciously like a return to the old policy of Whig courtship. It speaks well for the grit of the young men that they were still full of fight. But it must have been plain to them that the game was up unless they could sink the O'Connell ship at once. The tragedy was that they were part of the ship's crew, that the fat old man who was declining into senility was more ballast than captain, that the boat was becoming more and more rickety every day, and that there was no other.

In that quandary they found that the O'Connellites were scuttling the ship beneath their feet—a piece of treachery begun by the Young Liberator, who spread a typical Tammany story that the *Nation* was anti-Catholic, and its contributors "secret enemies of the Church." The now half-daft Old Liberator flung them into further disarray with a scheme for abandoning Repeal in favour of a kind of petty grand-jury system of local government dignified by the name of Federalism. Meanwhile Peel was left untouched; the precious moment was wasted; the people were bemused. Slowly the ship keeled over in the mud.

It would be futile to enter into details of the wasted days that wore out the spirit of everybody concerned in Conciliation Hall during those months. One example is enough—the lengthy discussion about whether they would give one Dr. Nagle, the Curator of the Manuscripts, a salary of £100 or £50. It began as part of the effort the young men were making to curtail ex-

penses, for the weekly collections were now, ominously, dropping and dropping. O'Connell was in Darrynane and his place
was filled by his slight simulacrum Johnny O'Connell, his son.
Sinecures established for his friends were wiped away. Fees bestowed on certain "patriots" were abolished. Committees of Inquiry were formed which, on his return, enraged him. One of
these concerned the Curator of the Manuscripts. This man's
duty had been to censor all publications on literary, legal, and
moral grounds, but his work had declined into receiving from
the Secretary a weekly list of proposed publications, which he
returned to the same gentleman without comment. When a motion dismissing Nagle was proposed, O'Connell was in the chair,
surrounded by all his sons. The motion was carried, and the
usual amendment was likewise defeated, but O'Connell, watching his triumphant opponents trail from the hall, quietly supported a further amendment to give Dr. Nagle £50. The voting was against even this amendment, but now the majority
amounted to only one. O'Connell, after further argument, established his right to fling his "casting vote," as well as his vote as a
member, and so equalized the voting. After further arguments,
heated and prolonged, the old man proposed, further, that in future a chairman should have two votes, and this also he managed
to establish. They now settled down to discuss the *affaire* Dr.
Nagle *con brio*, though all that was involved was whether he
should get £50 or the original £100; and at last O'Connell won.
"So," writes Doheny, with a pardonable savagery, "Dr. Nagle
continued to fill his office until his appointment to a more lu-
crative one under the Whig Government."

While these foolish men thus caracoled and pranced about
trivialities the Federal scheme hung in the air, and the writers of
the *Nation* continued to be abused as "infidels." Smith O'Brien
would do nothing. Doheny and the rest could do nothing. At last
in righteous anger, finely subdued, Gavan Duffy spoke for the
young men and denounced the Federal scheme. In outraged an-

ger Davis appealed to O'Connell, to his son, to Smith O'Brien, to stop the bigoted attacks. To Duffy came no reply but the whooping of the Tories at these signs of disunion, and of a weakening in O'Connell, not salvaged by an ultimate and quite unabashed *volte-face* from Darrynane about Federalism. To Davis came the replies of the country journals which had been "puffed" by the intriguers into repeating these sanctimonious fears of the honest *Pilot* that there were "men prominent in the national movement whose religious principles were not sound." There came, also, a blathering, plamausing letter from Darrynane, which alternately stroked and struck. Lastly, there were a few unctuous generalizations from the Young Liberator, Johnny O'Connell.

That O'Connell himself was quite willing (in the words of a modern Irish politician) to "cash in on Christianity," to use religion to beat an opponent, is clear from a squalid scene that occurred in Conciliation Hall. The origin of this squabble over religion—that particular "racket" is one of the least desirable bequests of O'Connellism to modern public life in Ireland—was Peel's desire to conciliate the clergy, firstly by giving an increased grant to Maynooth, and secondly by establishing three popular University Colleges. The bishops had no objection to the grant, and some of them, while rightly demanding certain alterations in the scheme, greeted the Universities scheme as practical and timely. But Archbishop MacHale was still adamant against popular education under secular control. The majority of the hierarchy went with him, and O'Connell—he cannot, in view of his expressed opinions about cheap education, have been honest in this—supported him rather than his more farseeing and accommodating colleagues. He possibly hoped by so doing to get a better bargain, but the event shows that he overdid it badly. In Conciliation Hall he called the proposed Queen's Colleges "godless"; he denounced the Universities Bill as "designedly evil"; and he was supported by Conway, one of his sycophants, in a speech that repeated the now familiar insinuations about the irreligion of the *Nation* Party.

In shame and anger Davis rose to repel the charge. "I have not more than a few words," he said, "to say in reply to the useful, judicious, and spirited speech of my old college friend, my Catholic friend, my very Catholic friend, Mr. Conway. . . ."

At once O'Connell was on his feet, and with his jaw out he growled furiously:

"It's no crime to be a Catholic, I hope?"

Abashed, poor Davis stuttered out: "No, surely—no, it could not be, for . . ." But O'Connell had no mercy.

"The sneer with which you spoke would lead to that inference!"

Miserably Davis protested that his friends, his dearest friends, were Catholics. (He could not say that his sneer had been directed at the hypocrisy of Conway, whose private character was known to everybody. O'Connell had cunningly diverted the sneer to something to which it was never intended to apply.) Smiting the young men hip and thigh, the old intriguer followed up his advantage:

"There is no such party as Young Ireland!" he bellowed. Cheers encouraged him. "There may be a few individuals. I'm for Old Ireland!" More loud cheers. "'Tis time this delusion should be ended. Young Ireland may play what pranks they please. I'll stand by Old Ireland!" Cheers. "And I have some slight notion that Old Ireland'll stand by me." Loud cheers.

Davis got up. He said they were all bound together by the cause of Irish nationality. He said that they were bound by affection for O'Connell. He said they . . . But at that he broke down in tears. Whereupon O'Connell, striding across to him, laid his paw on his shoulder, and, while the audience cheered him yet again, he said:

"Davis, I love ye! I thank ye sincerely and heartily. If you're overcome, I'm overcome too."

Mr. O'Connell, record the newspapers, appeared much affected.

It is probably the most disagreeable incident in O'Connell's career.

Smith O'Brien was a Protestant, but he made an astute comment on this exploitation of religion.

"Unless O'Connell is willing to act as mediator, we shall have a priest and an anti-priest party in Irish politics."

This controversy on the three popular University Colleges ended in a way that reflected ill on the wit both of the bishops and of O'Connell. He kept on persuading MacHale that if the hierarchy did not yield the Government would come to an arrangement with them.

You have everything in your own power. The ministry will yield.

If one did not know that MacHale hardly cared whether the bill was amended or not, and that O'Connell would have preferred it to be lost rather than amended (which the *Nation* desired), one might feel that O'Connell was not the only one whose wits were astray. The ministers did not yield. MacHale had nobody in his power. No arrangement was made with the bishops—most unhappily for the later history of Irish education. For when, long after, the democratic Ireland took over the University Colleges, it took a foolish revenge for that defeat, and vulgarized them beyond words, governing them by a fantastic mixture of county councillors, bishops, farmers, professors, Members of Parliament, veterinary surgeons, labourers, and what not.

Had O'Connell, MacHale, and the Tories been a trifle less intransigent in the 1840's, how much more intelligently might not the whole scheme have been planned, and worked, from the beginning. The effect, meanwhile, as Gavan Duffy sadly summarized it, was that part of Ireland's youth attended the Protestant University of Dublin—Trinity College; part, against the wishes of their religious advisers, attended the Queen's Colleges; most received no superior education at all. There are some things in which a democracy must, at its peril, recognize a hierarchy of intelligence. That, in his best days, O'Connell recognized—a man with a powerful sense of values.

8

He was now floundering about like a homeless Lear, between the Commons, Dublin, and Darrynane, insulting his friends, flattering his toadies, and in magnificent flashes of his former keenness, circumventing with a real brilliance those whom he mistook for his enemies. He told the entire French nation that he would rather surrender his country's cause than succeed with the help of France. His abuse of English editors was boundless; he attacked them with the rage of a drunken man. He told the Americans that if England sufficiently rewarded Ireland he would help to pluck down the American eagle in its highest pride of flight. The speech was a marvel of folly:

We tell them from this spot that they can have us—that the throne of Victoria can be made perfectly secure—the honour of the British Empire maintained—and the American eagle in its highest pride of flight brought down. Let them conciliate and do us justice, and they will have us enlisted under the banner of Victoria then, but give us the Parliament in College Green, and Oregon shall be theirs and Texas shall be harmless.

Even when he retired to Kerry the throne had its spectre—his feeble son John. "Johnny," as the *Nation* bitterly called him, was half-witted, even as a politician. He turned Conciliation Hall into a revivalist bethel, pontificating now on Negro slavery (as if his father had not already sufficiently antagonized America), now on the insolence of those who disagreed with him, now on the malignancy of some journalist who had said that the Holy Coat of Treves was not the authentic garment of Christ.

The Young Irelanders met stories of his ineptitude wherever they went. "Dillon," wrote MacNevin, "is sick of the abomination of desolation on Burgh Quay." And again: "By the way, where is the Repeal agitation? It never opens its sooty mouth now." "A decent man," wrote Dillon, "cannot frequent the public meetings." Doheny wrote from Tipperary that the *Nation* was in great disrepute among the priests. That was wholly thanks to Johnny, who had pushed the misuse of religion to its limit. Even when Davis died, that youth with the soul of a hero and the softness of a woman, and illness or want was scattering the rest, Gavan Duffy has to record that the intriguers were rifling the dead like canaille after a battle. At last, in a fury, he wrote of those who were maligning Davis in the grave, that "the humblest of his friends would, if the necessity arose, take by the throat the highest head that breathed a slander upon him."

John O'Connell surpassed himself when he drove Barrett of the *Pilot*, a man who had, in his day, done splendid work for Repeal, into an act as lunatic as any committed by his doting father. Flying into a temper when the Catholic primate said he would give the new colleges a fair trial, he first bruited the whisper that the primate was about to become a Protestant—and small wonder, seeing that this mother was a Presbyterian; and then had the pleasure of seeing the *Pilot* announce that the Archbishop was gone off his head, a sad occurrence which would easily explain to a perplexed people His Grace's extraordinary conduct in differing from Burgh Quay on this or any question.

Well might the *Pilot* speak of a perplexed people. It might have better called them a poor, loyal, wondering and wandering, uneducated, and not-to-be-educated, people, who were now asked to do but one thing only—and they did it with a pathetic stubbornness, to keep on subscribing money for their old leader, withering in Iveragh. In '44 and '45 they poured into Burgh Quay their poor pennies and shillings to a total averaging £20,-000 a year—of whose expenditure Burgh Quay refused to return them the slightest record. That was because Johnny O'Connell and his friends were afraid of shadows: it might cause legal trouble, they argued, if the Government had any knowledge of the manner in which this public money was spent. Perhaps the lowest depths they sank to in their timidity was when Mitchel wrote an article on the use the people could make of railways in time of rebellion. Gavan Duffy was prosecuted for printing the article and defended by Robert Holmes along the lines of O'Connell's defence of Magee nearly thirty-five years before; that is to say, he did not apologize for the sentiments expressed by Mitchel —he gloried in them—and, strange to relate, he induced the jury to disagree. It was left to the cowards of Conciliation Hall to condemn Duffy for something on which a British court had acquitted him.

With things thus wallowing in the Nile mud; the old leader pawing after his young girl; his son mouthing at the fighting men; the bishops in disagreement; the young men beaten to the wall—one might well think that defeat and disaster could go no further. But it did. Famine took the land by the throat. Slowly the foul-smelling breath of plague rose over their little patches of fields, preparing to exterminate the people by the million. The cabins became dens of death. That summer of 1845, cold and wet, the tips of the potato-stalks began to wither under their eyes, and under their eyes they dropped on their rotting stems until the stench from the decayed tubers underneath came like a gas into the hovels, a forewarning of the stench of death that was, later, to come out of them. That Forty-Five thousands starved, but nobody heeded. Instead O'Connell was hopefully forecasting a new Whig alliance, saying that Peel had doomed himself by his opposition to the repeal of the Corn Laws. O'Connell was wrong. Peel played his old trick of resigning, and on Lord John Russell's failure to form a Cabinet, returned to pass the law he had opposed. The repeal of the Corn Laws, incredible as it must sound to modern ears, did not apply to Ireland. There would be cheap corn for the English poor. There would be no corn for the Irish poor. For them Peel had something better— a Coercion Bill.

O'Connell, now over seventy years old, bowed and feeble, came out of his retreat that winter of '46 to make his last stand for his army of the poor. He had travelled over Ireland and seen the results of the famine of the summer before. He had begged Dublin Castle to do something, anything—open the ports, stop the export of Irish wheat, stop distilling, give employment on railways, use the Crown rents on the Irish woods—that had hitherto been used to decorate Windsor Castle and adorn Trafalgar Square—to repay a loan for the relief of the hungry. The Tories sneered at this endless Irish begging for alms, as if, groaned Mitchel, the exchequer was their exchequer. They told him there was no immediate cause for fear. O'Connell might, then at least, but then too late, have felt that the young men were right to think that a decent death on the field was better for any man than this slow mass-murder.

In the Commons he stood up to attack the Coercion Bill. His voice was not audible to the gallery, and Disraeli described his appearance as a performance in dumb show. The bill was passed by a huge majority. In June O'Connell took his final revenge on Peel. He allied himself with the Whigs and threw out the Tories on a motion to rescind the bill. It was his last victory: his race was done.

The crops again stank in '46, and while Meagher of the Sword was uttering his famous speech in defence of force in Conciliation Hall, and Johnny O'Connell was manœuvring him and the remaining Young Irelanders out of the Repeal Association, that old terrible smell of decay wafted final death down the valleys of Ireland. Now the young men saw their error; they had thought nobly, but they had prepared nothing. To Lord Bessborough O'Connell was saying: "the more troops the better," and the Government was accordingly flooding this country of walking skeletons with fattened soldiery. To the few fighting relics of the secret societies, like the Molly Maguires, who tried to soothe their agony with murder, the Chief Pacificator of all Ireland was issuing a manifesto such as might have come from the warden of Bedlam. It ended gloriously with:

I proclaim to you that you will be speedily taught by the lesson of a voyage in a convict ship, perhaps to Norfolk Island, which I have so often described to you, where you will be worked, chained together in gangs and without wages, under a burning sun and the lash of a merciless overseer. You will be taught by the bayonets of the policemen, and the cracking of your neck on the gallows. You outcast traitors. You who give strength to Ireland's enemies. Your country disclaims you. I abhor you.

Thomas Steele,
O'Connell's Head Pacificator and Head
Repeal Warden of Ireland.

For the last time the land blackened as if the frown of God had moved across it. Officials poured into the fields by the thousand, one to every twenty men employed on rashly and hurriedly conceived relief works, and the army, that had risen but three years before like the children of Israel called from their bondage, fell like dogs on the scraps of food flung them in charity. The priests served them but poorly in their misfortune. Won over by the O'Connellites, they ordered the people to pay their rents and hold themselves calm—to sell what little corn they had and pay their rents; and be calm! In Dublin O'Connell could only weep, and wail, and fling gibes at the Young Irelanders. They were now "the Little Ireland Gang." They were "the boys of the *Nation*." He did not care twopence for Young Ireland—but, no, slavered the poor, gibbering old cretin, jigging and laughing at his own pawky humour, "No! Twopence was too much. I don't care three halfpence for them!" And then, suddenly remembering his suffering wretches down in Kerry and Cork, he breaks down into sobs and cries that a curse has fallen on his beloved Ireland. Down he goes to Kerry again, and he is met in the silent little villages by handfuls of broken people. They listen to him, still eager for a word of encouragement from their Liberator, and with parched mouths they raise a feeble cheer. In some places they boo him. In Limerick city a band goes by his hotel playing "Remember the Glories of Brian the Brave," and his bullies, seeing a reference to Smith O'Brien, sally out and smash the instruments. He does not care. He does not care in Darrynane, where his people sit like statues under the gables, waiting for death. At his feet his hounds lie listless—there is no coursing now, there is hardly a hare left on the barren and rocky hills. Wearied out, moping, he comes back to Dublin in the January of '47, and that February he goes to the House of Commons. Tottering to his place, swaying as he rises, he mumbles out a pitiable appeal for mercy to his dying people. He stretches out his wavering palms and he says:

Ireland is in your hands. . . . She is in your power. . . . If you do not save her she can't save herself. And I solemnly call on you to recollect that I predict with the sincerest conviction that one quarter of her population will perish unless you come to her relief.

The House rose and cheered.

A few days after he fell sick. "Take me home," he begged, but the doctors said he must go to the south of France, and his chaplain persuaded him to it by telling him he could make his journey into a pilgrimage to Rome and the Holy Father. He set out, and a rest at Hastings did him good. He chuckled that all his family had been long-livers and he went on to Folkestone, where he said good-bye to his friend Fitzpatrick. So, on to Paris, greeted and honoured more than he had the strength to bear; on to Lyons, followed at every stage by cold and wintry weather that kept him for days to his rooms, where, like a child, he could not bear to be for ten minutes without his priest, Father Miley, by his side. Once Miley stole out for a breath of air, leaving him with his son and his valet. Within a quarter of an hour messengers were chasing through the streets in search of him, so nervous and so lonely was the old man lying helpless and fearful in his hotel bedroom, screaming for his priest.

The inevitable symbolism now became a curse. He was treated less as a man than a figure, and his pilgrimage less as a cure than a gesture, until he found himself hedged in by decorums and Miley began to complain of his (very natural and human) fractiousness. "Never had I such a struggle as from two to four last night to keep him in bed, or prevent the alarm being given to the whole hotel. It would have been most unfortunate that any but his own should have seen him." What picture more frightening and pathetic can there be than that hint of a grey-haired, slightly wandering old man, in his night-gown and his tousled hair, saying what, behaving how, we can only guess, while his priest and his valet try to lead him back to his bed, and the sleeping city of Lyons wraps that foreign hotel about in the quietness of indifferent sleep? And again:

By day I cannot leave him to walk in the open for fifteen minutes, and by night all his griefs and terrors are on me—for he will not be satisfied unless I am by his bed. By day and night nothing will he ever talk of, or speak, or think of for a moment but his own maladies and misfortunes.

And, at long last, when they have gone on to Avignon, and to Marseilles, and by ship to Genoa, and are on the threshold of the Holy City, the old man rebels; Miley sinks into despair; the pageant is ruined.

He would probably have died at sea had he stirred then. He could not swallow. They bled him at intervals, but his mind wandered. He clutched the counterpane and started up to shout defiance at Peel across the floor of the room. He fell back and he played in fancy with his children. He jumped up roaring:

"I have it! I have it! Here in a box!"

"What? What?" they begged him.

"The Repeal! I have it here in a box! I have it safely locked up in a box!"

In his quieter hours he talked of nothing with Miley but of eternity and his hopes and chances of heaven. From Thursday, the thirteenth of May, to Saturday morning he never opened his lips, Miley records, but to speak of his eternal interests. They gave him the Viaticum, bringing it solemnly in a little group through the streets of Genoa a few hours before the dawn broke over the city and the sea. The morning wore on into the close afternoon, and as he lay there, waiting, he became more and more at peace. Continually he murmured: "Jesus . . . Jesus. . . ." He called Duggan, his servant, and he thanked him. He said, at four in the afternoon, that they should send his heart to Rome. At six o'clock, with the ungullible knowledge of the doomed, he said to Miley:

"My dear friend, I am dying."

A murmur of Italian prayers wandered through the room from that on until about half-past nine. Then he said many times: "Jesus . . . Jesus . . . Jesus . . ." and made one last struggle that shook his great frame. At twenty-three minutes to ten they heard a noise like a tap running dry.

9

His body, embalmed, reached Ireland in August, on board the steamer *Duchess of Kent*. As it steamed up the Liffey a ship passed it by, outward bound. It was the emigrant ship, the *Birmingham*, laden with emigrants, and as they passed there rose from it the Irish keen, lamenting the dead chief. So the Irish Liberator entered Dublin city, and the exiles, more fortunate than most of those who remained, passed into the future.

They were leaving the blighted homes in their tens of thousands, leaving behind them plague, death, and despair. Many of them left too late to live, and by the hundred they lie at the bottom of the Atlantic, or they died in the hospitals of America. In that Famine period of the black forties a million creatures starved, and as many more emigrated to England and America, there to nourish an ancient love and an ancient hate, and build for themselves a life denied them at home. Their vestiges remain to this day in Ireland—a broken wall, a few ridges high on the mountain-slopes, grass-smooth or furzy now, a hearthstone cluttered with nettles or burst by a tree that grows out of it and blows in the wind, and in the winter sheds its tears for the homeless.

It might well have seemed that in his grave, and in those million graves of the poor he had led, they buried Ireland. Yet, already Parnell was alive, a child at the breast; and so was Michael Davitt. The chain goes on, from one poor generation to another, through James Stephens the Fenian, who was out on the hills with Smith O'Brien the year after they buried O'Connell, and through the Fenian Brotherhood that included Davitt, and involved the oldest signatory to the Proclamation of the Irish Republic in 1916. That was Tom Clarke, beside whom Michael Collins, a young man of twenty-five, jerked at his rifle from the loopholed windows of the blazing post office in—of all places—O'Connell Street.

10

WHAT he gave us is hard to tell. Much good, much bad, but one thing was priceless—the principle of life as a democracy. He taught simple men to have pride, and he taught them how to fight. He gave them the elements of life-cleverness and the seed of a civilization. He almost killed truth, and he warped honour; but he brought honour to the simple folk of Ireland and he exposed the lie of Empire. He gave them discipline and a great tolerance, and between them he moulded many divergent elements into something approaching a unity. He left an ineffaceable mark on the character of the Irish mind, so that no man after him but has had to accept its duality as a basic fact, and its ideals as a passion to be fanned at peril and controlled with difficulty. To what that idealism moves, who can say without reference to him who tried to define it? To a variety of life, won by love, and held by charity? As against the Anglo-Saxon ideal of security won by force, consolidated as comfort, held by tolerance? To an evasion of despotic fact, won by sheer cunning held by an emotional mutability? Or did he lean to a life where justice is always tempered by humour, and where subterfuge makes up for appetite openly denied? In whatever way one might try to define the ideal life of the Irish people, his image is likely to rise before the mind—always remembering that he came at the beginning and was only following his instinct in a groping use of the material to his hand. Lecky said that he studied men, not books; in studying men he found himself, and in finding himself he presented to his people a mirror of their reality. He is interesting in a hundred ways, but in no way more interesting than in this—that he was the greatest of all Irish realists, who knew that if he could but once define, he would thereby create. He did define, and he did create. He thought a democracy and it rose. He defined himself, and his people became him. He imagined a future and the road appeared. He left his successors nothing to do but to follow him. They have added precision to his definition, but his definition is not altered; they have added to his methods, but his methods remain. You may break gold but it is gold still, fashion wood but it is wood still. The content of Irish life is the content of the Irish character, the dregs and the lees and the pure wine of this one man's recipe—to be purified indeed, to grow more rich in the wood with time, but never to lose the flavour of his reality, the composition of his mind.

INDEX

Abercrombie, 92, 169
Age of Reason (Thomas Paine), 74, 76
Aksakov, Sergei, 44
Alvanley, Lord, 101–2, 276
Anglesey, Lord, 232–4, 246
Annals of the Irish Harpers (Charlotte Milligan Fox), 36 *n.*
Arago, Dominique-François, 302
Ardagh, Bishop of, 298
Ashley, Lord, 273

Balzac, Honoré de, 39, 69
Barrett, 252, 311, 322
Barrington, Sir Jonah, 34, 141, 144–7
Barry, 152–4
"Battle-Song of Munster," 35
Bedford, 172
Bellew, Sir Edward, 111, 129, 184 *n.*
Bellew, William, 184, 219
Bennett, Richard, 59, 63–4, 67, 197, 199, 247
Bentinck, Lord William, 191
Beresford, Lord George, 223
Bergin, Dr. Osborn, 26
Berkeley, 107
Bessborough, Lord, 324
Bexley, 102
Bible in Ireland, The (Asenath Nicholson), 141
Biggar, 299
Le Blanc, Justice, 200
Blennerhasset, John, 28

Bolivar, 215
Booth, Junius B., 202
Boynton, Bully, 258
Brady, Mr., 61
Bran, Daniel, 34
Brougham, Lord, 252, 259, 264
Brown, Colonel, 199
Browne, Dillon, 286, 311
Buonaparte, Napoleon, 66, 69, 189
Burke, 237–8
Burke, Eleanor, 17
Bushe, 104
Byrne, Colonel Miles, 303
Byron, George Gordon, 209

Caldwell, 141
Callanan, 292
Camden, Lord, 169, 172
Campbell, 152–3, 251
Captain Rock (Moore), 211
Carleton, 258
Carnot, 302
Casement, Roger, 203
Castlereagh, Lord, 95, 102, 137–8
Catholic Association, 219, 233
Catholic Board, 83, 148, 163 ff., 183–4, 194, 210
Catholic Committee, 121–3, 125 ff., 151
Catholic Relief Bill, 51–3
Caulfeild, 148–9
Chateaubriand, 130
Château-Renault, 19
Chesterfield, Lord, 25, 144

Index

Chronicles of a Russian Family (Sergei Aksakov), 44

Clare, Earl of, 92

Clarke, Mary Ann, 102

Clarke, Tom, 69, 329

Clifden, Lord, 184

Clinche, James, 121

Cloncurry, Lord, 247–9

Cobbett, William, 102–3, 211, 245, 285

Coercion Bill, 234, 263–4, 270, 324

Coffey, Father, 227, 231

Collins, Michael, 39, 69, 329

Connolly, James, 69, 272

Consalvi, Cardinal, 191–2

Convention Act, 122, 127

Conway, 318–9

Cook, Capt. James, 41

Coppinger, Stephen, 219

Corbet, General, 303

Corkery, Daniel, 23, 27, 221

Cormenin, de, 138

Corn Laws, 323–4

Costello, Mark, 252

Courtenay, Eleanor (Ellen), 201–3

Cox, Watty, 172

Crawford, Sharman, 84, 268 ff., 279

Croker, "Johnny," 137

Curran, John Philpot, 92, 99, 104, 136–137, 148

Daly, Judge, 98, 179

Darrynane Abbey, 41 ff., 66, 92, 190, 200, 236–7, 316

Daunt, O'Neill, 93, 97, 237, 285, 302

Davis, Thomas Osborne, 69, 107, 287, 289, 293–4, 309, 311, 318, 319–20, 322

Davitt, Michael, 39, 329

Day, Judge, 117, 180

Democracy and the Gaelic Tradition (Frank O'Connor), 29–30

Desart, Lord, 179

D'Esterre, 196–8

Devonshire, Duke of, 218, 224

Dhuiv, Máire ni. *See* Duv, Máire

Diderot, Denis, 130

Dillon, John Blake, 293, 322

Disraeli, Benjamin, 265, 276–7, 324

Dogherty, 238–9

Doheny, Michael, 141, 287, 290, 293–4, 303, 309, 311–4, 317, 322

Doneraile Conspiracy, 238–9

Donoughmore, Lord, 207, 218

Downes, Lord, 166, 179

Drapier's Letters (Jonathan Swift), 52

Drumgoole, Dr., 75, 121, 186

Drummond, 266

Dublin Evening Post, 154 ff., 225–6

Dudley, 102

Duffy, Charles Gavan, 287, 288–90, 292, 297, 313, 317–8, 320, 322

Duffy, James, 295

Duggan, 328

Duigenan, 92, 176

Duncannon, Lord, 244, 248, 261

Duv, Máire, 41, 44–5, 89

Edgeworth, Maria, 141, 195

Edinburgh Review, 132

Ejection Laws, 194

Eldon, Lord, 101, 218, 235

Eliza, 65

Elliot, 153

Emmet, Robert, 69, 111, 181, 281, 288

Esmonde, Sir Thomas, 217

Étoile, L', 215

Fagan, 56, 117, 270, 271

"Farewell to Patrick Sarsfield" ("*Slán le Pádraig Sairséal*"), 30–1

Faria, de, 63–4

Farrell, 246

Felon's Track, The (Michael Doheny), 141–3, 293–4, 312

Ffrench, Lord, 111, 126–7

Fingall, Lord, 111, 122, 125, 127–9, 131–2, 184, 188, 209–10

Finlay, James, 154–5, 188

Fitzgerald, Lord Edward, 69, 90–1, 104, 288, 291

Fitzgerald, Sir John, 14, 19

Fitzgerald, Vesey, 225 ff., 232

Fitzpatrick, Hugh, 151–4, 172, 184

Fitzpatrick, P. V., 40, 84, 254–6, 265–6, 278, 285–6, 326

Fitzwilliam, Lord, 172, 218

Fletcher, 99

Forbes, Lord, 244

Ford, 313–4

Fox, Charles, 111–2

Fox, Charlotte Milligan, 36 *n.*

Fullarton, 62

Garnier-Pagès, Louis-Antoine, 302

George IV, 209, 235

Gifford, Jack, 137, 176

Index

Godwin, William, 73, 75–6, 130
Goldsmith, Oliver, 68
Goold, Sir Francis, 184
Gore, 229
Gorman, Dick, 219
Gould, William, 24–5
Grady, Harry, 103
Graham, 284
Grant, 102
Grattan, Henry, 92, 95, 112, 118–9, 122, 135, 137, 183, 185, 188, 207, 281
Grey, 259, 263–5
Griffin, Gerald, 93
Griffith, Arthur, 290

Habeas Corpus Act, 111–2
Hardinge, Sir Henry, 246, 284
Hardwicke, 172
Hardy, 73
Hare, 127–9
Hay, 126, 207
Hayes, Father Dick, 192–3
Healy, Tim, 230
Hibernian, The, 187
Hickman, 227
Hidden Ireland, The (Daniel Corkery), 23, 27, 36, 221
Higgins, 89, 92
Hobson, 62
Hogan, 314
Holmes, Robert, 323
Houston, Dr. Arthur, 73
Hunter, Mrs., 61
"Hunting Cap." See O'Connell, Maurice
Hussey, Peter Bodkin, 121, 126, 131
Hutchinson, Colonel, 134
Hutton, Robert, 122–3

Irish Avatar (Byron), 209
Irish Emancipation Act, 241–2

James II, 19
Jeffrey, 210
Joinville, Prince de, 203

Keller, Jerry, 96, 98, 103
Kenney, 231
Kenyon, Lord Chief Justice, 111
Keogh, John, 32, 111, 120–2, 131, 196, 289
Kirwan, 127, 131, 151, 172

Labour in Irish History (James Connolly), 272
Lake, General, 91
Landor, 66
Langrishe, Sir Hercules, 52, 53
Lawless, Jack, 121, 148–9, 219, 228, 231–4
Lecky, William, 25, 67, 141, 144, 177, 221, 330
Ledru - Rollin, Alexandre - Auguste, 302–3
Le Fanu, Joseph Sheridan, 141
Lenihan, Maurice, 299, 301
Lennox, Charles. See Richmond, Duke of
Letters from Ireland (William Cobbett), 211
Letters of Peter Plymley (Sydney Smith), 211
Lever, Charles James, 195
Leveson-Gower, Lord, 232
Lidwell, George, 197, 199, 200
Life and Times of Daniel O'Connell (Thomas Clarke Luby), 184 n.
Life and Times of O'Connell (Christopher Manus O'Keeffe), 133 n., 184 n.
Life of O'Connell (Michael MacDonagh), 299
Litta, 191
Littleton, 264
Liverpool, 135
Lorton, Lord, 244
Louis XVI, 56
Luby, Thomas Clarke, 184 n., 204
Lytton, 296–7

Macaulay, 259
MacAuley, "Billy," 137
MacCarthy, Eugene, 43
MacCarthy, Theigue, 24
MacCooey, Art, 33
MacDomhnaill, Sean Clárach, 26
MacDonagh, Michael, 299, 301
MacDonnell, Aeneas, 207–8
MacDowell, Rose, 312
MacGhearailt, Pierce, 23, 33–5
MacHale, Archbishop John, 87–8, 214, 268–9, 278, 318–20
Macnamara, Major, 197–8, 202
Macpherson, 192
Magee, John, 70, 151, 154 ff., 187
Maguire, Father, 231

Index

Mahon, Charles James Patrick (The O'Gorman Mahon), 187 n., 226, 231–233, 236–7
Mahon, Nicholas, 187 n., 188, 219
Mahony, Darby, 56, 65
"Mallow Defiance, The," 300–1
Maloney, 228
Mangan, James Clarence, 287–8
Man of Feeling (Henry Mackenzie), 65
Manton, 225
Marat, 56
Marrast, 302
Marshall, 67
Martley, 100–1
Mathew, Father Theobald, 297
Mauriac, François, 81
Mayne, 99
Maynooth Grant, 217
McCarthy, Felix, 62
McClelland, Baron, 97
Meagher, Thomas Francis, 287, 324
Meath, Lord, 247–9
Meehan, Father C. P., 288
Melbourne, Lord, 264–5
Middleton, George, 64
Miley, Father, 326–8
Milner, Dr., 185
Mitchel, John, 69, 80, 117, 181, 187, 206, 272, 287, 290, 311, 323
Moore, Tom, 76, 169, 211, 292, 300, 314
Morpeth, 266
Mulgrave, Lord, 266
Murphy, Arthur, 62
Murphy, Father, 226
Murray, Archbishop, 192, 271

Nagle, Dr., 317
Napoleon. See Buonaparte, Napoleon
Nation, The, 291, 309–10, 316, 318, 321–322
Netterville, Lord, 129
Nicholson, Mrs. Asenath, 27, 49–51, 140–2
Norbury, Lord, 98 ff., 152–4, 199
Norfolk, Duke of, 218

O'Brien, Sir Edward, 226–7
O'Brien, Smith, 181, 226, 290, 309, 311, 317, 320, 326, 329
O'Bruadair, David, 14 ff., 23, 28–30, 290
O'Callaghan of Clare, 26–7
O'Connell, Count Daniel (uncle of Daniel O'Connell), 40–1, 43, 48, 53, 57
O'Connell, Daniel, childhood, 40 ff.; family, 41 ff.; education, 51 ff.; student life in London, 57 ff.; religious attitudes, 70 ff., 279–81; early career as lawyer, 96 ff., 114–8; political philosophy, 104 ff.; marriage, 108–11; activities against the Union, 123 ff., 245 ff.; Chairman of the Catholic Committee, 125 ff.; legends about, 138–40; Fitzpatrick trial, 152 ff.; Magee trial, 154 ff.; Relief Bill controversy, 187 ff.; duels, 196–200; Eleanor Courtenay, 200–4; Doneraile Conspiracy, 237–8; career in Parliament, 242 ff.; decline of popularity, 270 ff.; Lord Mayor of Dublin, 287 ff.; Monster Meetings, 294 ff.; trial and imprisonment, 307 ff.; senility, 312, 316; illness and death, 326–9
O'Connell, Henry, 201–2
O'Connell, James, 196, 198
O'Connell, John, 202, 298, 314, 317–8, 321–4
O'Connell, Mary, 67, 108–10, 198–9, 204, 208, 267, 279
O'Connell, Maurice ("Hunting Cap," uncle of Daniel O'Connell), 40–1, 43, 45–6, 48, 51, 53–5, 57–60, 89, 108–9, 111, 201
O'Connell, Maurice ("Moss," brother of Daniel O'Connell), 39–41, 51 ff., 89, 93
O'Connell, Maurice (son of Daniel O'Connell), 111
O'Connell, Morgan, 40, 41, 43, 46–8, 76, 89, 201
O'Connell, Morgan (son of Daniel O'Connell), 215
O'Connell, Mrs. Morgan, 51
O'Connor, Feargus, 262–3
O'Connor, Frank, 29–31
O'Connor, Jerry, 197
O'Flaherty, Roderick, 18
O'Gorman, Nicholas Purcell, 121, 187, 192, 215
O'Heóghusa, Eochaidh, 25–6
O'Keeffe, Christopher Manus, 71, 83–6, 133 n., 158, 184 n.
O'Mahony, Donal, 44
O'Malley, Father, 271
O'Mara, Tom, 247–8, 251

Index

O'Meara, Barry, 189
O'Murchú, Sean, 33
O'Murphy, Art Mór, 36
O'Rahilly, Egan, 20, 23 ff., 289
Osborne, 179–80
Ossian (James Macpherson), 65, 74
O'Súileabháin, Eóin Rua, 23
O'Súileabháin, Tomás Rua (Thomas Roe O'Sullivan), 23
O'Súilleabháin, Dómhnall, 200

Paine, Thomas, 61, 74–5
Parnell, Charles Stewart, 61, 107, 203, 243, 293, 329
Peel, Lord Robert, 102, 155 ff., 178, 194–5, 198–200, 229, 235, 242–3, 247, 259–60, 284, 298–9, 304, 306, 313, 315, 318, 323–4
Perceval, 124, 133, 135, 229
Phillips, 186
Pierce, 256
Pilot, The, 146, 270, 322
Pindar, 74
Pitt, William, 111–2
Pius VII, 191–3
Plunket, 102, 104, 187, 207
Political Justice (William Godwin), 73, 76
Poynter, Dr., 191–2
Protesting Catholic Dissenters, 185

Quarantotti, Monsignor, 191–2

Racine, 81
Raparees, 14, 19, 29, 289–90
Ray, 285
Relief Bill, 182–3, 185, 187
Repeal Association, 251, 308
Richmond, Duke of, 134–5, 154 ff., 172–174
Rigby, Mrs., 60–1
Rights of Women, The (Mary Wollstonecraft), 73, 76
Ross, Martin, 195
Rousseau, 73, 130
Russell, Lord John, 251, 323
Ryan, 111

Sarsfield, Patrick, 30–1, 291
Saunders' Newsletter, 217
Saurin, William, 104, 151 ff.
Saxton, Sir Charles, 199, 200
Scully, Denis, 111, 154, 187

Shaw, 137
Sheares brothers, 56, 181, 288
Sheehan, Father, 231
Sheil, Richard Lalor, 82, 97, 101, 121, 123, 196, 207–8, 211, 215, 217–8, 220, 224, 226–8, 231, 252, 261–2, 282–3, 292, 313
Shelley, Percy Bysshe, 130
Sheridan, Dr., 127, 130–1, 151, 172
Shrewsbury, Lord, 125
Simpson, Henry. *See* O'Connell, Henry
Sinn Fein, 105, 107
Sirr, Major, 104, 127
"*Slán le Pádraig Sairséal,*" 30–1
Sligo, Marquis of, 261–2
Smith, 48, 104
Smith, Sydney, 210–1
Society of Precursors, 278
Somers, 286
Somerville, E. O., 195
Stanley, Sir Edward, 197, 247–8, 254, 259, 260–1, 264, 284
Steele, Thomas, 108, 225, 286, 299, 314, 325
Stephens, James, 69, 329
Stephenson, Oliver, 17
Sterne, Henry W. G. B., 99–100
Strafford, 166
Stuart, Villiers, 223–4

Taaffe, 127, 151
Tablet, 310
Thackeray, William Makepeace, 295
Thelwall, 73
Thompson, Douglas, 62–4
Thornton, General, 233
Toler, John. *See* Norbury, Lord
Tone, Wolfe, 32, 43, 63, 65, 69, 78, 92, 107, 119, 121, 288–9
Tooke, 73
Trimleston, Lord, 184 *n.*, 189
Troy, Archbishop, 208
Tyler, John, 302

United Ireland (John Mitchel), 272

Vandeleur, 230–1
Vignier, de, 63–4
Voltaire, 74

Wallace, 182
Waterford, Marquess of, 224–5

Index

Wellesley, Lord, 264

Wellington, Duke of, 102, 232–3, 235, 244–5, 247, 284

Westmorland, 167–8, 172

White of Bantry, 43

Whitworth, 156

Whyte, 227

Wicklow, Lord, 244

Wollstonecraft, Mary, 73

Woods, Dr., 36

Wynne, 102

Wyse, Sir Thomas, 223–4, 313

Yeats, W. B., 107

York, Duke of, 218

Young Irelanders, 291 ff.

Zapata's Questions (Voltaire), 74, 76